The Governance of Policing and Security

Crime Prevention and Security Management

Series Editor: **Martin Gill**

Titles include:

Mark Button
DOING SECURITY
Critical Reflections and an Agenda for Change

Bob Hoogenboom
THE GOVERNANCE OF POLICING AND SECURITY
Ironies, Myths and Paradoxes

Kate Moss
SECURITY AND LIBERTY
Restriction by Stealth

Forthcoming:

Joshua Bamfield
SHOPPING AND CRIME

Paul Ekblom
THE 5IS FRAMEWORK FOR CRIME PREVENTION AND COMMUNITY SAFETY

Crime Prevention and Security Management
Series Standing Order ISBN 978–0–230–01355–1 hardback
978–0–230–01356–8 paperback
(*outside North America only*)

You can receive future titles in this series as they are published by placing a standing order. Please contact your bookseller or, in case of difficulty, write to us at the address below with your name and address, the title of the series and the ISBN quoted above.

Customer Services Department, Macmillan Distribution Ltd, Houndmills, Basingstoke, Hampshire RG21 6XS, England

---

The Governance of Policing and Security

Ironies, Myths and Paradoxes

Bob Hoogenboom
VU University Amsterdam and Nyenrode Business University, The Netherlands

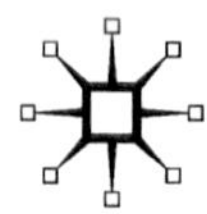

First published 2010 by
PALGRAVE MACMILLAN

Palgrave Macmillan in the UK is an imprint of Macmillan Publishers Limited, registered in England, company number 785998, of Houndmills, Basingstoke, Hampshire RG21 6XS.

Palgrave Macmillan in the US is a division of St Martin's Press LLC, 175 Fifth Avenue, New York, NY 10010.

Palgrave Macmillan is the global academic imprint of the above companies and has companies and representatives throughout the world.

Palgrave® and Macmillan® are registered trademarks in the United States, the United Kingdom, Europe and other countries.

ISBN: 978–0–230–54265–5 hardback

This book is printed on paper suitable for recycling and made from fully managed and sustained forest sources. Logging, pulping and manufacturing processes are expected to conform to the environmental regulations of the country of origin.

A catalogue record for this book is available from the British Library.

A catalog record for this book is available from the Library of Congress.

10 9 8 7 6 5 4 3 2 1
19 18 17 16 15 14 13 12 11 10

Printed and bound in Great Britain by
CPI Antony Rowe, Chippenham and Eastbourne

For Maurice Punch and Gary Marx

Contents

Introduction

In John Irving's novel *The World According to Garp,* we encounter two scenes in which a young child is warned before taking a swim in the Atlantic Ocean: 'beware of the undertow', for undertows are dangerous for the unwary. The book analyses 'undertows' in policing and the broader security structures in our societies.[1] I have made my way through what is generally called police research with crossovers to criminology. The conventional policing and criminal justice systems that I first started with have become part of a far broader 'security architecture' involving new transnational policing structures, military influences, an emerging private security market, a wide variety of regulators for different market segments and, last but not least, after 9/11, the growing role of security and intelligence services. Moreover, policing and this new 'security architecture' are affected fundamentally by innovations in science and technology. Today's buzz words are *restructuring, reconceptualisation*, and *reframing* of policing and security. It is important to realise that this is *not* institutional tinkering but could very well indicate a covert and undebated paradigm shift. In all this, a permanent key question is 'what is truly real'? In this wilderness of mirrors, do we see what we think we see and can we believe what we are told? Can we feel the undertow before it carries us away? Or, is this viewpoint too dramatic?

In this book, I intend to go beyond piecemeal institutional change: beyond changes in segments within separate parts of 'the system'. I wish to explore issues and themes related to the growing process of interweaving taking place in the field of policing between regulators, military forces, private security and security and intelligence agencies. Sometimes called 'hybrid' policing and security arrangements, these grey areas raise fundamental questions with regard to the rule of law, democracy, human rights, privacy and basic societal norms and values in an advanced, Western democracy.

The question concerned here is a seemingly technical one: given what has just been said, what do we actually know, what is it that we do not know and how can we get to know about it? This in turn raises issues about the perspectives adopted throughout police research and criminological discourse. In my view, these are too limited to tackle the issues raised: it is necessary to return to the notion of social science as penetrating façades and exposing hidden realities (Goffman, 1959).

In 1985, I started working as a researcher in the field of policing in the Dutch Home Office's Directorate of Policing. At the time, a small group of social scientists were conducting research on the introduction of the new concept of community policing. I must admit that the initial choice of regulatory agencies and specialised investigative units as my first research topic was slightly coincidental, but then my interest in policing as a process was grabbed immediately. In much of the policing research conducted in those days – and even today – policing is defined in organisational terms (*the public police*) and in terms of what the public police do: maintaining order, controlling crime and serving the general public. But at the time, there were also 67 different public administration agencies doing 'policing'. Studying policing as a process, I found many of the regulatory agencies and specialised investigative units doing exactly what the public police do: keeping law and order, but mainly in the economic domain (Hoogenboom, 1985). In our mental system, surveillance, control, information (or intelligence) gathering and even the investigative process itself are so closely interlinked in being considered equal to *The Police* that it is very difficult to break away from this notion. The 'mental prison' we live in with regard to policing has all the characteristics of what Kenneth Galbraith calls *conventional wisdom*: a term used to describe ideas or explanations that are generally accepted as true by the public or by experts in a field. The term implies that the ideas or explanations, though widely held, are unexamined and, hence, may be re-evaluated upon further examination or as events unfold.

Subsequently, my research moved into the realm of privatisation and private investigations. My fascination with the limited scope of police research (and criminology for that matter) increased even more. Since then, I have tried (successfully) to break away from 'traditional science' (Kuhn, 1962) every now and then – but without ever losing sight of public policing. I have lectured at the Dutch Police Academy since 1988. In my PhD dissertation entitled *The Police Complex. On the Interweaving of Policing, Regulatory Agencies and Private Investigations* (Hoogenboom, 1994) I not only pursued my interest in developments taking place 'outside' the criminal justice system, but I also became interested in the slow but steady process of interweaving taking place.

At the same time, I could not 'believe' the degree of 'slow-motion' thinking still prevailing in police research and criminology: community policing was – and still is – high on the research agenda. I was fortunate to visit international conferences on policing, criminology and, in the last decade, (private) security. Policing and criminology in these meetings are dominated by the criminal justice system and public policing. Currently, there is an abundance of conferences and publications on (private) security, and their numbers have increased dramatically since 9/11. Their academic level, however, is lacking in many ways. Many of the presentations are aimed at selling (new concepts, consultancy, hardware, software and other toys for the security girls and boys). This is not meant to sound degrading: I have the highest regard for 'old school' police researchers and criminologists, and certainly for private entrepreneurs. I used to be one myself. In 1997, I teamed up for a period of four and a half years with an accountancy firm that, to paraphrase Don Corleone from *The Godfather,* made me an offer I couldn't refuse if only I would be so kind as to set up a forensic accountancy practice in the Caribbean, working from the Dutch Antilles. This I accepted, and for three years I travelled the Caribbean. I educated myself in consulting, teaching and forensic investigation cases in matters such as money laundering, international fraud, business ethics and public–private cooperation.

Not only had I broken away from 'traditional science' by knocking on the doors of regulators, specialised investigative units and private security, but in doing so I also developed an interest in white-collar crime. Most of the rule breaking addressed by regulators, specialised investigative units and the private security sector is not at all related to the stereotypical thugs, hoodlums, organized crime figures trying to imitate Marlon Brando or 'scumbags and assholes' (Van Maanen, 1987) with whom traditional science seems to be so obsessed. I entered the offices of financial institutions, the Amsterdam Stock Exchange, oil and gas companies, trading companies, accountancy firms and the offices of other assorted everyday businessmen and public officials dealing with economic violations. 'Crime' in this neck of the woods – as we have all known ever since the publication of Sutherland's quintessential work (1939; 1946; 1986) – is not perceived as crime at all. The one-sided focus on traditional crime in police research and criminology – understandably so because one very much leans on the official criminal records and statistics – is all about 'nuts, sluts and perverts' but that focus blinds us to the structural and pervasive nature of 'crime' in a bona fide context (Punch, 1996).

Every now and then, some chagrin on my part slips into my teaching, my writing and my commentaries. Although I often use the Mafia movie quote 'nothing personal, just business' when charging into a traditional science situation, I sometimes feel that little progress is being made in policing and security studies. In 1999, when I was living and working in the Dutch Antilles, I came across an advertisement advocating writing a chapter on the future of criminology. The occasion was the twenty-fifth anniversary of the Dutch Criminological Foundation (NVK). I dipped my pen in vitriol and wrote *On Old Folks and Things That Pass Away. Criminology in 2018*. The chapter – also in this book – discusses 'Dinosaur Institutions' in criminology missing out on changes taking place not only in society, but also in institutional responses to crime. The undertows are not seen, not sought after and not found interesting it seems. True innovations, I argued, are taking place in information and communication technology (ICT), forensic accountancy, business administration, ethics, architecture and political science.

My interest in developments 'outside' public policing also took me in to the world of the intelligence communities and the academic field of intelligence studies. In the early 1990s, I became a member of the Netherlands Intelligence Study Association (NISA). Founded by social scientists and former political intelligence officials, NISA members study the history of intelligence (World War II, the Cold War). Again, intelligence is an undertow in policing and security that is hardly ever covered by academics. In cooperation with my friend and colleague Marc Cools, *Vulnerable Knowledge* (Kwetsbare Kennis) was published in 1996. The book – for the most part written by public officials from the Dutch intelligence community and security managers from multinational corporations – addressed economic and corporate espionage. Intelligence has always been connected in one way or the other with public policing as well as private security. I recently completed a publication on the growing interweaving (cooperation) between Dutch policing and the Intelligence and Security Service (AIVD) based on empirical research – interviews, internal sources and literature studies. But, in general, the second oldest profession in history does not get that much attention in mainstream normal science.

I strongly believe in crossing boundaries: moving in and out of academic disciplines. Intellectual life is far too organised along vertical lines. We have become specialists in limited policing and security topics, using our 'own' language, theories, concepts and definitions to safeguard our autonomy in this specialised area. We have become specialist within specialist domains, speaking specialised languages for specialised audiences in small theatres. As for myself, I am not all that much interested in all the individual parts of the broader puzzle. I quoted Ericson and Carriere (1992) at the end of my PhD dissertation: 'the only viable academic sensibility is to encourage people to let their minds wander, to travel intellectually across boundaries and frontiers and perhaps never to return to them.'[2] Disciplines are necessary evils. Necessary because of the body of knowledge they produce. Disciplines may turn into an evil because of their hierarchy and the accompanying ego and power games being played (Foucault, 1974; Kuhn, 1962). Also, disciplines can be considered evil through their immanent rigidity in terms of theories, methodologies and research subjects.

Almost by chance, and later in actually venturing into blind alleys, dark caves and other relatively uncharted territories, I became somewhat disenchanted by academic silo thinking. My feelings were enhanced even more when I came under the 'spell' of Gary Marx in the early nineties. I read his '37 imperatives for young and aspiring sociologists' (Marx, 1997): 'don't linger on one subject for too long', 'speak truth to power', 'write all the time, on everything' and, last but not least, 'don't read books, write them'.

David Halberstam, the American author who more or less danced his way through politics (*The Best and the Brightest*, 1974), baseball (*Summer of 49*) and military history (*The Coldest War*, 2007) is another role model in this respect, as is Robert Reiner (2002) for much of his work, but especially for his fine work on the way in which the police have become an integral part of our popular culture in movies, television series, novels and literature. There are many ways to satisfy my curiosity in policing and security, and I am convinced that popular culture is vastly underestimated as a source for our understanding of social reality. *Crime and Literature. Sociology of Deviance and Fiction* by Vincenzo Ruggiero (2003) is a fantastic example, as is the movie *Serpico*, based on the true story of police corruption in New York in the early 1970s. Somewhere along the lines to follow, I will bring in Tony Soprano to make this point even stronger.

Plan of attack

First, I wish to challenge traditional science by stressing that the interweaving of social control and policing systems requires a new perspective: new intellectual lenses, so to speak. In the first two chapters, I confine myself to the traditional research object of police studies and criminology: public policing. In these two chapters, I trace historic dynamics and patterns in the (political) function of the police, the gradual centralisation stemming from the political function, and I stress the differentiated character of policing on the ground. Much of the police research was – and still is – on the blue-coated worker and concepts like community policing, reassurance policing and, more recently, restorative policing. The point I'm making in the first two chapters is that for us to understand 'governance of policing and security' we first must return to some of 'the classics' in policing and rethink and reanalyse what the functions of policing are. Because of the one-sided nature of police research (and criminology) looking into the most visible aspects of policing, other police functions – from order keeping, gathering intelligence (infiltration, informants) and the criminal investigation process – are 'neglected'. The ongoing blurring of boundaries and interweaving taking place between different 'policing' actors can be understood only in the context of the history and theoretical function of the public police. Some commentators argue that policing is in the process of large-scale fragmentation and the public police is becoming but one among many organisations, agencies and/or nodes (Bayley and Shearing, 2001). I will dive into some undertows looking for empirical signs, examples, triggers and on-the-ground examples of the opposite idea: increasingly the state (and the police) is 'reinventing' itself along new hybrid structures and processes involving new 'policing' and security actors, agencies and private security companies. Fragmentation of policing is making some waves in the current literature while new alignments are constantly being created among a multitude of agencies.

Therefore, in the following chapters, I trace undertows in other parts of the new security architecture. Structures, functions, cultures and the blurring of boundaries and accountability issues will be analysed on a structural basis within the various security domains. I will touch on regulatory agencies, inspectorates, private security and private investigations but also the intelligence and security communities. Throughout the book, I will address the blurring of boundaries between the police and regulatory agencies, between the police and private security, between the police and the intelligence and security community and between the police and the military. One of the undertows in all this is the security technology cutting through traditional barriers. Policing is becoming more intensive and extensive than previous forms and transcends distance, darkness, physical barriers and time; its records can be stored, retrieved, combined, analysed and communicated with great ease; it has low visibility or is invisible; is often involuntary; emphasises prevention; is capital rather than labour intensive and involves decentralised control and triggers a shift from targeting a specific individual to categorical suspicion (Marx, 1988).

Second, I intend to introduce ironies, paradoxes, double-loop arguments and irrationalities within the emerging new security architecture. Although, as my arguments go, we can trace increasing cooperation – and even interweaving – between different security domains or 'silos', we also find many contradictions, tensions and conflicts of interests. Privatisation, militarisation, internationalisation and, for instance, securitisation are in many ways based on broad and sweeping generalisations (Bowling and Newburn, 2006). The story of the new security architecture unfolds itself at different levels, in different time frames, and it involves many paradoxes. What do we know about the effects of the war on drugs, the war on crime and all the security measures, programs, technology and manpower involved? Does it 'work' or are we made to believe all the 'necessity languages' involved? What is real, what is stage acting?

Third, questions are raised related to accountability and governance issues within this new landscape that could have profound implications for human rights, privacy and civic society. The rule of law, due process, accountability and democratic control have a long-standing tradition in police research and criminology, but, so my arguments run, if public policing is becoming part of a new security architecture, do the traditional checks and balances still function well? Or are we on the brink of policing and security arrangements crossing and fudging blurring accountability boundaries? Is there any truth in Sartre's question: 'do you think you can govern innocently'? Can governments keep their hands clean, or do they endeavour to evade accountability?

On the one hand, we find much 'necessity language' (justifications related to rising crime and fraud, the threat of organised crime, the war on drugs and the war on terror), but at the same time significant organisational and corporate deviance is taking place (for example, Abu Ghraib and police corruption), as are megafraud cases that threaten the very future of financial markets (Enron, Parmalat, Ahold, the financial crises of 2008/2009 and new Ponzi schemes on an unprecedented scale by entrepreneurs like Bernard Madoff), cases involving collusion ('revolving door' argument) of public officials moving into private security companies and using their contacts for contracts and widespread bending of the rule of law (private justice arrangements) and cases of illegality by private military companies (PMCs).

I would certainly not wish to go as far as the Rolling Stones in stating that 'Rough Justice' (2005) is all around, but I will address undertows in the 'business' of justice that challenge conventional wisdom. For this reason, I use the concept of 'unsafe and unsound practices'. Can undertows be discerned within the new security architecture indicating criminogenic factors in themselves through new concentrations of power with unclear accountability structures? *Quis custōdiet ipsōs custōdēs*? is a Latin phrase from the Roman poet Juvenal that translates literally as 'who will guard the guards themselves?' and is variously quoted in colloquial English as 'who watches the watchmen?', 'who watches the watchers?', 'who will guard the guards?', 'who shall watch the watchers?', 'who polices the police?' or other similar translations.

The modern, democratic state is based on the separation of powers, professional legal-rational bureaucracies, transparency with respect to an elected parliament and inquisitive media, accountability under the rule of law with respect to the courts and finally an independent judiciary, based on the pivotal principles that no one is above the law and that the state will protect the citizen from the arbitrary use of authority. This system is an ideal, conveying the idea of a clean, legitimate state as opposed to a totalitarian police state where authority is arbitrary and people in power are unaccountable (as could be witnessed in the Soviet Union under Stalin). *Das Leben der Anderen*, the modern classic movie about the Staatssicherheitsdienst (the state security service Stasi) in communist East Germany, offers a frightening glimpse of an unwanted near future.

The closer a government moves towards this ideal system, the larger the degree of legitimacy it is likely to enjoy. It is assumed that, without legitimacy, there cannot be sound government, effective policing, feelings of safety or a belief in a 'just world'. Doubtlessly, there are many politicians and officials who endeavour to abide by the ideals and precepts of legitimate, accountable democracy, yet it is unavoidable that the scrutiny of undertows will reveal some grey areas of cooperation, perversions of the truth, covert activities and efforts to evade accountability. This is more than traditional Machiavellian manipulation: the stakes are higher as a result of globalisation, increased complexity and the new and different threats facing us today.

Finally, a few words are needed here to elaborate on my approach. I will sketch the contours of the new security 'architecture'. The metaphor suggests that there is an architect with a building plan, but this is open to debate. Some of the material presented here will give the reader more detailed background information and additional insights into current trends. I will draw on police research in the Netherlands and some of my own research conducted in the Netherlands and also on (inter)national literature covering the changing nature of policing and security.

Finally, to 'complicate' matters more, I will draw somewhat on popular culture. For instance, Tony Soprano is introduced in one chapter, not only as my witness for the defence of some of the ironies witnessed at work, but also because social science is in dire need of a bit of humour every now and then. As Gary Marx puts it: 'have fun: enjoy what you do'. This is exactly what I planned to do from the outset of the current project in addition to making the reader more sensitive to certain new issues by pinpointing new themes and new research questions.

In all this, I wish to stress the essaylike character of the book. In moving beyond the 'traditional science' of policing and security, I enter some uncharted territories lacking safe and sound empirical bases. Indeed, the phrase 'underresearched' pops up many times in the limited number of writings on PMCs, regulation, militarisation, security technology and, for instance, the intelligence community. Of course, many different explanations are available here. They partly lie in the very nature of the work itself: regulation is carried out by regulators, loss prevention by the private security sector and antiterrorism measures by security and intelligence services. These tasks, however, are exercised with considerable variation and with different levels of discretionary power, with secrecy and/or confidentiality and with difficulties of access. In many ways, this may take place strictly within the rule of law.

Yet at the same time, the logs and files concerned here – simply because they often fail to find their way into the regular criminal justice system – are not systematically scrutinised by the public, investigative journalists, lawyers, Parliamentary Oversight Commissions, judges and, of course, police researchers and criminologists. They remain offstage, and this is intimidating for young researchers seeking grants and access to sites and publications. Still, it is even more widely noticeable that research topics that touch on the powerful, the mighty and their abuse of power – governmental deviance, the rapaciousness of multinationals and corporate crime, to name but a few examples – represent minority interests that are closely scrutinised only by the handful of scholars who continue to research these areas.

From time to time, I move from the Netherlands to the United States and the United Kingdom. For instance, chapters on technology and political intelligence lack substantial empirical sources in many countries. The strength – if any – in my approach is the charting of new territories, exploring emerging trends, markets and 'coalitions of the willing' in the ongoing process of interweaving taking place. In doing so, I aim to gradually develop new ideas and new research questions that pinpoint ironies, myths and paradoxes. From a philosophy of science perspective, in many ways I'm in the exploratory phases of doing research. This strength is at the same time the weakness of the book because certain chapters cannot reasonably be labelled as 'international comparative' or 'empirical'. Moreover, political systems and cultures, legal systems and law enforcement systems in the countries I describe (because of the availability of sources) can be compared in some ways, but in many ways they differ – not to mention the countries and political systems not dealt with at all. Undertows are interesting intellectually but caution is necessary lest we draw too many parallels. I recently attended an international police conference in the Netherlands, and I wrote down a quote from an Australian police officer sitting next to me who, in a heated debate, said: 'Perhaps I'm not God's gift to police research, but still I've got something to offer'. In this mind-set, I wrote the book.

Finally, let me mention two valuable concepts that are addressed in the final parts of the book: varieties of the 'myth system' and the 'operational code'. The former refers to the formal front that governments and corporations present to the outside world and the latter indicates the actual informal – and sometimes covert – rules of the game: what really happens on the shop floor, in operations and in implementation? For instance: governments bribe, corporations form cartels, the police torture and security services set up illegal operations. Somehow, the interface between the two 'systems' has to be managed, and only when this has been exposed can we obtain a glimpse of the true lie of the land.

With the empirical obstacles outlined above, I invite the reader to join me on a journey into a bewildering hall of mirrors in which the criminal justice system is but one of the 'one hundred tiny theatres of punishment' (Foucault, 1988). The story about to be told is diverse, sometimes contradictory and perhaps in some ways covering too many subjects, but in my view, it offers one way of formulating new research questions. The challenge involved here lies in avoiding the distortions, in clarifying the images and in establishing some coherence. And of course, one should have fun while doing it – and perhaps while reading parts of it, too.

1

Within Public Policing: Gradual Centralisation

Introduction

In this and the following chapters, I trace historic dynamics and patterns in the (political) function of the police, the gradual centralisation stemming from the political function, and I stress the differentiated character of policing on the ground.

Policing: Functions and historical dynamics

In 1979, two theses were published in the Netherlands that analysed the political function of policing and the historical dynamics of the police system: *Overheidsgeweld* (Governmental Violence) by Van Reenen and *Opdat de macht een toevlucht zij?* (So that power be a refuge?) by Fijnaut. Van Reenen is a police functionary who later studied sociology in Rotterdam. Fijnaut is a former police inspector who went on to study philosophy and criminology in Leuven. In their research concerning the evolution of the police system and the police function, these two police researchers have developed invaluable new concepts. Both authors, like Robert Reiner (1992), develop a theoretical framework to understand policing in which the distinction between 'the group of words, police, policy, polity, politics, politic, political (and) politician is delicate' (Reiner, 1992). Indeed, the subtitle of Fijnaut's study is 'The history of the police as a political institution'.

The (historical) discussion of the police system takes place at two levels: the political/administrative level and the organisational level. Both are inextricably linked.

On the political/administrative level, considerable – and sometimes even fierce – discussions have so far taken place concerning the degree of command and control demonstrated by the police since the mid-nineteenth century (*City and County Legislation* and the *Federal Police Decree*, both dated 1851). This discussion about command and control is closely linked to the (desired) level of police care: locally, provincially, regionally or nationally.

Since 1858, the police force has consisted of a locally organised municipal police force, the municipal constabulary in smaller municipalities, the military police and the federal constabulary. The year 1919 saw the inclusion of the Corps of Police Troops. Cooperation among the various forces was relatively poor, and their areas of operation overlapped.

Various government committees (1852, 1858, 1881, 1883, 1898, 1931) formulated proposals not only to ensure uniformity, but also to organise police care on a national level. In 1852, for example, it was proposed that a federal police force be set up under the responsibility of the Ministry of Police. In 1883, it was suggested that the municipal police merge with the federal police, resulting in a combination that would then fall under the Ministry of Justice. In 1898, it was suggested that a general federal police force be set up, and in 1931, the government committee envisioned a municipal police force under the authority of the Royal Commissioner.

Following the Police Decree of 1945, a division was made between federal and municipal police. The military police no longer formed part of the police system. Command over the police was divided between the mayor of the municipality concerned and the state attorney. Mayors were responsible for maintaining public order, while the state attorney was charged with investigation tasks. Management tasks were distributed between the Ministry of Internal Affairs and the Department of Justice.

The 1993 Police Act ceased to distinguish between municipality and the federal police. Today, the police system consists of 25 regional police forces and a corps offering national police services known in the Netherlands as the KLPD. In 1998, management of the KLPD was transferred from the Department of Justice to the Ministry of Internal Affairs.

In his *IJzeren politiebestel* (The Iron Police System), Van Reenen discusses the historical dynamics of the police system. Time and time again, supposedly decisive proposals were formulated to create a good and effective police system once and for all and, in so doing, end all discussion and strife. These attempts were never successful. The main reason for this is that the police system was not originally a rational arrangement made by people with the help of certain resources and set up to achieve particular predefined goals. Rather, it was a system that developed over time: it had to grow. In addition, the police system was characterised by the existence of established interests: the mayor's (public order, local crime problems and the relationship with civilians), the state attorney's (criminal investigations) and interests held by ministerial departments (for example, coordination, standardisation, appointments and training/education). Also, established interests existed within the police system itself. Talking about a particular period, Van Reenen points to a 'battle between federal and municipal police'. Fijnaut analyses the 'institutional battle' among and within police services. The various established interests entail 'a powerfully conservative element in the discussion without it generally being clear that it concerns the representation of general interests' (Van Reenen, 1978).

Three types of dynamics

According to Van Reenen, the police system is subject to three types of dynamics: marginal change, system change and revolutionary change.

Marginal change

Marginal change forms part of the normal dynamics within the existing political and administrative order. Changes are called marginal because, from a political perspective, they do not – or only barely – change the existing balance of power. They are generally 'technical' adaptations, such as a cooperative agreement between forces.

System change

This type of change relates to changes in the police establishment that go beyond marginal alterations, but that nevertheless to an important degree remain within the existing political–administrative framework. The recent establishment of the national investigation squad is an example of this type of change. This involved more than marginal changes to the structure, although the positions of authority figures and managers have more or less remained as they were. The establishment change is a compromise between new and old concepts.

Revolutionary change

Revolutionary change occurs in the event of a radical deconstruction of the existing political and administrative order in which a new political order is created. In such situations, an entirely new 'revolutionary' police system needs to be built up. 'Old' elements remain recognisable as a result of the need to take on expertise, manpower, auxiliary resources and organisational methods from the old system in order to maintain at least a minimum of effectiveness. During the German occupation of the Netherlands in World War II, a revolutionary change occurred because the police force was integrated within the German police system.

Criticising the police: Of all times

Inefficiencies in the police system have been criticised since the mid-nineteenth century. In the period ranging from 1850 to 1940, the relationship between federal and local policing was questioned regularly, with many references to 'the inefficiency of the police organization' (Van Reenen, 1978). In this period, the discussion addressed poor cooperation and overlapping areas of supervision and tasks. Without exception, proposals to solve the issues were founded on a federal or state police system. Another remaining issue concerned the question whether the system was indeed inefficient and thus what decisions in this matter should be based on, or whether in fact a political argument was concerned.

After the World War II, the issue of enhancing efficiency through reorganisation continued to play a similarly large role. Proposals for solutions again moved towards increases in scale. In 1993, the objective behind the formation of the regional police system was to 'end the existence of a fragmented, inefficient and proportionally expensive police apparatus' (Fijnaut and van Helten, 1999).

The memorandum *Criminaliteitsbeheersing. Investeren in een zichtbare overheid* (2001) (Managing crime. Investing in visible public administration) addresses the 'criminal enforcement shortage' and calls for an improvement of the 'quality and control of criminal investigation'. The memorandum strongly emphasises investigative activities and the associated necessary improvements in acquiring criminal information ('information position').

A historical constant: The gradual increase in scale

Central to Fijnaut's thesis is that, from a historical perspective, an ongoing process of 'nationalization of a repressive apparatus' has been taking place: a question of gradual increases in scale among police systems in Western Europe. Fijnaut distinguishes between 'rapid and slow phases' as far as changes in the establishment are concerned. In periods of political instability and threats, it is possible to change the existing order fundamentally and extensively. As some examples, Fijnaut mentions the social unrest witnessed during and shortly after the French Revolution, the (imminent) revolutions in 1848 and in 1917–1919 and finally the police reorganisations during and after the World War II. This 'basic pattern' as Fijnaut describes it can clearly be illustrated by international developments following 9/11. Especially in the United States, reorganisations were introduced with the objective of improving cooperation on a national level (in particular the exchange of information) between police and investigation and safety services. This included the foundation of a new federal department: the Homeland Security Department.

We also find Fijnaut's 'basic pattern' of lengthy and gradual scale increases in the foundation of various police units: in arrest and observation teams in the seventies employed throughout the Netherlands, in the organisation of supralocal investigation teams as criminal investigation teams in the eighties, in the foundation of supraregional core teams following the regionalisation of the system in 1993, in the foundation of a national investigation team and, more recently, in the foundation of a national investigation squad that includes the core teams mentioned above.

Fijnaut's basic pattern is also found in the maintenance of public order. In the last 40 years, large-scale police actions have been subject to further supralocal and national regulations. In the 1992 outline memorandum *Riot Squads* (Mobile Units), the organisation is introduced into the new police system. The main issue in large-scale police actions is the so-called 'up-scaling' issue: when, how and by whom is this type of large-scale police action to be organised?

Finally, the basic pattern can be found in the growing desire, witnessed over recent decades, to store and process criminal information. Although this information is primarily collected on a national level (crime analysis), it is also to an important degree collected de-centrally. Historically and within the 'iron police system', we see a basic pattern of partial changes, a gradual centralisation of command and control. These partial changes to the establishment have primarily taken place within investigation services and criminal information operations. This historical analysis of policing and the political function of public policing have somehow been 'neglected' in Dutch police research. The more structural analyses of undertows in the police system ('basic patterns') that are related to traditional core tasks of policing – order keeping, law enforcement, intelligence gathering and the exercise of the monopoly of violence – have been 'diluted' in academia because of the overwhelming attention being given to 'community policing', reassurance policing' and, more recently, 'restorative policing' (SMVP, 2004). In the next chapter, I will look underneath the 'waves' of fashionable police language to restore somewhat the balance between the political function of policing outlined in this chapter and some of the undertows in public policing nowadays.

2
Within Public Policing: Fictional and Factual Policing

Introduction

In this chapter, public policing is again the main topic, but this time I will put the historical dynamics aside and look more closely into what is actually happening on the ground. That is, the police system is not the object of research, but policing itself. In doing this, I will discuss undertows in policing related to the gradual strengthening of the traditional law and order tasks of the police and the fact that police research (and criminology) increasingly studies parts of public policing that are actually diminishing in terms of manpower, priorities, budgets and political relevance. For this I use the concepts of fictional and factual policing. My argument here is that fictional policing accounts and academic studies neglect factual realities of policing. The factual realities of policing, I argue, fit the function and historical dynamics discussed in Chapter 1, and a distinction is made between five levels of policing. My argument here is that the first level of policing (community policing and other visible policing) – the main object of social sciences – actually is becoming less prominent vis-à-vis policing on other levels (riot squads, infiltration, criminal and political intelligence, forensic investigation, international cooperation and so on).

Undertows in policing

Reassurance policing is one of the concepts introduced during the past decade. Change seems to be omnipresent. My aim here is to try and make some sense of the continuing stories of change being spread, of which reassurance policing is but one of the latest. I am fascinated by the cycles of reform that seem to have proliferated in the past decade. Old-fashioned order keeping through the (threat) of non-negotiable force – for many police researchers the quintessential function of policing – has today made way for elegant well-formulated oral and written reports of 'nodal policing', 'community policing', 'intelligence-led policing' and all sorts of policy lingo heavily permeated with fashionable new public management notions of 'targets' and 'planning procedures'. Visible characteristics of neighbourhoods in decline, which have always been the locus of police work all over the world, are now called 'signal crimes' in the reassurance perspective. What could possibly explain the almost continuous emergence and short-lived sustainability of new policing concepts?

In trying to make sense of this 'manic pace of change' I came across Klockars's article 'The rhetoric of community policing' (1988), which struck me for its originality. Klockars dismantles many fictional accounts of policing and touches upon factual realities encountered in the business of policing. Klockars, in the late 1980s, used Bittner's concept of circumlocution to analyse the movement towards 'community policing'. Circumlocution is the use of an unnecessarily large number of words to express an idea: the term refers to evasive speech. From his perspective, 'community policing' is best understood as the latest in a fairly long tradition of circumlocutions whose purpose is to conceal, mystify and legitimate police distribution of non-negotiable coercive force (Klockars, 1988).

In essence, any organisation – not only the police – uses its own language, rhetoric and myth systems. The various types of language are used to give meaning to the organisation, the core tasks it performs and their very *raisons d'etre*. It is of no importance at all whether these narratives do not – or partly – represent reality because they serve a symbolic purpose. In the social sciences, we find references to 'ritual organisations'. Ritual organisations also use language, signs, symbols and images to conceal factual realities. Other police researchers like Loader and Reiner have also touched upon the more ritualistic or symbolic dimensions of policing. In his article 'Policing and the Social: Questions of Symbolic Power', Loader (1997) analyses the police in the context of ideas and concepts taken from political science related to the symbolic function of power. Loader opens his 'tale of two police forces', a symbolic (fictional) and factual tale, with the following quotation:

> The political system performs a function of symbolic protection far beyond its specific role as an apparatus of the selective regulation of

> social risks (...) It is most of all on the symbolic level that the institutions of authority, with all their show, ritual, prescriptions, and even codes of manners and etiquette, satisfy a latent need for social protection and spread a gratifying sensation of order and security. (Loader 1997)

Loader argues that sociological enquiry needs to devote more of its attention to understanding the social meanings of policing and outline a framework within which the role and significance may be investigated of policing as a cultural category. According to Reiner (1992), policing has fictional and factual dimensions: 'Most police work is neither social service nor law enforcement, but order maintenance – the settlement of conflicts by other means than formal law enforcement'.

What I do *not* intend to do next is write on reassurance policing. The reader can find excellent treatises on the subject in the literature. What I would like to do instead is place reassurance in the broader context of the seemingly unlimited supply of new policing concepts. My interest lies in stressing the growing divide between fictional and factual policing. For this reason, I have to go back to some of the classics in our body of knowledge on policing. First, the concept of circumlocution as used by Bittner and Klockars is explained more in detail. What is it, why is it important and how is it applied? Second, I will briefly sketch how Klockars applies the concept of circumlocution to community policing. Third, I will discuss certain new concepts introduced in (Dutch) policing during the last decade.

The police seem to be locked up in a 'manic pace of change'. The introduction of community policing has been followed by an ever-increasing number of new concepts and strategies varying from new public management techniques to 'broken window', intelligence-led policing and, more recently, reassurance policing. I will argue that Klockars's analysis can also be applied to many of these 'new' policies, strategies, tactics and operational activities suggesting change, innovation and constant adaptations of policing. Although we may witness in some ways 'a manic pace of change' with the introduction of new concepts, policing on the ground does not generally change that much. Continuities in policing are neglected. Underneath all the rhetoric of change, reproducing order has not fundamentally changed since the introduction of the bobbies by Sir Robert Peel.

Next, I will argue that the explanations for the circumlocution (or fictional or symbolic dimensions) demonstrated by many involved in policing and put forward by Bittner and Klockars can be extended and in some ways refined by incorporating police-related cultural notions and concepts, but especially also by means of a set of techniques used by police leaders to retain relative autonomy. As much as society has a need for fictional police stories, so police leadership has a need for different narratives – and even myths – to keep authorities and the public at bay with the sole purpose of safeguarding its autonomy. Reassurance policing from these perspectives has meaning mostly on the fictional (symbolic) level and relatively less on the factual levels of policing.

Finally, I will formulate my remarks on the rather narrow basis of police research with its dominant focus on the visible blue-coated worker. The almost exclusive focus on these blue-coated workers, 'working the streets' in their continuous search for signs and signals to respond to public needs, in community and reassurance-like strategies is but one single facet of multifaceted policing arrangements and strategies. In many ways, factual policing is a 'neglected' subject.

Fictional policing or circumlocutions

Central to the Bittner/Klockars argument is the notion that police are a mechanism for the distribution of non-negotiable coercive force. This entails a 'difficult moral problem', because we live in a civilised society and condemn violence. Yet, even within civilised society, the existential function of the police is 'to make available a group of persons with a virtually unrestricted right to use violence and, when necessary, lethal means to bring certain types of situations under control' (Klockars, 1988). Deep down, this offends core values cherished in Western societies, yet at the same time this situation is unavoidable and unchangeable. Even democracies need to resort to violence from time to time. Thus, democracies have a need for the monopoly of violence and thus for the police. This is a necessary paradox that needs some degree of comforting and wrapping up in narratives called 'circumlocutions' by Bittner and taken a step further by Klockars.

In order to reconcile itself with an institution whose means are irreconcilably offensive to it, society must cloak that institution with signs, symbols and images that effectively conceal, mystify and legitimate actions (Klockars, 1988). The police are an institution that is constantly being 'wrapped up' in this way (Bittner, 1970; Klockars, 1988). The 'irreconcilably offensive' nature of policing refers to the monopoly of force the police represents and at times exercises. The core capacity to use force, according to Reiner, underlies not only the diversity of problems in policing but also the means of policing. 'This does not mean that the police typically (or even often) use coercion or force to accomplish the resolution of the troubles they deal with. The craft of effective policing is to use the background possibility of legitimate coercion so skilfully that it never needs to be foregrounded' (Reiner, 1992). Reiner arrives at this conclusion on the basis of observational police studies conducted from the 1960s onwards. His argument follows the line of reasoning presented in the chapter entitled 'Demystifying the police'.

According to Bittner (1970), we must arrive at a favourable or at least acceptable form of judgement about an activity that, in its very conception, is opposed to the ethos of the polity that authorises it. Is it not well nigh inevitable that this mandate be concealed in circumlocution? The definition of policing as 'to make available a group of persons with a virtually unrestricted right to use violent and, when necessary, lethal means to bring certain types of situations under control' resonates with much theoretical and empirical research into policing.

According to Ericson, real police work is not crime-related in the sense in which policing is represented and perceived in the media, the popular culture and in many books. This popular view 'has remarkable currency, given that the public police actually spend a tiny fraction of their time dealing with crime or something that could potentially be made into a crime' (Ericson, 1982). The essence of public policing is 'reproducing order', according to Ericson. Policing involves a wide range of nonrepressive strategies dealing with a variety of behaviour. Certain types of situations must be brought under control: making the road safe for traffic after a car crash involving 14 automobiles, the security of Schiphol Airport or Heathrow Airport after a terrorist threat, or separating husband and wife after a call of domestic violence, to name but a few examples.

Day-to-day policing is not about crime or services rendered to the public but about reproducing order in social interactions. Reproducing order in many instances is done by means of the threat of violence and/or the use of violence, with examples varying from attempts to end a pub brawl, arrests made by specialised SWAT teams or the use of military-style order maintenance units during large-scale public events. Other illustrations include the 1984 miners' strike in the United Kingdom and, more recently, the large-scale deployment of riot police to patrol Seattle and Geneva during G7 summits.

Public policing on a local level essentially means a 24/7 task dealing with 'the asshole – creep, bigmouth, bastard, animal, mope, rough, jerk-off, clown, scumbag, wise guy, phoney, idiot, shithead, bum, fool or any of a number of anatomical, oral or incestuous terms – a part of every policeman's world' (Van Maanen, 1978). The 'asshole' is policed by the threat of violence or removed (with legitimate violence) from the location.[3] Reproducing order has very little to do with the rhetoric of building community relations. Policing in this respect is not about talking with 'the public' but with intervention.

Conventional wisdom equates police work with crime work: a myth perpetually reinforced by the police themselves, by moral entrepreneurs, politicians and some academics, and of course by the media and popular culture images in movies, television series and novels (Reiner, 1992). A sound – comparative and cross-cultural – empirical basis exists for the primary noncrime-related character of everyday policing.

Patrol police work is not primarily or essentially about crime prevention or law enforcement (Kelling et al., 1974; Wilson and Boland, 1978; Chan and Ericson, 1981; Ericson 1982). In fact, very little of the work of patrol officers has to do with crime. British, U.S. and Dutch research has consistently shown that not more than 25 per cent of all the calls to police are about crime; more often the figure is 15 to 20 per cent (Bayley, 1994). Moreover, what is initially reported by the public as crime often turns out to be no criminal matter at all. In addition, most of the genuine crime the police are called upon to handle is minor. And crimes that the general public tend to associate policing with, such as homicide, aggravated assault, robbery and forcible rape, in fact form a mere fraction of policing reality. In 1990, violent crimes accounted for approximately 1 per cent of all reported crime in Australia, 9 per cent in Canada, 5 per cent in England and Wales and 1 per cent in Japan. Policing is not about crime control but about restoring order and providing general assistance: 'the function of the police is to stop something that ought not to be happening and about which someone had better do something now' (Bittner, 1970).

Policing is strikingly similar around the world if we compare organisational assignments. Among the forces studied, about 60 per cent of police personnel patrol and respond to requests for service, 15 per cent investigate crime, 9 per cent regulate traffic and 9 per cent administer. Because most crime suspects cannot be identified readily, most crimes go unsolved. Only 22 per cent of the most serious crimes in the United States are solved, 35 per cent in England and Wales, 45 per cent in Canada and 30 per cent in Australia (Bayley, 1994).

A more recent illuminating perspective to illustrate the relative impact of policing on actual levels of crime comes not from police studies or criminology but from economics. In 2003, Steven Levitt received the John Bates Clark Medal, awarded every two years to the best American economist under the age of 40. Levitt claims that he does not have much knowledge of economics and that he looks at things not as an academic but as a curious explorer, or perhaps rather as a documentary maker, a forensic scientist or a bookkeeper. The *New York Times* profiled Levitt in 2003 and received many comments reacting to the unconventional way of thinking he demonstrated.

Levitt's underlying rationale is his deep-rooted conviction that modern life is quirky, complicated, in many ways corrupt and therefore almost unfathomable. In a way, he is also 'struggling' with many fictional (academic) narratives and real life, the things happening on the ground far away from the Ivory Towers of 'regular science'. If we ask the right questions, modern life (and science) is even more intriguing than we can imagine. Levitt is fascinated by the term *conventional wisdom*, which was coined by Kenneth Galbraith to describe certain ideas or explanations that are generally accepted as true by the public. However, conventional wisdom is not necessarily true. Conventional wisdom is also often seen as an obstacle to introducing new theories, explanations and so as an obstacle that must be overcome by such revisionism. This is to say, that despite new information to the contrary, conventional wisdom has a property analogous to inertia, a momentum that opposes the introduction of contrary belief, sometimes to the point of absurd denial of the new information set by persons strongly holding an outdated (conventional wisdom) view. This inertia is due to conventional wisdom being made of ideas that are convenient, appealing and deeply assumed by members of the public who hang on to them even as they grow outdated. The unavoidable outcome is that these ideas will eventually completely fail to match reality, and so conventional wisdom will be violently shaken until it stops conflicting with reality so blatantly.

This is exactly what Levitt does in *Freakonomics* (Levitt and Dubner, 2005). One of the questions raised is this: "why do drug dealers live with their mothers?" In a fascinating argumentation, using empirical facts and figures from a variety of disciplines, the authors argue that most of the drug dealers lead a marginal existence, barely making enough money to live a decent life and that they therefore have to live with their mothers. Conventional wisdom equates drug dealers with the high life. Reality has them going shopping for their mothers.

Levitt and his coauthors, fascinated as they are with crime issues and challenging conventional wisdom in this field, also raise the following question: "where have all the criminals gone?" In New York City, crime rates began to go down in the early 1990s. This happened so fast that it took everyone, including the self-proclaimed specialists (mostly in criminology), by surprise. From everywhere, (new) specialists came to the intellectual rescue. In their book, Levitt and his colleagues present an overview of conventional wisdom explanations: innovative police strategies, more and longer prison sentences, changes on the crack market and other drug markets, tougher weapon laws, more police, a stronger economy and a variety of other explanations (more death penalties, buying back of weapons by the government and so on). All of these explanations were put to the test and rejected by means of solid arguments based on facts and figures.

Evidence of conventional wisdom being violently shaken is also offered in their analyses of the gradual legislation of abortion dating back to the late 1960s and early 1970s in American states such as New York, California, Washington, Alaska and Hawaii. In 1973, the Supreme Court ruled on legalising abortion in the Roe vs. Wade case. In 1974, 750,000 women underwent an abortion (equalling one abortion to every four children born). The legalisation of abortion mostly benefitted unmarried women, women below the age of 20 and women living in poverty. In many cases, all three factors were involved. In 1980, the number of abortions amounted to 1.6 million. Levitt and his colleagues argue that if these women had not had an abortion, 50 per cent of the children would probably have lived in poverty and 60 per cent would probably have grown up without one parent: two factors contributing to the criminal careers of young people living in the inner cities. In the early 1990s, crime rates started dropping. The first generation of children born after Roe vs. Wade had entered their late teens, early twenties: the age at which young men usually get involved in crime. Legalised abortions lead to fewer unwanted births; unwanted births lead to more crime. Ergo: legalised abortion leads to less crime.

Levitt and his fellows show that states with the highest abortion rates in the early 1970s demonstrated the strongest decline in crime rates in the early 1990s. Also, in states with lower abortion rates, the decline in crime rates was less strong. New York State was one of the first states to legalise abortion and demonstrated a high abortion rate as well as a sharp decline in crime in the 1990s.

Circumlocutions and community policing

The term *community* in community policing implies some form of reciprocity between the community and the police. Policing in 'community policing' carries with it the strong implicit and explicit presumptions that crime control will be enhanced and will become more efficient and effective if the community is more involved in policing. Reciprocity is assumed to lead to less crime and some of its connotations have become part of the vocabulary used in reassurance policing.

Klockars deconstructs the reciprocity argument. Community policing and especially the reciprocal mechanism are to a large extent a 'mystification'. To make his argument, he criticises *The New Blue Line* (Skolnick and Bayley, 1986) that, in his view, is too 'uniformly cheerful about the (community policing) movement and wholly without critical reservations' (Klockars, 1988).

Why does Klockars talk about 'mystification'? First, '*the* community' does not exist. The notion 'implies a group of people with a common history, common beliefs and understandings, a sense of themselves as "us" and "outsiders" as "them", and often, but not always, a shared territory' (Klockars, 1988). This is a strong argument. I am convinced that police research is in dire need of much more differentiation. Too often, we talk and write about '*the* police' and '*the* citizens' as single, uniform groups – which they are not.

The inner cities of Birmingham, Amsterdam, Brooklyn North and London are 'communities' divided along ethnic, religious, cultural and socioeconomic power lines. These inner-city communities are fragmented in many ways. Social stratification is highly visible: beggars find themselves next to SUVs and the middles classes hire Polish working-class people for housecleaning jobs and painting while the yuppies fly down to Ibiza and back again. In between, we find different youth cultures rocking, hip-hopping and breakdancing their way into maturity. Klockars poses the basic – and in some ways troublesome – questions: 'Just what is it that the community policing movement has chosen to police in their name?' What part(s) of the community does community policing actually relate to? Next, he climbs down the hierarchical lines and formulates the argument that police officers who actually do the work in these inner cities 'see themselves policing people and incidents, perhaps "corners", or "houses", a "park" or a "street"' (Klockars, 1988). The notion of a 'community' is far too abstract to have any meaning for individual police officers who are dealing with incidents and reproduce order (Kelling et al., 1974; Wilson and Bolland, 1978; Chan and Ericson, 1981; Ericson, 1982; Reiner, 1992, 2002).[4]

On top of factional policing, layers of fictional policing are placed with the help of words, signs, metaphors, symbols and rituals that cloud policing on the ground. Klockars argues that community policing becomes a 'rhetorical device for high-command-rank police officers to speak to organizations or groups in areas that are at once, geographically, too large to be policed and, politically, too large to be ignored'.

A second reason why Klockars talks about 'mystification' is because policing in 'community policing' has strong connotations with crime fighting or crime control. Community policing – as did reassurance policing more recently – has come in line with the expectation that it will reduce crime. Again, Klockars deconstructs this argument. 'Despite the fact that for the past 50 years the police have been promoting themselves as crime fighters, devoting enormous resources to the effort, taking credit for drops in the crime rate and criticism for rises in it, the best evidence to date is that no matter what they do they can only make marginal differences in it'.[5]

Fijnaut and his colleagues (1985) formulate the same argument in examining research on the effects of policing on crime rates. The community policing movement incorporates these connotations, but also references to the preventive aspects of the strategy and the supposed coproduction aspect of working with communities as a 'semantic' construction, according to Klockars. In terms of Bittner, this is an example of circumlocution. Not only have some police researchers argued for realistic approaches to policing, but also this realism can sometimes be found within the police itself. In the 1980s, a number of Dutch chiefs of police challenged the underlying assumptions in the war on drugs and the consequences it had on manpower, resources and priorities. In the United Kingdom, former Chief of Police Newman of the Metropolitan may be cited as an example. 'It is important', Newman argues, 'that members of the public should have a realistic appreciation of what police can or cannot achieve (...) so too it is necessary that police officers' expectations (...) are shaped upon the reality of the present and not upon some imprecise aspiration of perfection based on either past or present fantasies' (Reiner, 1992).

A manic pace of change versus continuity

After the introduction of community policing in the United States during the 1980s, the United Kingdom 1990s and a number of Western European countries 1990s, the police now seem to be constantly introducing new strategies and operational tactics. New Public Management methods, programmes and accountability structures have been introduced. In the 1990s, a quality measurement tool (INK-model) was introduced in the Netherlands, and regional forces became the subject of evaluation studies by the Home Office. Ideas were introduced on intelligence-led policing and zero-tolerance and on financial investigations. The role of the police in environmental crime and intelligence-led policing was determined, as well as in nodal policing and more recently reassurance policing.

I will discuss this 'manic pace of change' by analysing the different phases through which these new concepts 'mature'. Next, I will probe into the matter more deeply and draw attention to *continuities* in policing. Much of today's factual policing still remains the same and has not changed significantly over the last 250 years. Neither the nature of day-to-day policing nor the problems dealt with by the rank and file have changed much. The distinction between fictional and factual policing enables us to distinguish *'two tales of policing'*: a narrative tale, using many written words, and a factual tale, in which police officers in the street are hardly influenced – or at least to a much smaller extent than the change narratives seem to suggest – by the these written words, but in which they still use their oral and manual capacities to reproduce order.

Change

Each of the 'new' concepts follows more or less the same pattern as the others. In the first phase, 'a buzz' emerges in which enthusiastic police professionals share their experiences and impressions gained during visits to the police in Kent (intelligence-led policing) or attending "breaking ball" (Compstat) meetings at Police Plaza number 1 in New York City. Or they become interested in specific topics such as leadership, counterterrorism, fraud or new management techniques after attending conferences, listening to lectures or reading a book. Many of the new ideas come from abroad. Punch (2006) calls this 'policy transfers': police officials from different Dutch regional forces, sometimes accompanied by government officials and/or public prosecutors, travel around the globe and constantly pick up numerous new trends and concepts. In the second phase, initial consolidation takes place. The new concept is used in public speeches, people write articles about it in different police magazines and some police leaders start experimenting with a new concept.

In both phases, there seems to be genuine interest in and true attachment to the new concept or idea. A small number of police officers involved generate a lot of energy and seem to be convinced that this new concept can and must be introduced and implemented in Dutch policing. No proper plan or strategy would seem to be involved, and I would argue that the real trigger in these two phases is the intrinsic value individual officers attach to the concept. In some ways, these officers may be termed 'moral' policy entrepreneurs who at a certain point in time strongly believe in the new innovation. As we all know, a central feature of police culture is the sense of mission shared by police officers. In embracing a new concept or strategy, this sense of mission seems to become part of the drive to take the concept/strategy to the next level.

In the first two phases, a relatively small circle of police officers is involved. They share information and experiences and seem to be reinforcing each other in the value and necessity of the new concept. They also use the same words, signs and idioms. This process creates strong bonds among them and is useful to communicate the concept to a wider (police) audience. What is striking, however, is the fact that no clear-cut and accepted definition exists of what 'community policing', 'broken window', intelligence-led policing, leadership or reassurance policing exactly is, or means, and what its function is or could be.

In phase three, wider circles of acceptance are to be found, and in many cases, the policy entrepreneurs are successful. The new concept or strategy becomes *salonfähig* (presentable) within the police and in government circles. The possible advantages for the effectiveness or greater legitimacy of policing related to the new concept thus become part of the narrative. Because uniform definitions remain lacking, the attractiveness and 'selling quality' at this stage seem to lie more in the emotional appeal and/or the informal leadership qualities of the (police) officials involved. For instance, if a high-ranking police or government official embraces a new concept and starts talking about it, greater credibility is attained.

In this particular phase, 'alliances' are created between public officials and the small group of 'moral entrepreneurs'. These entrepreneurs can be found in policy circles, on police management levels, in the consultancy business and in academic police research. Different objectives formulated by different groups of people are brought together and people seek – and negotiate – new projects (conferences, articles, training programmes and [evaluation] research). The various different objectives could be political – when the new concept fits into current or planned policy programmes - or they could be of a bureaucratic nature. For instance, policy advisors working for the Ministry of Interior, the Justice Department or regional forces may see opportunities for new projects or policy programmes. I firmly believe that the bureaucratic internal dynamics at work in putting new concepts and strategies on the agenda have so far been grossly overlooked and neglected in research.

Consultants have financial interests and academic researchers combine their intellectual interests with funding interests to set up new research projects. In some ways, co-optation takes place and the small group of police officials – the moral entrepreneurs – become part of a wider network of officials who together, but for different reasons, nourish a growing interest in pursuing this new path of introducing performance and quality measurement systems, intelligence-led policing, leadership programmes, nodal policing and, more recently, reassurance policing.

In phase four, reification takes place on account of the growing budgets that are used for the funding of programmes, seminars, conferences and foreign trips to get access to specialists and other experienced insiders. Reification refers to the process in which new concepts and strategies – still somewhat abstract in nature – become fixed realities. The people involved do not really question any of the underlying political, theoretical or policy assumptions or the added value to policing itself. Assumptions and added value seem to be taken for granted – so let's roll out the new concept.

What is fascinating in this phase is the fact that a number of these concepts went through all of these stages at the same time (1995–2007) but independent of each other. Although community policing and reassurance policing, or intelligence-led policing and "signal crime", or "broken window" and "tegenhouden" (stopping crime in its early stages) basically share the same policing fundamentals (getting the right information in time to act in such a way that problems can be handled), only a narrow interface exists between the different change programmes. The different concepts and strategies seem to have their own dynamics, narratives and interests. Hardly any communication takes place between the different 'change silos'.

Phase five is the decisive phase in which the concepts and strategies are implemented in factual policing. After all, the proof of the pudding is in the eating, as the popular saying goes. Little research has been done on the actual integration into police culture and operations. In 2005, I carried out a research project for the Dutch Police Academy on the effects of management contracts between the government and regional police forces specifying targets such as arrest rates for certain crimes. For the first time in a number of years, I was involved in fieldwork in five regional forces (ten districts), and I was impressed by the number of organisational changes. Compared with the early 1990s, I noticed a greater sense of direction, more involvement of leadership, a larger degree of transparency and greater accountability. The title of the ensuing book refers to these changes: *Operational Involvement* (Hoogenboom, 2006a). However, at the same time, I concluded that the pace of change – and the constant introduction of new changes – was such that questions could be raised with regard to the actual implementation on any substantial level. Of course, in a number of forces, successful implementation of a number of concepts has taken place so far. But between forces and even within forces I found clear differences. Thus, the basic question is this: does factual policing really change?

Continuity

Ponsaers and Enhus (2005) analyse three crises in Belgian policing. The first was triggered by the dramatic events in the Heizel football stadium where, during the European Cup final in 1985, 28 people died as a result of riots and the mismanagement exhibited by police leadership. The second crisis was triggered by a number of shootings at shopping malls in the 1980s. The perpetrators were never arrested and Belgian society was rocked by a public outcry not only on the perceived mismanagement by the judiciary and the police but also by discussions about a political cover-up. The third crisis involved the investigations related to the murder and sexual exploitation of a number of young girls.

All three crises led to public outrage, parliamentary enquiries and subsequently to reforms of the Belgian police structures, the rule of law and the educational system. As Reiner argues for the United Kingdom in the aftermath of the Scarman and Newman reports, the police system became the subject of 'cycles of reform'. Nevertheless – and the conclusion drawn by Ponsaers and Enhus is at once fascinating and bedevilling – in spite of these cycles of reform, neither the factual nature of police work nor the police culture have changed. In addition, Reiner points to the very gradual nature of factual changes.

The Ponsaers and Enhus and Reiner positions resonate with the position held by Bittner and Klockars: underneath all the changes, underneath the introduction of new strategies and tactics and underneath all the restructuring and reform, neither police work nor police culture actually change much. And, if changes are taking place, they are very gradual and will take many years to actually wield a large impact.

Continuities in policing can be explained in the context of what some of the classics in police research have indicated is the quintessential (political) function of the police: reproducing order. In his monumental history of Western policing from the seventeenth century onwards, Fijnaut (1979) agrees with Bayley on the political function of modern policing. The origins of modern policing and, subsequently, every major structural police reorganisation find their rationale in *la raison d'etat*. In the transformation from feudalism to the nation state and as a result of political, social and economic unrest, the state needed a modern police force to reproduce order. This has been and still is the factional reality of policing.

Fijnaut argues that 'reorganizations of the police were never aimed at improving the fight against crime, or improving the way the police carries out assistance or even service to the public. Nor has traffic control ever been a trigger for police reforms or internal organizational issues'. Van Reenen (1979) analyses the historical dynamics in policing and also stresses the need to understand (reorganisations) in police structures and police practices in the context of political and social turmoil.

So, our story of change and continuity is in fact more complex. As Reiner (1992) argues, in public policing we find 'fictional' and 'factual' presentations of what policing is all about. Actually, although public policing develops through 'cycles of reform', there is – according to Reiner too – perhaps more continuity in policing than we might think. It is precisely this continuity that Bittner and Klockars describe in terms of the need and functions of signs, symbols and images that effectively conceal, mystify and legitimate actions. The police as an institution are "wrapped up" in narratives of crime fighting, crime control, prevention, community relations, reassurance and the like. These are fictional accounts of policing and not factual representations of policing. These fictional accounts do not so much represent reality but rather construct reality.

The narratives create the impression of action, of change, of movement, of innovation – while at the same time factual policing does not change much, or perhaps not at all. In fact, this is not a problem at all because the core function of policing is reproducing order. And this is still being done 24/7 on the factual level of policing. In talking to the rank and file during the research activities for *Operational Involvement*, the well-documented and analysed cynicism (Reiner, 1992; van de Torre, 1999) of the police culture still remained prominent. As one police officer with 25 years of experience on the job stated: 'What has changed in all these years? Nothing! I do what I have to in the same way'. Or to quote two police officers (male and female) "on the beat" in one of the more problematic neighbourhoods in Den Haag when I explained what I was researching: 'That's all a lot of crap'.

Updating Bittner and Klockars

The principal explanation Bittner and Klockars offer for the many symbols, signs and images that the police are 'wrapped up' in is the function it has in concealing the fact that deep down policing is about the exercise of force. They believe this creates a moral dilemma in society, and hence the need for fictional policing accounts.

Like Klockars, who analysed community policing from this perspective, I wish to extend this perspective to other new policing concepts and strategies as well. It is my opinion that much of the factual realities of policing are constant over time – or at least much more constant than all the change narratives seem to imply. Although different 'mods and fads' of course have an effect on policing and the police organisation, I feel that these effects are exaggerated. So, we are facing 'a Grand Canyon' of much fictional policing on the one hand and factual continuities on the other.

The remaining – fascinating – question is this: what is the explanation? Although I believe that Bittner's and Klockars's explanation is valid, it is at the same time very broad and general (societal uneasiness with the exercise of force). I will demonstrate that this societal need is intertwined with other related phenomena:

- The 'streetwise' character of police leaders in dealing with conflicting political, (inter)organisational and public demands;
- Traits of the police culture, especially its conservative nature and;
- The semi-autonomous factual realities of the police as a frontline organisation with relatively many discretionary powers.

Keeping up appearances and playing the game

Police leaders, too, are in dire need of narratives full of rhetoric, symbolism and images to create the impression of constant action and adaptation to different needs in their attempts to retain autonomy.

This is one of the conclusions formulated in *Progress or Raindance? Evaluation of the Planning and Control Cycle of Dutch Policing* (in 't Veld et al., 2002). In 1999, the Dutch government created a national policy plan with a set of fixed priorities that the 25 regional forces had to 'translate' into their respective organisations and operations. *Progress or Rain dance* chronicles this process.

In 't Veld and his fellow authors describe the implementation as a ritual in which all participants 'obeyed' the rules of the bureaucratic process. Government officials, police leaders, public prosecutors and mayors, in short all the actors involved, 'played the game'. They performed necessary tasks and duties (consultation, drafting plans, monitoring progress and carrying out evaluation studies). Hardly any debate – let alone any heated debate – took place on the premises and/or consequences related to the planning and control cycle. Moreover, barely any relationship could be discerned between regional plans and their operational consequences as perceived on the shop floor. In the terms used by Reiner, we may speak of 'fictional' rather than factual police narratives.

Underneath the language of change (the introduction for the first time in history of a national mechanism to define police priorities on regional and local levels), in 't Veld et al. lay bare what they call "a black hole" in which police leaders attach hardly any meaning at all to the planning and control cycle. Yet, at the same time, they loyally and constructively produce all the necessary documents, attend necessary meetings and give necessary presentations – internally as well as externally.

Three explanations are put forward to address this phenomenon. First, the dominant position held by the police may be mentioned here, both in national and regional policy networks. This is especially relevant in the context of information on crime. Many actors depend on the police for crime statistics, crime analyses and other operational information on crime.

Second, the highly developed degree of sensitivity demonstrated by police leaders serves as an example with respect to the demands, wants and needs facing the various different actors involved. In time, each of these actors will be 'served', but from time to time the police say 'no' to requests with reference to other priorities as formulated by other actors. Because of the relative monopoly on crime information, this is rather easily done.

Finally, these explanations come together in what in 't Veld et al. call the capacity for 'immunisation' exhibited by the police. This term refers to the choice of words, phrases and idiom that the police use and that are carefully chosen to be in alignment with those expressed by the (national) authorities. In doing so, regional police forces create the suggestion that the regional planning and control cycle is in line with the national goals and priorities.

In strategically using and applying these three factors, the police are able to balance different demands and at the same time retain its autonomy. In 't Veld et al. conceptualise this process in terms of 'ritualisation', because everyone involved 'plays the game' and does not use the instrument in practice. Here, we witness a perfect example of the intermingling of fictional and factual realities. Although Bittner and Klockars could argue here that this 'immunisation' is no problem at all, because the ritual of planning and control fits their analyses, I believe that police leaders primarily wish to retain their relative autonomy.

Of course, high transaction costs are involved in 'keeping up appearances'. Investments must be made in manpower, time, project budgets and setting up consultation structures – not to mention in hiring consultants and academic researchers to develop plans and later evaluate the planning and control cycle. The authors offer the following quotation at the beginning of their report: 'if the elite in control is favored by preserving the status quo they will foster inactivism by engaging in all sorts of ritualistic behaviour like rain dancing' (in't Veld, 2002).

Cop culture

To understand continuity in policing, we must also incorporate cultural dimensions: 'Cop culture is crucial to an analysis of what they do' (Reiner, 1992). One of the characteristics mentioned – next to a sense of mission, pragmatism, action orientation, cynicism/pessimism, isolation and solidarity, among others – is conservatism: both political and moral. But I would hazard a guess that, in all these cultural dimensions, individually and in combination, no truly fertile ground exists for real reforms and large-scale innovations. Cop culture is incident and action driven and directed to reproducing order. This primary function has not changed, nor has the culture in which it is exercised.

How to incorporate the rank and file?

It is possible to use Loader's 'tale of two police forces' for the distinction between 'management and street cops', too. Much of the narratives of change, different authors argue, have meaning in a relatively small circle of police managers and different 'moral entrepreneurs'. In the final analysis, following Klockars and in t'Veld et al., factual policing remains largely unaffected and, in my view, part of the explanation also lies in the fact that the police itself incorporates two realities: 'The problem which bedevilled so many previous innovations: how to incorporate the rank and file' (Reiner, 1992).

Chan (1996), in discussing possibilities to change police culture, makes a distinction between the formal structural context of policing and police cultural practice. Changes in the formal context (rules and regulations, but in our case new concepts and strategies) 'inevitably alter the way the game is played (...) but the resulting practice may or may not be substantially or even discernibly changed' (Chan, 1996). Chan uses the illustrative metaphor of sports. If the rules of the game are changed or the physical markings of the field, Johan Cruyff will still play football like he always did. The game itself, the techniques and tactics do not fundamentally change. 'Experienced players', Chan argues, 'may be able to adjust quickly to the new rules and hence show no sign of changing their performance'.

The manic pace of change and continuities

In a recent study of citation practices in British criminology, Paul Rock (2005) demonstrated the prevalence of what he calls "chronocentrism" – the doctrine that what is currently adhered to must somehow be superior to what went on before, and that ideas, scholars and scholarship inevitably become stale and discredited over time.

Continuities in policing are neglected by most of the police scholars as well as by prominent figures in policy circles or the general public. In the classic movie *Finding Nemo*, the adorable little fish Dory offers her guidance in helping to find Nemo. Shortly after this offer, she shakes her head, turns to Nemo's father and asks: "Who are you, where are we going"? It turns out that her short-term memory is affected. I have used the story here to illustrate the lack of institutional memory in law enforcement and regulation (Hoogenboom, Bakker and Pheiffer, 2006).

Neither in politics, the corridors of bureaucratic power, nor in the academic community can a deep and thorough knowledge of the classics be found. For more than 20 years, I have conducted research on policing, and during this period, 'new' questions pop up every five or six years and new policy makers enthusiastically start 'new' dossiers. Sometimes I am invited to offer advice, and I am often struck by the lack of basic knowledge on recent policing history and even by the lack of well-established and long available knowledge – both in the Netherlands and abroad. A couple of years ago, with a slight touch of irony, I said I would honour a request for advice on one condition: before the interview, I intended to test the civil servant concerned on some of the classics, so that we would not have to waste much time and get straight to 'business'. I never heard from him again. In a culture like this, new concepts fall on fertile ground and the combination of the above-mentioned four explanations will in one way or another explain why fictional narratives are functional in many respects.

The undertow in policing (reproducing order) is clouded and mystified by fictional narratives of which reassurance policing is but the latest example. I agree with Jones and Newburn (2002) when they write: 'Much current criminology tends to exaggerate the degree of change, and underplay the extent of continuity, in seeking to explain the transformations taking place in contemporary policing systems'. Reiner, in his book review of Newburn's *Policing. Key Readings* (2005), uses the word *neophilia*, which is defined as a love of novelty and new things. A neophile is an individual who is unusually accepting of new things and excited by novelty. Many new concepts have been introduced in policing, and I observe a lot of love and excitement for newness, most recently in reassurance policing – as this volume proves. Still, I prefer some of the classics.

Community/reassurance policing: Part of larger and much more differentiated policing arrangements

Although rich in many ways, the empirical and theoretical body of knowledge on policing is at the same time limited. First, it is dominated by Anglo-Saxon perspectives and does not reflect policing developments in other parts of the world. In this respect, it is useful to differentiate to a larger extent between the contexts in which policing is taking place. For instance, we can differentiate between democracies, countries in transition, failed states and dictatorships. Policing in China and Burma or in Darfur differs from policing in Stockholm. In contextualising policing in this way, we can also make ourselves more sensitive to the core function of policing as discussed earlier.

Second, our body of knowledge in fact concerns a small part of policing. During the past 25 years, much research has been done and considerable theoretical progress has been made, as the excellent readers edited by Newburn (2003a, 2005) show. However, much of the police research tradition is limited to the most visible aspects of policing: foot patrols, motorised patrols and all sorts of issues related to 'community policing' (relationship with citizens, street-level aspects, policing styles and so on). The blue-coated worker may dominate research, but the areas that remain under-researched include the factual levels of policing in criminal investigation, riot control, specialised observation and arrest teams, infiltration and the whole gamut of criminal and political intelligence work or traffic control, and police capacity involved in VIP protection, to name but a few. In some ways, we have become 'blinded by the light'. The overall result in the eyes of many (researchers, the general public) is that policing equals patrol, community policing and, more recently, reassurance policing.

Five levels of policing

Factual policing takes place on five different levels. On the first, policing is all about 'blue-coated workers' involved in patrol, surveillance and the different forms of 'community policing'. But in writing so much about 'community policing' – and thus creating and sustaining a narrative answering Bittner and Klockars's argument – one tends to forget that the actual manpower active in community policing is much more limited than suggested. For instance, 24/7 shifts in Dutch police districts are primarily organised around reactive patrolling by car and on the streets. Their function is called 'noodhulp' in Dutch (emergency response or addressing calls for help). Community police officers are organized within a separate unit and basically work day shifts. Underneath the community policing narrative, factual policing – even on the first and most visible level – does not come close to the images created by the overwhelmingly large body of literature focused on 'community policing'[6] The argument becomes even stronger if we include other organisational levels of policing:

- Traffic control, criminal investigation departments (and criminal intelligence), crowd control (riot units), environmental crime units and digital crime units on the regional level;
- Surveillance and arrest teams on the interregional levels, but also interregional investigative teams and interregional riot-unit structures;
- Centralised criminal intelligence service on the national level, national intervention teams (combining police and military specialists in armed combat) and the national investigation organisation as well as the Dutch Military Police (grown from 2,200 staff in 1993 to 6,500 in 2007) and finally;
- The transnational organisation units and processes for cross-border cooperation, rogatory commissions, working with liaisons and Interpol, Europol, Eurojust and so on.

'Community policing' is but one facet of differentiated, multilevel and multifaceted policing. There are numerous Dutch organisational units, ranging from the regional police force level to the national level, that incorporate activities and responsibilities varying from investigation, infiltration and criminal intelligence to national crisis organisations and specialised units for the placement of electronic bugs or the specialised force for diplomatic protection. Three observations are relevant here.

First, on the different levels, many of the policing tasks mentioned above involve tasks that some of the researchers have included in what they consider to be the core task of policing: reproducing order – if necessary, with (the threat of) violence. The monopoly of force, according to many and starting with Max Weber on the very essence of the state, is organised on these levels. Hardly any of the underlying assumptions of 'community policing' or 'reassurance policing' (citizen involvement, reassurance gap) is applicable here. A specialised arrest team is trained to take someone out of the public domain as swiftly as possible using a minimum of force, but it will kill the target if he or she uses firearms. Many of the organisational units mentioned in the addendum and the tasks they perform do not fit the community policing ideology, yet they are an essential and integral part of policing.

Second, manpower, budgets, powers, career perspectives and training capacities involved in all these levels are becoming increasingly important and growing. Police research is currently researching a part of policing that is actually in 'decline'. We seem to be missing these transformations in policing by clinging to the 'safe' narratives of community policing and other similar concepts.

Third, in the context of ongoing 'militarisation' and 'securitisation' of policing (Bowling and Newburn, 2007), considerable attention is being given to 'community policing' and 'reassurance policing' – seemingly ignoring the broader picture of factual policing.

3
Blurring Boundaries and the Unbearable Lightness of Criminological Discourse

Introduction

After mapping the political function of policing and the dynamics within the police system itself and the way policing is carried out, I will from now on turn my attention to developments taking place outside the criminal justice system and public policing. This I will do for two reasons. First, I am looking for undertows in policing; more specifically, I will be analysing 'policing' taking place 'outside' the police. But second, and relevant for my 'governance of policing and security' perspective, I will explore how this all relates to public policing, what blurring is taking place and how this can be explained from the theoretical points being made in the first two chapters.

Autobiographical notes

It was in the mid-eighties when I took my first steps in the domain of police studies research. I published work on special investigation services (1986), private security (1987) and private investigators (1988). And it was no mere interest that I pursued. I was simply fascinated by the limited character of the research topic traditionally featured in police studies and criminology: the criminal apparatus. In my PhD dissertation, *The Police Complex: On the Cooperation between the Police, Special Investigation Services and Private Investigation* (1994), I pointed out two contradictory processes.

First, I addressed the growing fragmentation of the police function, increasingly often brought about by a large number of (semi-)public organisations (inspections, special investigation services and supervisors) and private organisations. Second, I pointed out the political desire to establish greater coherence between the various organisations that execute the policing function. A particular inspiration for the latter was the prediction formulated by Fijnaut (1985) in which he states that, in the future, we will witness the creation of a 'nationally integrated police complex of special and private police around a differentiated regular police apparatus that encompasses the whole of social life'.

As a result, there is a scientific need to expand fundamentally our knowledge objects in the field of police studies, or more broadly, the whole of criminological research. Today, 15 years down the line, this need is more acutely felt not only as a result of the increasing internationalisation of police care, but also due to the increasing role of the army. Finally, we are currently making huge leaps in terms of technological developments. What is happening at the edges of the 'iron police system': which boundaries are blurring?

In this chapter, I will discuss the works of a number of authors who developed the intellectual basis for a more multiagency-oriented framework for policing and security. Core concepts include the fragmentation of the police function and blurring boundaries between police organisations.

The concept of blurring boundaries is subsequently applied to the traditional police system. My position is that, in the coming decade, the boundaries between the following will become increasingly vague:

- National and international policing;
- Civil and military policing;
- Public and private policing;
- Physical and digital (or technological) policing; and
- Criminal, financial, political and private intelligence.

Intellectual basis

For some time now, the daily practice of scientific activity has been characterised by a repetition of very much the same moves. Thomas Kuhn called this *normal science*. It is the core concept in his *Structures of Scientific Revolutions* (1962). Within any scientific discipline, there is an important degree of consensus about the research object, and within that framework there are a limited number of theoretical principles.

Kuhn speaks of paradigms. Most scientific research is carried out within the limits of these paradigms. New paths are not sought, let alone set foot upon. One does not challenge or stray from existing theoretical limits. Experiments in form, content, style or language are not encouraged. Empirical characteristics are interpreted within those paradigms that, in a certain period of time and/or among a generation of scientists, are accepted as the norm.

The object of police research and criminology is the state's criminal system and, particularly, public policing, the judiciary, the prison system and rehabilitation. Over the last 200 years, an impressive body of knowledge has been built up regarding this knowledge object in these scientific disciplines. However, this generally remains limited to the criminal system itself. It would be fair to talk of a criminal paradigm. This paradigm no longer suffices. The concepts of policing, enforcement and investigation are no longer exclusive to the standard police force. Conflict resolution by means of criminal law is just one of many instruments of social control.

Criminological discourse is unbearably light in its perspective, content, shape and neophilia. On the occasion of the twenty-fifth anniversary of the Dutch Association for Criminology (1999), I wrote an essay on the future of criminology entitled *On Old Folk and Things That Pass Away. Criminology in 2018* (Chapter 4 in this book). In the essay, I pointed out the development of knowledge on criminality within other disciplines: corporate ethics, architecture, the ICT world, forensic accountancy and so forth. According to Kuhn, paradigm shifts first occur when it appears that empirical insights can less and less often be explained by means of existing theoretical thought frameworks. Kuhn calls these anomalies. It is only when these anomalies occur for longer periods of time that a scientific revolution can occur. Internationalisation, militarisation, privatisation and the development of modern technology are virtually unheard of in modern criminological theory formation, let alone in empirical research. There are as yet an insufficient number of anomalies.

In his *L'orde de discourse* (The order of speaking), Michel Foucault goes a step further. He strongly emphasises – in powerful, literary language – the political dimension of scientific activities. A power struggle is taking place. The scientific ideal of seeking knowledge for the sake of knowledge is naïve. Scientific thought, speech and writing are subject to disciplinary powers. Foucault argues his point with the help of highly evocative language ('muzzling'). Superb. In my PhD dissertation, I used a slightly longer quotation: 'There is a sort of muffled fear of those events, those thoughts expressed en masse, the appearance of all those expressions of all that make it violent, discontinuous, quarrelsome, disorderly, and risky. Of the incessant, powerfully chaotic buzzing of the discourse'. There must be order – also among enlightened scientists.

A few years ago, at a conference on the privatisation of security, I stated that private security organisations would soon be bearing arms. I had just returned from the Caribbean where, in a city such as Caracas, there is seemingly no distinction to be seen on the streets between private security and the regular police. Everyone is armed. The same holds true for private security in southern European countries. The 'reward' for my comment was a suppressed but indignant buzzing from some of the participants around the table – and certainly in the audience.

I recently took part in a closed meeting with private and public functionaries involved in tackling credit card fraud. The meeting was held at the head office of a credit card company. I pointed out the symbolism of the meeting: more than a hundred people had gathered – of which approximately 75 were law enforcement officers and public prosecutors next to private security people – all present in the catacombs of a financial institution. I asked the (slightly provocative) question: who is in charge here when it comes to tackling white-collar crime? The meeting was opened by the managing director of a multinational company, not by the chairman of the College of Attorney Generals nor by a chief of police. The environment differed markedly in terms of luxury and treatment from that of the public prosecutor's house in Utrecht.

The existing paradigm leaves no room for extensive privatisation of the police function. As early as 1987, Shearing and Stenning wrote that it is sometimes a shock for public officials to see just how great the role of security companies has become, 'yet that shock is minimized and redefined in terms of the existing paradigm': the security market is our 'junior partner'. The same seems to be true for the expanding role of the army, certainly after 9/11.

This type of 'incessant, powerfully chaotic buzzing (critique, contrary thought, discussion) is therefore in direct opposition to established thought and therefore suppressed': it is 'muzzled' according to Foucault. Foucault is even more ruthless than Kuhn in his analysis of scientific censure. The acceptance of articles in professional literature, submitted research proposals, funding for research and job appointments in a scientific community are dictated by established interests, which in turn are linked to unyielding paradigms. Editors of reputable normal science journals screen for politically correct articles, and appointments of new staff and professors take place on the basis of the level of respect one has for established frames of thought (and interests).

Foucault, however, fundamentally breaks away from the criminological paradigm. The criminal system is just one of the many 'hundreds of minor theatres of punishment' in our society. Behavioural control takes place in the 'front and back yards of the criminal justice system'. Foucault calls this the 'disciplinary power'. This he localises in numerous institutions: the workplace, bureaucracy, the army, even in the school system – and certainly in scientific activity. There shall be order!

In his *Visions of Social Control*, Stanley Cohen (1985) consistently uses the concept of 'de-institutionalization'. In addition to changes in the criminal justice system, there is an increase in social control. Cohen, influenced by Foucault, points to psychiatric care workers, welfare workers, youth social workers, pedagogues and psychologists 'forcing their way' into the family: policing the family. On the basis of observations, checks and tests using various diagnostic instruments, people are assessed, classified and grouped. Cohen also points out the increase in the number of alternative punishments (community service), half-open institutions and cases involving electronic house arrest. He also notes the increasing role of the private security industry.

The social control net is being cast over ever-growing areas in society, and the mesh is getting finer and finer. Increasing numbers of institutions and officials are active at the junctions of these social control networks. Cohen refers to this phenomenon as penetration. The process generally takes place under the guise of good intentions. Stated objectives include prevention issues, the treatment and reintegration of citizens with mental complaints, difficult students, rowdy children, rule-breaking employees and finally criminals. More recently, Jonathan Simon (2007) writes from the same perspective in his *Governing Through Crime. How the War on Crime Transformed American Democracy and Created a Culture of Fear.* Crime has now become a significant strategic issue. Across all kinds of institutional settings, people are seen as acting legitimately when they act to prevent crimes. Technologies, discourses and metaphors of crime and criminal justice have become more visible features of all kinds of institutions, where they easily gravitate into new opportunities for governance. Policing and security discourses and practices become more and more integrated into domestic relations, education and the workplace.

The police and the judiciary are no longer the dominant institution (or governmental monopoly) responsible for behavioural regulation and the administration of punishment. The major difference between Foucault and Cohen on the one hand and the criminal law paradigm on the other hand lies in the endless variety of proactive techniques available. Behavioural steering occurs 'in the front and back yards of the criminal justice system' where criminal justice plays but a minor role, although society at large, criminal justice policy makers and functionaries within the criminal justice system still cling to the notion of a monopoly on policing, justice and the penal system.

Cohen continues to point out the ongoing 'blurring of boundaries'. Police and the judiciary have become enmeshed in this wide array of welfare workers, social workers, private security staff and alternative techniques. It is a case of mutual influence. For the benefit of their 'clients', referrals are organised, joint projects initiated and information exchanged.

The question that follows asks what this conception of blurring boundaries means in practice for the police system and the police function. Before we can offer any satisfactory answers, let us first consider the traditional police system.

Blurring boundaries

In the first two chapters, the political function and the historical dynamics stemming from this were discussed. In the rest of the book, I'm looking into the undertows of 'the governance of policing and security'. For me a central concept is ' blurring of boundaries'. Police researchers and criminologists not only study a public policing fictional reality (Chapter 2), but they also are structurally neglecting the factual reality of the governance of policing and security in which lines are blurring.

National/international perspectives

In his book *Policing the World* (1989), Anderson points to the fact that the police and the judiciary are by definition bound to a national, united state. An important component of a state's legitimacy is the governmental monopoly with regard to physical violence. Anderson argues that, as a result of proliferation in international cooperative associations between the various police areas, national sovereignty comes under threat. Thus, a police and judiciary vacuum is created between national and international or even global levels that is 'far reaching, (and) not widely understood'. Anderson wrote these prophetic words as early as 1989.

Cops across Borders is an impressive book on the internationalisation of public policing. In a fascinating description of developments, he shows how, since its independence in 1776, the United States' influence on police and justice systems around the world has grown. A long road has been travelled since the first liaisons with the Secret Service in Rome, the legal attachés of the FBI that are linked to embassies, the various training programmes for foreign police functionaries and multinational police organisations such as the Drug Enforcement Agency (DEA) and Customs. And what is more, the end is not yet in sight. In the current post-9/11 period, we are witnessing a further internationalisation of American services.

The two reference works mentioned above go back some time. A more recent publication is *Keizer in lompen. Politiesamenwerking in Europa* [Emperor in rags. Police cooperation in Europe]. All in all, the internationalisation of public policing to an important degree still remains a white spot in criminological research. What exactly do we know about cross-border police cooperation, of Europol, the international exchange of information, the multifaceted training activities in the former Eastern block and the role of the United States, to mention but a few issues? Research is still (too) limited and hampered by the national united state. In the light of the internationalisation of both (organised) crime and its control, this is greatly to be regretted.

Public/private perspectives

In the classical vision of the state (Weber, 1962), the government is granted authority (command and control) over policing. This is no longer the case today. It even remains an open question as to whether governments are still the primary caretakers of police care: an increasing number of nongovernmental parties have placed the responsibility for safety upon themselves, over which governments have no authority. The concepts of command and control that are embedded in the collective consciousness of criminal law experts, politicians and criminologists are 'only' meaningful for the state's criminal apparatus. Within the traditional paradigm, one speaks of command and control over the public policing. But with the fragmentation of the police function, an ongoing and simultaneous fragmentation of command may be witnessed (Bayley and Shearing, 2001).

The new, fragmented police function is currently executed under the auspices of five authorities and controllers.

Economic authorities

Multinationals often place their safety requirements with corporate security services (in-house security) or they use the security market ('contract security') for uniformed surveillance, security equipment and/or research. In addition, coalitions are being formed along geographical boundaries (shopping streets, company premises) and functional boundaries (banks, petrol stations, jewellers, bars and cab drivers, for example) within which companies or security officers work together to safeguard joint interests. In parallel, there has of old been an illegal security system in which organised crime organises its own security. Examples include the United States (Mafia), Russia and Japan (Yakuza).

Residential authorities

Residential authorities (residential and shopping complexes) may close themselves off from the public space by means of uniformed guards and technology ('gated communities'). One variety here is a coalition between residents of a residential area who jointly sign a contract with a security firm for surveillance. Neighbourhoods may also set up advisory councils to address security issues.

Cultural authorities

Cultural authorities may communicate joint values, ideologies or religious conceptions and organise their own (physical) security. A classic example is the Vatican, which not only has its own security service (Swiss Guard), but also its own professional information service. In the United States, the Nation of Islam has its own marshals, as do Islamic and Jewish groups in Europe.

Individual authorities

Individuals may hire (personal) security for 24/7 surveillance or for certain occasions only. The Rolling Stones have their own security service, and captains of industry employ bodyguards. I had a wonderful experience in de Kuip (a Dutch football stadium) during a concert by Jagger and his band. Although I had a backstage ticket with which policemen and private security guards allowed me to go just about everywhere, the police and I were nevertheless refused access to the band's 'inner sanctum' by their security people. There are, simply speaking, limits in trying to reach public figures: not only in de Kuip and not only for pop musicians, but in major sections of today's society.

Government authorities

Government authorities have command and control with respect to public police care, but also contribute greatly to its fragmentation by

- Stimulating the personal responsibility of citizens and companies (Report Society and Criminality, 1985, and all ensuing policy reports);
- Employing 'contract security' for former public police tasks such as guarding and transporting detainees, guarding police and judiciary buildings, or parking control;
- PPS-constructions in which private parties cooperate with the public police;
- Permitting police officers to perform security tasks off-duty;
- Passing on police costs and
- Allowing an increasing number of civilian public servants to perform tasks within the police organisation ('civilization of the governmental monopoly') related to traffic regulation, recording reports, researching traffic incidents and, for example, providing information on prevention.

The restructuring process cannot simply be understood in terms of 'privatization' only; much rather, it is a question of police care becoming more multifaceted ('multi-lateralising'), also known as the 'hybridising' of the police function. Hybridising means that it is no longer immediately clear whether the police care is executed by sworn public police officers, the government that has hired private security, a private firm that uses private security, a company that has hired public police officers or a government that has charged public officials with police tasks.

The following list explores reasons given for this restructuring:

1. *Limitations of the public police care* Public faith has dropped as a result of (a) the belief that procedural rules present (too) many limitations to effectively combat crime (b) increasing cost awareness following governmental spending cuts whereby a legitimate reason has been found to offload certain tasks and stimulate third-party and PPS constructions; and (c) the public perception of structural corruption, certainly in major cities in the West, but particularly in Third World countries.

2. *Crime increases* In this respect, the following arguments may be presented. (a) In the last forty years, crime statistics have risen around the

globe, leading to both objective and subjective feelings of insecurity. Crime is particularly violent in Third World countries. (b) The introduction of the free market principle has led to the rise of commercial (that is, no longer government-controlled) media: negative news gathering and associated crime sell well. The media exaggerate sensational crime incidents and thereby reinforce perceived feelings of insecurity. (c) Competition within public police care itself, within private police care itself and between public and private police care combined leads to 'exaggerations' of threat analyses. Increasing numbers of new annual reports and surveys are appearing today that magnify (new) forms of criminality (cyber crime, internal fraud). These reports partly reflect reality, but are also based on political, agency-political and commercial interests (egos, budgets, pleas for new rules and regulations, to name but a few). The result is a self-enforcing dynamic that leads to greater demands for security. (d) The more citizens and companies protect themselves, the more (ironically) the feeling of insecurity grows: the offer of safety creates the demand for more safety. (e) As a final result, an increasing demand for safety may be witnessed coming from citizens and businesses. At the same time, beliefs and feelings that the public police care cannot (any longer) meet its expectations have gained momentum. Ergo: an ever-greater demand for private security develops.

3. *Changes in the economic system* Relevant changes in this area can be formulated as follows. (a) There have been enormous scale increases in the private domain. Residential areas, shopping malls, recreation grounds and production areas are increasing in size. On these large-scale private domains ('mass private property' the same need for safety exists as it does in public domains. Ergo: the demand for private security goes up. Parties with significant economic interests therefore increasingly often organise their own security. (b) The market economy involves increasing volumes of valuable and often easy-to-steal products appearing on the market (cars, mobile phones, laptops). Criminals as well as consumers are increasingly aware of this fact. For consumers, this leads to a greater demand for safety with respect to these kinds of products.

4. *Changes in the political system* The introduction of the market principle in many public policy areas (transport, telecommunications, utility sectors, education and so forth) is currently leading to great fragility and therefore to the demand for private security.

The above reasons for restructuring police care can be supplemented with the increasing transfer of authority over police care and its execution by supranational institutions. This applies to public as well as private police care. Authority (command and control) is increasingly often practiced by international public bodies such as the United Nations ('peacekeeping operations'), the European Union (Europol, Eurojust) and trans-national police organisations (FBI, U.S. Customs, DEA) but also by multinational private security organisations.

Civil/Military Perspectives

The state and the police are closely linked. The police lay claim to the sole use of violence with respect to and on behalf of society (Fijnaut and van Helten, 1999, 3), but only as *ultimo ratio*. This method is necessary to exact decisions taken by government. The functionality of the police within society and the authority of the state are therefore closely linked. In addition to its *internal* safety, the state also deals with *external* safety. In this case, the state is not threatened from within, but from abroad. External safety has of old been the domain of the armed forces (Fijnaut and van Helten, 1999, 6). However, this traditionally clear boundary is currently blurring.

The Stichting Maatschappij, Veiligheid en Politie (SMVP) (Dutch Police Foundation for Society, Security and Police) recently concluded a project studying the relationship between the police and the armed forces. In its recommendations, the SMVP's board declares the time ripe for 'creative minds within the police and the armed forces' to think about structural forms of cooperation between the two parties. Some degree of cooperation had already been established as soon as it was considered necessary. For example, the military policy traditionally offers assistance during major public order disturbances. In the event of disaster control, the armed forces are charged with cordoning and supervision. The police, in turn, support the military police in border control. The SMVP board, however, indicates that a larger degree of cooperation is in fact possible. It expresses its expectations that the regional police will increasingly often become involved in international peace operations. In fact, the Netherlands should be obliged to have police staff available for international peace missions because the military police can in no way provide the required staffing levels itself.

In practice, these things are already happening. One evening, the military police and the regular police worked together on a preventive search campaign in a Dutch city's entertainment district. Six military policemen participated. In total, the operation involved some thirty staff from the police, the military police and the criminal investigation department. A number of current social developments are contributing to the traditional distinction between police and armed forces becoming blurred (*Militaire Spectator*, 2002, 462).

Armed forces in peacekeeping operations

In complex, foreign conflicts involving citizens in sudden intense outbursts of violence, the armed forces sometimes fulfil police tasks, or at least tasks that very much resemble them. Moreover, there is increasing cooperation in these missions in the context of civil military cooperation (CIMIC). As a result, the barriers perceived by citizens as factors distinguishing the police force from the armed force are currently also blurring.

Terrorism

Since the 3/11 attack in Spain and the 9/11 attack in the United States, the demand for safety far exceeds the supply of the police's traditional violence potential. As a result, the army is starting to play an increasingly important role in the battle against terrorism. The most visible feature of this process is the increased presence of armed forces in guarding objects (airports, embassies and so forth). Large-scale incidents, catastrophes and the threat of terrorism lend themselves to the intrinsic expansion of structural cooperation between police and armed forces, even if it is only because the armed forces have well-trained anti-terror units. Deploying these units in cooperation with police tasks is effective and efficient.

It is very well imaginable that the role of the army commando troops (KCT) will be expanded in the Netherlands. Combating terror (for example, in the event of hostage situations or hijacking) is part of their brief. In addition to the KCT, the brigade of special security assignments of the military police (BSB KMar) and the armed forces' special assistance unit of the Marine Corps can also be deployed whenever necessary. Their cooperation during the supposed incident of terrorism relating to a traffic tunnel in Rotterdam that took place shortly after 9/11 and in which these units were used may well be a portent of the changing face of police care.

Intensification and internationalisation of organised crime

The army and navy have been involved in the war on drugs for some time now. Especially in the Caribbean, the navies of a number of European countries – and of course the American navy – have of old had specific assignments. The Netherlands has also contributed to this effort.

Military assistance has also been provided in combating crime on Curacao. Militarisation is therefore not only limited to sea operations. There has also been intensive cooperation – for some time now – between military and civilian organisations in the American war on drugs. In Colombia, for example, the distinction has actually become less clear-cut. In the summer of 2000, the U.S. Congress approved a proposal to invest 862 million dollars in the war on drugs in a number of South American countries. As part of the package, the Colombian army was given 16 Black Hawk helicopters and 30 Huey transport helicopters for their three anti-narcotics battalions (Rabasa and Chalk, 2001).

Dispersal of military technology: 'Nonlethal weapons'

A pioneering report commissioned by the European Parliament sketches a picture of the military technology that may find its way into the public maintenance of peace. In addition to electronic surveillance technologies, the distribution of so-called nonlethal weapons goes unhindered. It sounds like science fiction, yet it has become modern reality. Targets can be temporarily disarmed with the help of kinetic, chemical, acoustic or microwave technology.

A number of examples can be listed here. High-frequency waves can disturb the ear's balance organ, causing nausea, vomiting, spontaneous defecation and general disorientation. It is possible to direct this weapon at a specific individual in a group. Disturbances of the peace can be tackled by dispersing chemicals that are rapidly absorbed into the bloodstream through the skin, causing paralysis. One variation is the dispersal of chemicals that cause pain or spread an awful stench, or the use of chemicals that screen off certain areas ('area-denial chemicals').

Weapons have been developed that expel a gluelike substance, pinning a target's feet to the ground. Laser pistols can blind their targets. So-called thermal guns can penetrate walls so that targets' body temperatures rise to high levels – with all the unpleasant associated consequences. Certain rifles emit microwaves, as a result of which targets feel as if they have been struck by a very hard blow to the head. Much of this technology has been developed for and by the American army. Certain commentators believe that this new technology will find its way into standard police care.

Paramilitary policing

In the American context, people talk of paramilitary police care. Military elements are becoming entwined with police care, particularly in maintaining public order and in the equipment and actions of arrest teams (SWAT teams). Kraska and Kappeler (1997) are often quoted in this context. They noted that in 1982, 59 per cent of all forces included a paramilitary unit. In 1995, this had increased to almost 90 per cent. In 1982, records showed that, on average, SWAT teams in the United States were used once a month, primarily for arrests and sometimes to deal with kidnappings. In 1995, they were used seven times each month.

Over the years, these so-called SWAT teams in the United States have also developed a function in basic police care. More than 20 per cent of the forces use SWAT teams for surveillance duties. This is changing the face of police care. As a result of their clothing and equipment, SWAT teams have a military appearance. They are heavily armed with automatic weapons. In a number of cities, the teams use armoured vehicles.

The Dutch Ter Beek Committee has developed four possible scenarios with respect to the future relationship between the police and the armed forces (*Militaire Spectator*, 2002, 463). These are described below.

- *Separation*: The police and armed forces remain separate, and any resulting inefficiency is accepted for what it is;
- *Ad hoc cooperation*: The principle of cooperation is not unacceptable in cases where cooperation is considered necessary, but things must not go too far. The individual organisations should remain recognisable and separate;
- *Structural cooperation*: Where necessary, police and armed forces work together on a structural basis. The different roles are maintained, as is political accountability;
- *Merger*: A minister for social safety is appointed. The two parties involved are integrated with an eye to increased efficiency and effectiveness.

Which of these options is to become reality will to a large degree be determined by the perceived lack of security in the Netherlands and, in particular, by the question of whether or not terrorist attacks will occur.

Physical/digital perspectives

Over the past few years, a number of influential reports have been published in the United States, Great Britain, Australia and Canada based on studies into the future of technology in maintaining law and order. By means of an inventory of the latest developments, policies have been determined with the objective of organising the maintenance of law and order in such a way that optimum use can be made of this cutting-edge technology.

In his preface to *Police Science Technology Strategy Report 2003–2008*, John Denham, minister of state for policing in Great Britain, comes straight to the point: 'I want to ensure that the police is equipped with the best means and technology available, so that it is capable of achieving maximum effectiveness and efficiency'. To that end, structural cooperative ventures are being organised in the above-mentioned countries between central government, the police and the judiciary, private enterprise and finally also the scientific community.

In these ventures, the primary objective is to integrate science and technology in maintaining law and order. This integration is seen as essential. It will enable experts in science and technology to make an important contribution to the achievement of crime prevention objectives as formulated in the national criminality policy plans. The countries involved share more or less the same aims:

- The identification and neutralisation of public disturbances of the peace whereby an increasing amount of attention is devoted to terrorist threats;
- The effective deployment of intelligence-gathering technology;
- The exchange of information between forces and other relevant partners in the maintenance of safety;
- The introduction of mobile data systems;
- Maximising probative value;
- The effective management of the investigation process, including crime scene investigation management;
- The introduction of automated management support systems;
- The monitoring of potential perpetrators;
- The integration of technology in surveillance strategies;
- The effective localisation and securing of traces, and therefore evidence, and
- The protection of police functionaries and vulnerable citizens.

In addition, four categories of work are distinguished: operations, deployment, development and research.

The integration of science and technology in operations also affects the possibility for the police in its daily work to gain direct access to national criminal systems and access to local, regional and national support services, the national DNA databank and also to automated fingerprint systems.

Additionally, the integration of science and technology in deployment relates to the further development and introduction of new digital information systems that link forces, facilitate wireless communication, expand the automated number plate registration system as well as the Video Identification Parade Electronic Recording (VIPER) system for the identification of individuals in large groups. Finally, the integration of science and technology involves the further introduction of portable drug-testing equipment for immediate, on-the-spot analyses.

As far as development is concerned, the integration of science and technology also involves middle-term and long-term investments for the (outsourced) development of automated and portable equipment for DNA analysis and other forensic investigations (including fingerprints and explosives) on a portable device ('lab-on-a-chip'). Investments are also needed with respect to national forensic databanks, the application of technology used in surveillance (night vision, movement detectors) and, for example, the improvement of video surveillance for the generation of images to be used as evidence.

Finally, the integration of science and technology is also strongly motivated by investments in scientific research areas covering biometrics, DNA, chemical tracing and, finally, more advanced detection systems for drugs and explosives (for example, those to be deployed at entrances or along the road).

Police, financial, political and private intelligence

The above-mentioned blurring barriers are likely to lead to a gradual decline in the existing fragmentation of information systems, within the police force and certainly among international police organisations (for example, Europol), private security organisations and the armed forces. Increasing (inter)national pressure is currently being exerted on the existing, fragmented information systems and positions held by the various organisations, particularly after 9/11.

In this vein, the SMVP has stated that possibilities exist for cooperation between police and armed forces as far as information sharing is concerned. In combating international terrorism, the police as well as the armed forces operate with their own information services, both showing an increasing degree of overlap. Bundling forces will enable the parties involved to realise significant efficiency gains and thus to improve results, certainly when – as may be expected – technological innovations are introduced. It will, however, require continuous efforts to enhance the professionalisation of information service activities, according to the SMVP.

Criticism aimed at the information systems used within the Dutch police force has been around for years. The General Accounting Office has researched the exchange of investigation information between the KLPD and the police regions. On several recent occasions, officials have pointed out that the exchange of investigation material between the police organisations proved inadequate. The investigators' most important conclusion was that the minister of foreign affairs and the KLPD had, until that moment, not done enough to improve the situation. The KLPD currently lacks a specific information system for terrorism, although it is legally obligated to have one.

The General Accounting Office has recommended the development within the KLPD of an information system that is specifically targeted at terrorism and that is available to the investigation services for easy and ready use. Much is now being done to integrate information systems. In response to the report, the ministers of the Dutch Foreign Affairs and Justice Departments indicated that several projects were actively carried out [(Bestek ICT 2001–2005, Landelijke Informatie Coördinatie DNP) (ICT Plan 2001–2005, National Coordination of Information)] to tackle the issues involved in the various basic registration systems in addition to the coordination of information within the police organisation. The Public Order and Safety Inspectorate will be addressing the issue of supervision more systematically. To process information related to terrorism, the KLPD uses an information system entitled BRZ or the Register for Special Investigation Cases. Whenever combating terrorism is concerned, regular alignment takes place between the public prosecutor, AIVD, police and KLPD. The various progress reports on combating terrorism consistently devote attention to the exchange of information between various public organisations.

Unbearable lightness

The object of study in criminology and police science (the criminal law system) is too limited, and policing and criminological discourses have become 'unbearably light'. The traditional police and judiciary apparatus is becoming part of a far broader 'security architecture' – one that is becoming more and more enmeshed in international developments and processes and that is driven by rapid developments in science and technology. Yet the traditional, 'iron' police system is still subject to 'marginal changes' or (minor) changes to the establishment (Van Reenen, 1979). These reflect the historic 'basic patterns' of gradual nationalisation and gradual judicial policing (criminal investigations) (Fijnaut, 1979). The question is whether the boundaries of the 'iron system' have in fact been reached and whether political space will become available for the emergence of a radical reorganisation: 'a revolutionary construction' (Van Reenen, 1986).

Further research will be required to provide these issues with sound and solid theoretical and empirical foundations. We have not completed our mission yet. Criminology studies the field of (registered) crime that constitutes the main focus of the police and the judiciary. Police studies address the organisation and the political-administrative embeddedness of the police and the judiciary. Other areas remain underresearched and are in fact sometimes not even studied at all. Here, relevant fields include the internationalisation of police care, the private security industry, the changing relationship between the public policing forces and the armed forces, the influence of technology on the exercise of policing by the regular police and private security firms, the armed forces and information and investigation services and, finally, the study of information exchanges.

4
On Old Folks and Things That Pass Away: Criminology in 2018

Introduction

In previous chapters, I sometimes referred to this chapter. It was written on the occasion of the twenty-fifth anniversary of the Dutch criminological association. I was working at the Dutch Antilles at the time, 'temporarily selling my soul.' But after two years of selling out, I returned to academia and wrote this piece. It was published in the anniversary book and has hardly ever been referred to since. Looking back, it was one of the moments when I wrote about things taking place 'outside' the 'mental prison' of police research and criminology and one of the occasions when I charged into 'normal science'. In retrospect, I can see that it is also one of the works in which I tried to break away from the common sense of policing and security. Factual policing and security no longer fit 30-year-old routines and one-sided social science. Therefore, I imagined myself at a criminological conference in 2018. This experiment also – at least to me – was one of the earlier ventures into narrative knowledge. As mentioned in the introduction to this book, I love working at the intersections between social science and literature or, more broadly, popular culture. I recommend Vincenzo Ruggiero's (2003) *Crime. Literature. Sociology of Deviance and Fiction* as a fine example of this type of work. In literary writing, we are not restricted by the rules and regulations of normal science. We just speak our minds: no stifling and meticulous waste of time with references and the like. Echoing the line in one of the Rod Stewart's early songs, I 'stood on the table with my glass of gin, and came straight to the point'. An essay like this – as well as *The Sopranos* chapter to come – enables me to make points, raise questions and start a debate. I'm not into science for methodologies only; I'm in science because I am curious and want to find out how things work. There are many ways to tell social science stories, and this is one of them.

2018: Let your mind wander

Imagine that today is 2018 and that a 'criminological' conference is under way. A global audio and video system links the participants. Now I may use the term *criminological* here, but the word *criminology* is in effect no longer used. The keynote speakers include a professor of forensic genetics, a senior lecturer in forensic IT, a professor of human rights abuse, consultants in corporate ethics, scholars involved in preventive architecture, a number of forensic accountants and, finally, corporate security officials. A senior lecturer in actuarial insurance studies is present as well as the crème de la crème of business professionals specialising in risk management and organisation studies (human resource managers). The conference is entitled 'Knowledge – to help us predict and to help us control'. All participants serve multinational corporations and hold part-time positions at universities.

Universities around the world have by now made a full transition to the market economy. Business reengineering entered academia around the turn of the century and rapidly gained ground. Today's curricula are determined on the basis of market demand. Research schools, scientific staff and professors are sponsored by insurance companies, medical institutions, financial organisations, political parties and foundations with idealistic objectives – such as the Foundation for Architecture and Safety, the Foundation for Forensic Computer Studies and the Foundation for Forensic Auditing. So what happened to criminology at the end of the twentieth century?

Simply speaking, the prediction formulated by Ericson and Carriere (1994) came true. In their challenging chapter 'The Fragmentation of Criminology', Ericson and Carriere describe a process of fragmentation in social sciences and extend this process to include criminology. Their descriptions and analyses of deviant behaviour, criminality and conflict resolution are to an increasing degree expected to become the subject of study in academic arenas outside criminology.

In this chapter, I follow Ericson and Carriere's lead and describe developments within traditional criminology, and especially within a number of alternative disciplines. I end on a sombre note with respect to the instrumental use of criminological knowledge and its ethical boundaries.

Back to the future of criminology

Ericson and Carriere's prediction did not stand alone, but formed part of a somewhat broader crisis witnessed in criminology at the end of the twentieth century. Along the sidelines of criminological discourse, several authors pointed to the fact that criminology no longer addressed relevant developments in crime and punishment outside its own disciplinary boundaries. Criminology had ended up in a dead-end street, which criminologists did not grasp at all. They were blinded by their own theoretical lights. The critical voices of the above-mentioned authors and also those of people like Loek Hulsman, Nils Christie, Michel Foucault, the formidable Stan Cohen and others remained completely unheard in mainstream criminological debates, let alone in any research programmes.

Intellectual gatekeepers were active all the time: intellectual barbarians were stopped at the gates of intellectual progress. In *The Futures of Criminology*, for example, Nelken describes the *fin-de-siècle* feeling within criminology in which 'little of innovative value seems to have been created, and what is worse, it has failed to keep up with and track new developments elsewhere' (Nelken, 1994). It was not merely a particular stream within criminology that had found itself in the line of fire, but rather the future of criminology as a whole, Nelken states. He refers to Gouldner, who as early as 1973 pointed out the need for a re-evaluation of criminology's ambitions in the light of increasing fragmentation threatening the pretensions of the science as a whole.

Nelken repeatedly wonders whether all this is not slightly exaggerated. Has criminology really failed to keep up with developments elsewhere? Of course, high-quality and fundamental research was still being performed at the time, but it would seem to be more devoted to a further refining, re-evaluation and integration of existing historical insights into the causes of crime (Braithwaite, 1989). Pavarini wonders whether 'criminology is worth saving?' In his view, it is confronted by an identity crisis so profound that serious doubts are expressed about its survival (Pavarini, 1994, 43). What happened?

Criminology became caught up in its own topic of research: the criminal justice system and the question of the 'effectiveness' of the government's crime policies. The traditional attention devoted by criminologists to the 'nuts, sluts and perverts' – the most visible aspects of crime – continued to exist. Other institutions, other forms of criminal behaviour and other (groups of) perpetrators were generally ignored. Not only did research limit itself to the criminality that is the focus of the criminal system, but within the field of research, intellectual laziness was rife, too.

In 1998, the Dutch police researcher Fijnaut formulated the following conclusion about police investigations: 'The image of the research, including future research, (...) would seem to be not very daring, rather conventional, and virtuous' (Fijnaut, 1998). He believes the issue is 'primarily about research that is to a great extent simply in line with research performed in years gone by, which itself was primarily focused on optimising the organisation and operation of standard police forces, internally and externally' (Fijnaut, 1998). Fijnaut wonders whether a need exists for an entirely different type of research. He not only misses economic, psychological and historical research, but also feels that institutions such as the military police, national intelligence and security services and private police forces themselves should be the subject of study (Fijnaut, 1998). One of the comments presented at the end of Cohen's *Visions of Social Control* (1985) runs as follows: 'Indeed, the difference between state and market control might well be the crucial theoretical issue for the future.' Shearing (1990) also proposes an expansion with respect to the topic of research, so that criminology can be brought in line with the emergence of private police forces – which fall outside the strict domain of criminology.

Within criminology, only rarely do individuals break away from the traditional vision: 'In the process of analysing myriad institutional responses to crime, criminology confronts fragmentation within and among social institutions. It is precisely this institutional and organisational fragmentation that makes an expansion of the research focus of criminology and police science superficial or at best highly specialised in a very narrow domain. According to Ericson and Carriere, this fragmentation is a chronic condition: an irreversible process that, as a whole, is not seen as a threat or scientific knowledge issue, but rather as a normal state of affairs. It is in fact more than that. It is considered desirable because, on the boundaries of disciplines, a revival in scientific thought on crime and punishment lies ahead. But then criminology has to be open to the idea. This, however, was not the case.

Beyond the dinosaur institutions

Today, in 2018, the dinosaurs of traditional criminology have either disappeared from the stage or have adapted to changing conditions. In the Netherlands, the group of dinosaurs includes well-known institutions such as the WODC, the Netherlands Study Center for Criminology and Maintenance of Law and Order (NSCR), the IPIT, the Bonger Institute, the Crisis Research Team (COT) and, for example, the Police Centre at the Vrije Universiteit in Amsterdam. Internationally, almost all institutions of high repute can be placed within this category. The renowned professional journals and book series are now mere historic artefacts. Unnoticed and unwanted, these dinosaur institutions were caught up in a vortex of change too great to handle within the relative safety of their own four walls.

For a long time, criminological research was able to justify its existence with its research into organised drug criminality. Nevertheless, funding for this type of research came to a complete standstill in 2013 when the war on drugs was abandoned on a global scale. The institutional fragmentation of attention paid to criminal behaviour in a large number of organisations, corporations and institutions was already well on its way at this stage. An important explanation for this process lies in the global process of privatisation of supervision, control and criminal investigation. Christie (1993) did actually raise the alarm bell for the criminological community with his first sentence in *Crime Control as an Industry*: 'This book is a warning regarding recent developments in the field of crime control'. In Chapter 7, he addresses the fundamental developments resulting in criminality control becoming a product on the order and safety market. Christie condemns this development and places many a major question mark. However, his warnings and questions fell on fallow ground. Privatisation bypassed mainstream criminology.

Starting in the 1970s, the number of private initiatives increased markedly, and by the end of the twentieth century, the number of staff in the industry was huge. In the United States in 1994, the private–public ratio was 2:1. At the start of the first decade of the twenty-first century, employee numbers in the private initiative sector increased vastly around the world. On the one hand, this led to more staff; on the other, to a large degree of product differentiation. First, growth could be witnessed concerning the number of uniformed guards at company gates, in office complexes, in industrial centres and in residential areas. This development was followed by the foundation of corporate security services within multinational firms: mainly banks, insurance companies and credit card companies. In addition to security staff responsible for physical security, former detectives and intelligence officers were used in investigations into internal and external fraud.

Further professionalisation took place at the end of the twentieth century through the foundation of compliance departments, the appointment of risk managers, the development of forensic auditing, the rise of IT security departments and the development of business or corporate intelligence departments. By the end of the twentieth century, a number of these departments and organisations employed numbers of staff that left criminal investigation departments of a medium-sized police force sadly wanting (Hoogenboom, 1994). The institutional map of supervisory and control services had changed fundamentally. The 'old world' of the penal system and the associated organisations and services had become supplemented by a 'new world' of functionaries and organisations. The major trends in this 'new world' included staff expansion, professionalisation, internationalisation and finally automation and the increased use of technology.

Sutherland revisited

The 'new' security structures are no longer, or barely, occupied with the 'old world' criminology of street crimes, organised crime or public order issues. In the 'new world', fraud and corruption issues are the prime focus. They occur within organisations and institutions such as the political-official apparatus, (inter)national business and other institutions. The 'conflict' in which the new security structures are involved no longer relates to the 'lower (dangerous) classes' of society, but rather with society's middle and upper classes. In the last decade of the twentieth century, financial corruption scandals were exposed that proved far too great in scope and complexity for the 'old world' to deal with: the savings and loan scandal in the United States, stock exchange fraud in New York, Tokyo, Vancouver and Amsterdam, environmental fraud, illegal weapons trade, corporate espionage and international insurance fraud. And then we saw political corruption within international (political) organisations such as the European Union, the World Bank and the IOC. Finally, the financial crises in 2007–2009 not only revealed the structural collapse of international regulation, but also gave us a glimpse of amoral undertows in the management of financial institutions, laying bare wide-scale looting, fraud and cooking the books.

Traditional criminology did not – or could only barely – follow this institutional fragmentation nor did it investigate the 'other' types of criminal. Within the WODC, a start was made on investigating the nature and scope of organisational criminality and, as a follow-up to the SMVP investigation in the mid-1990s, research was performed into mapping the market of illegal financial service provision. This development was continued at the start of the twenty-first century, but many of the other institutions' research programmes did not – or could only barely – keep up with the changes.

Financing criminological research was (too) slow, as a result of which other social organisations, institutions and interest associations entered the market. The NIBE, NIVRA, Nyenrode, the Association of Insurance Companies, IT institutions as well as interest associations, accountancy firms, the medical world (pharmaceutical industry, bio-technology and gene-technology companies) and multinationals: they all stimulate research and the distribution of knowledge through courses and training programmes and by appointing professors for a revival of thoughts on fraud and corruption. Internationally, these developments were clearly demonstrated in the creation of the National Computer Security Association, the Association of Certified Fraud Examiners and the Insurance Fraud Institute. At the end of the twentieth century, the number of semipublic and primarily private organisations and foundations that focused on another form of criminality increased strongly.

Political science and social administration

The increasing amount of attention devoted to fraud and corruption was also driven by the fact that a greater focus was placed on political and official corruption within political science and public administration. In many places around the world, (inter)national business is closely tied to (inter)national governmental bureaucracies that have a large degree of discretionary decision-making power whether or not to allocate subsidies and/or impose levies.

In those days – and now I am going back a bit to recall the old days at the end of the twentieth century – and then also slightly in the margins of criminological discourse, we came across the occasional call for a greater focus on international tax fraud, EU subsidy fraud and the perversion of Third World financing programmes. The amounts of money involved in these types of fraud, or at least assumed to be involved, are well nigh unimaginable. In Maastricht, at the end of the twentieth century, a lone scientist – Grat van den Heuvel (1998) – developed the concept of collusion, but again this did not lead to a fully fledged research tradition within mainstream criminology. Normal science prevailed.

In the 1990s, the United Nations, the OECD and the World Bank initiated global programmes to combat corruption and the abuse of power. These and other organisations asked political scientists, development sociologists, economists and organisation experts to investigate the backgrounds, guises, nature and the scope of corruption. Another important impulse was the foundation in 1992 of Transparency International (TI). This organisation aimed to suppress corruption through (inter)national cooperation and the formation of coalitions involving organisations and individuals. TI has developed extensive, primarily applied, programmes for the development of anticorruption policy and more generally to establish transparency in governmental actions.

TI has also stimulated the foundation of so-called national chapters around the world in which – per country – lawyers, scientists, journalists, government functionaries and representatives from business hold a position. In many countries around the world, the national chapters have led to increased attention for corruption, and in particular to the inclusion of preventive mechanisms. By the end of the twentieth century, some 70 national chapters had been founded. Today, in 2018, this number has tripled. So far, TI has gained powerful support. Hundreds of organisations around the world are currently active in their (inter) national fight against corruption. Governments, TI and similar other institutions are stimulating scientific research and have appointed professors of ethics in government. The knowledge of corruption and the abuse of power have increased dramatically around the world. Never before in history have the back stages of the political–governmental system and the collusion of government services been mapped so clearly.

Business and management studies

Today, in 2018, criminological studies are a standard element in business studies and all manner of management schools. For the development of preventive measures, known concepts such as risk management, human resource management and security management are supplemented by criminological knowledge of individuals, opportunity structures, group processes, motivation and cultural characteristics demonstrated by organisations. In Belgium at the end of the twentieth century, Dr M. Cools, eminent criminologist and head of Alcatel Corporate Security, was appointed professor of corporate security at the Vrije Universiteit Brussel. He was one of the first in a long line of criminologically educated academics to find their way into the world of corporate security. His knowledge on the development of criminological thought, and in particular the cause of crime, was used to perfect specific internal processes. The prevention of deviant behaviour – both in recruitment and selection, and in daily practice – is the prime focus here.

In 1990, Gary Marx wrote a satirical article about the above-mentioned development, focusing in particular on the technological components involved. Marx talks about a fictitious company in which the all-perceiving eye has been perfected. Employees are watched continuously throughout the day by means of advanced video and audio systems. Urine tests are compulsory in screening the use of alcohol and drugs, and the use of computer networks is monitored on content. All these components had already existed for some time at that stage, but had not yet been fully integrated in business practice. Marx's vision became a reality in the first decade of the twenty-first century.

Forensic auditing

In February 1999, the Dutch Erasmus Universiteit started the post-doctorate programme in Forensic Auditing, an initiative developed by the Faculties of Economics and Law. The curriculum consisted of a combination of know-how in the fields of general economics, accountancy, controlling techniques, auditing, corporate-legal criminal law, investigation techniques and criminology. The latter was not defined as such, however, but referred to as fraud diagnostics instead. The reason for this postdoctoral programme was the strong increase in both the scope of fraud and the sheer interest in the phenomenon. Within government as well as business sectors, a growing awareness could be seen with respect to the dangers and risks that fraud entails in its increasing complexity.

In the programme's first year, knowledge deficiencies among the various participants are eliminated, while in the second year students are offered lectures on subjects ranging from administrative organisations, controlling studies, EDP Auditing, fraud diagnostics and ethics to investigation and research techniques and finally tax fraud. In that same year, a similar programme started at Nyenrode Business University. Both initiatives have indicated that the professionalisation of fraud prevention and research is advancing by leaps and bounds. Developments are expected to continue until well after the first two decades of the twenty-first century.

At universities, professors and senior lecturers have been appointed in the field of fraud diagnostics who not only build on the mental legacies of Sutherland, Braithwaite and others, but who also develop their professional arena based on their daily practice of fraud investigation within government and business. Where criminology was not truly successful in extracting itself from the fetters of 'street crimes' and the daily operation of the criminal system, here we see a tremendous and wonderful revival of theoretical and primarily practical research into organised crime and into the more general field of white collar crime.

Information sciences and security

In the 1980s, some thought was reluctantly devoted to the consequences of automation for criminal threats. Subsequently, waves of new threats were reported in the literature, although they were hardly ever mentioned in the criminological journals. Thoughts regarding computer criminality (its nature and scope, developments, prevention and repression) were primarily developed within the industry itself. This led to the formation of special departments within companies for the prevention of cyber crime; the birth of interest associations and computer security magazines; the organisation of many conferences, and it also led to a massive boom in books on cyber crime, encryption, privacy, corporate and economic espionage, and open source intelligence.

The transition from the 'old' to the 'new' world and the associated changes in the ways of criminality as well as in the development of new safety structures is most notable in the area of cyber crime. An entirely new type of jargon had developed at the end of the twentieth century with respect to criminality in the information society – including words such as spoofing, backdoors, denial of service and many others. Computerisation led to the gradual redefinition of warfare, marketing, competitive relationships, territorial threats and finally internal and external fraud. The increasing level of complexity and interconnectivity on the part of information systems led to new potential threats, the subsequent formation of computer security departments and the appointment of specialists. In the world of cyber crime and (private) cyber cops, a multidisciplinary approach to computer criminality has been developed in which organisational-sociological knowledge is combined with knowledge on the nature and scope, modus operandi and perpetrator profiles (formerly known as criminology). The resulting approach, in turn, has been combined with specialist knowledge of computer programming and other electronic know-how related to computer functionality and communication networks.

Genetics and criminology

At the end of the twentieth century, virtually no social or scientific debate took place on genetic experimentation. The majority of doctors, scientists, ethical specialists or lawyers had no idea of the technological advances made at the time. They did not know how genetic tests were performed nor did they fully grasp their findings, let alone what these could be used for. Now, it is technically possible not only to perform genetic research on a foetus, but also to subsequently operate on the unborn child and adapt its genetic structure. Truly dramatic developments are foreseeable for the following decades. Gene diagnostics and gene therapy have become standard practise and part of the medical system and the pharmaceutical industry sector. Gene therapy, including implantation and operations, has become an integral component of medical care. In the twenty-first century, 'attendants of the genetic gene pool' monitor the public and private care systems by means of genetic tests. The attendants link knowledge on criminal behaviour to medical science. The method of choice is the genetic test. This is made compulsory by government services and the private initiative.

In the twenty-first century's first decade, the impulse is coming from the medical world, insurance industry, world health organisations and government services, including supervisory and investigation services. It is leading to guidelines and gene policies that include a wide range of demands. Some people have pointed out the risks of this process through arbitrary choices and downright discrimination. The forerunners in this discussion presented themselves as early as the 1990s, and today the medical world may well be termed a runaway train.

In 1992, a conference on genes and crime was disrupted and cancelled (*Science* 262 [1993]: 23–4), but science nevertheless emphasised the necessity of research into, for example, the relationship between genes and criminal behaviour. Work in this field has to be done with caution. Nevertheless, knowledge on the relationship between genetic make-up and behaviour is increasing steadily. Dutch research has reported on the localisation of what is assumed to be an 'aggression gene' (*New Scientist* [October 30, 1993]: 6). Kohn expunged his worries on the development in *The Race Gallery: The Return of Racial Science*. The relationship between genes and crime are discussed in *Nature Medicine* 1 (1995): 1108–9; *Probe* (December 1, 1995): 7. The president of the Behavior Genetics Association was criticised by board members for his wish to place the subject on the research agenda (*Science* 270 [1995]: 1125). In his view, relevant research was also to include mental 'deficiencies', and subsequently an interest group for mental patients reacted by publishing a pamphlet: Protecting Human Dignity and Human Rights.

The use of alcohol and drugs has also been mentioned frequently in relation to various forms of deviant behaviour. In gene research, specific determinants have been found for alcohol, cocaine and nicotine addictions. Genetics and crime are discussed in *Politics & Life Sciences* 15 (1996): 83–110. Today, in 2018, research institutes are locked in mutual competition in the race to localise particular genes expressing a relationship with what we now term 'deviant behaviour'. Multidisciplinary scientists who have been educated in part in what was then called 'criminology' are currently playing an important role in research programming.

Architecture and security science

The relationship between architecture (that is, broader urban planning) and security has been known for some time. A classic example is the penitentiary design developed by Jeremy Bentham (the panopticon): a round prison with a tower in the centre from which everything and everybody may be observed without the detainees knowing they are being watched. The end of the twentieth century saw the heyday of prison architecture. In *Correctional Facility Planning and Design* (1986), Farbstein develops prison infrastructure in great detail. He devotes his attention to the perception of the environment (light, view, colour, sound, temperatures and sensory deprivation), social spaces (communication and social interaction, group size, privacy and stress), behaviour and activities and finally prison security. In its study *Design Guide for Secure Adult Correctional Facilities* (1983), the American Correctional Association Committee drafts a summary of construction designs and lists the equally detailed background ideas that these designs are based on.

In 2018, the relationship between architecture/urban planning and security has been perfected. In the twenty-first century, specific penitentiary architecture has become part of mainstream architecture. In the construction of residential areas, recreational facilities, offices and industrial spaces and in laying out public spaces, 'criminological' knowledge on inhabitants, visitors, employees, clients, patients, suppliers and so forth is used to design and lay out literally everything that has to be built. In the process, 'criminological' knowledge is described as risk management and generated through demographic studies and what has been termed 'dataveillance' (the registration of incidents and behaviour, linked to personality characteristics and personality predictions, which in turn are generated by closely interlinked computer data).

This development started in the second half of the twentieth century: not only in the construction of resorts in many parts of the United States, South America and South Africa, but also in the increasing number of technological resources that were used in the architecture of offices, recreational spaces and public spaces (video systems, access control through iridology, handwriting comparison, face recognition systems and electronic signatures). Although it was standard procedure to lock up deviants in the nineteenth and twentieth centuries, risk groups and individuals are now kept out – or only allowed entry under strict supervision by means of digital systems. The eminent criminologists Stenning and Shearing (1987a) actually posited this utopian vision in their analysis of Disneyland, although mainstream scientists at the time ignored their reconnoitring into the future.

Literature and mass media: Dostoevsky criminologist?

The distinction between scientific and literary knowledge no longer exists in 2018. The myth of the rational scientific model has made way for the narrative story. In 1990, Foqué and 't Hart attacked the roots of the euphoric embrace of science. In their work entitled *Instrumentaliteit en rechtsbescherming. Grondslagen van een strafrechtelijke waardendiscussie* (Instrumentality and protection of rights, bases for a discourse on the values of criminal law), the authors present a superb chapter on narratives and deregulation: 'The literary story would appear in many historical instances to have the capacity to point out initiated changes in the awareness of norms and values, and the associated reactions of people, whereas scientific analyses, philosophical reflection, and legal frameworks are incapable of doing so'.

We gain insight into the level of certain feelings. 'One often tends to put the latter down and thereby make it harmless by qualifying it as 'fiction' (...), thereby suggesting that, in contrast to law and social sciences, it addresses matters that did not 'really' happen and therefore is not 'real' (en Foqué and 't Hart, 1990, 344–69). Literature breaks through 'the reticence of a dominant and petrified human and social image that on the one hand has the pretension to be able to ascribe the patterns of everything and everyone a place, while on the other hand demanding a price for the box model: the suffocation of conformism'.

In the twentieth century, only a few lone wolves in the criminological community pointed out the importance for criminology of literary works. In his *Basic Models*, Bianchi writes about Genet, Sade and Sartre to indicate that the 'scientific' labelling model had been described years before in literature (Genet) and in philosophy (Sartre). Gutwirth (1985) uses these examples in *Dostoevsky: A Criminologist? A Historical and Biographical Quest into the Criminological Insights of the Russian Writer.* The author concludes that Dostoevsky's oeuvre 'is and remains relevant for criminology and that (his work) proves that literary and philosophical works may in no way be ignored by a science such as criminology on the pretext that they are not 'scientific'. Thanks to their paradigmatic and methodological freedom, they are not infrequently better placed to distance themselves from inaccurate evident matters that applied scientists believe they can assume as an irrefutable and indubitable epistemological basis.

In the 1990s, Linda Davies, a former banker, wrote financial thriller novels in which the international world of *haute finance* is intrinsically linked with corruption, internal fraud, incompetent supervisors, machinations by information and intelligence services, murder and homicide. Her first book, *Nest of Vipers,* is about corruption in the banking world. Its heroine, Sarah Jensen, is a brilliant and beautiful banker who is recruited by an intelligence service and becomes involved in a global conspiracy that puts her life in danger. In *Wilderness of Mirrors,* drug smuggling, the diamond trade and gun running are all interwoven. In studies by Powis (1992), to mention one example, or in final reports such as that of the American Congress on the BCCI affair – which fully came to light at the start of the 1990s – we find the same combinations, only then observed from opposite perspectives: oblivious accountancy firms, stumbling and incompetent supervisors, corrupt lawyers, (former) government officials, and the criminal system itself. The U.S. Central Intelligence Agency (CIA) used BCCI to finance illegal operations and refused to share its knowledge of extensive fraud and laundering operations with other American supervisory institutions and/or intelligence services. Apart from the BCCI case – and a handful of other financial scandals – the complexity of international fraud neither gets through to the mainstream criminological debate nor to the broader public.

At the end of the twentieth century, some people managed to break through the boundaries of science and literature. Ericson and Carriere (1994) pointed out the effects of literary studies that influence criminology. In their work, they mention Burke, Gursfield and Wagner-Pacofici, all of whom use literary analyses to analyse the public debate on crime and criminals. In 2018, knowledge of crime is to an important degree obtained through novels and films. Al Pacino movies like *Scarface* ('You need fucking people like me') and *Donny Brasco* are regularly shown on pay-per-view channels. At a corner of Washington Square in New York, a small statue of Al Pacino is visited daily by hundreds of fans. Al Pacino stares across the square to statues of Marlon (*The Godfather*) Brando ('we all wanna be Marlon') and Jack Nicholson in *The Departed*. People are no longer interested in nineteenth and twentieth-century issues as narrowly delineated definitions of organised crime, white collar crime or (political) corruption, nor in methodologically justified yet boring exposés on the nature and scope of this, that and the other – either in statistics or well-wrought theses. They don't believe this crap anymore. Hell is sitting on a hot stone reading your own academic paper. Daily media coverage of widespread corruption on Wall Street, industrial espionage, identity theft and the like give the public an ample idea of what social and corporate life is all about. They don't need 'sanitised' and quasi-intellectual scientific publications that are top heavy from quotations of what someone else already wrote in a slightly different way.

The end of the debate

In 2018, institutional fragmentation is still in full swing. What was known in the nineteenth and twentieth centuries as criminological knowledge has become entwined with other scientific disciplines: political science, corporate economics and management studies, the medical world, accountancy, computer sciences and architecture. Within these domains, some sort of control thought pattern emerges – for which matters such as criminological knowledge are used – while issues such as the protection of rights and those relating to power are lost sight of. Efficiency, coordination and a systematic approach are the new key words. Conclusions, however, are not new. In the early twentieth century, the rise of the social sciences was questioned for its utilitarian character. Criticism regarding Saint Simon's positivism ('all social issues can be solved through planning and organization based on science') right up to Comte relates to exactly this pretension and the 'abuse' of scientific knowledge in exerting social control.

Foucault is explicitly negative about the use of the social sciences in disciplining human behaviour. Cohen (1985), inspired by Foucault's analysis, sighs: 'We have heard enough about the criminologist as a technician, hired hand, and servant of the state, as an informer and supplier of alibis, as a producer of knowledge which legitimates power.' Nelken (1994) also points to the fact that criminology 'is regularly accused of degenerating into a public, practical, policy-oriented science.'

The most powerful intellectual countermovement to this type of instrumental thought in the twenty-first century is the revival of ethics. Within all the (multi-)disciplinary initiatives mentioned so far, academic chairs in ethics and associated research programmes have been created to a greater or smaller extent. At the end of the twentieth century, multidisciplinary discussions were held on the ethics of governmental behaviour. This is now also taking place in business. The process is illustrated by the European Business Ethics Network or, for example, the involvement of business in activities such as those set up by Transparency International.

Within the privatisation of supervision, control and investigation, these opposing forces have been slightly less well developed. The discussion on ethics in the medical world concerning the limits of gene technology may still be ongoing, but in various parts of the world there are no ethical limits as far as experimentation or applications are concerned. Within management and corporate security, guidelines and (complaint) procedures have been formulated. The same is true for forensic auditing and architecture. Compared to the democratic control mechanisms of the 'old' world (penal code and code of criminal procedure), the legally protective elements of the 'new' world's security structures are still less stringent and coherent, and possibility limits are increasingly often stretched on the pretext of threats to social order, safety and productivity.

In 2018, ethics specialists still raise questions, but their numbers, prestige and influence have dwindled. Some of them play the (paid) role of court jester and are tolerated on the basis of political-symbolic considerations. Others leave the ethical domain altogether, in sheer frustration. Rare individuals submerge themselves in writing literature, occasionally leafing through antiquated criminological writings and still, for a fleeting second, feeling charmed by the passionate debates on abolitionism, Left Realism, neo-Marxism or – in retrospect – the in effect desperate and incomprehensible discussions on postmodernism. Old folks and things that slip away....

5
The Governance of Policing and Security

Introduction

How does this chapter fit into the 'grand scheme of things' of the book? First, I am again moving outside the framework of the first two chapters. Factual policing and security nowadays involve a multitude of actors. The traditional perspective on all of this in police studies and criminology no longer suffices. It is a recurrent theme in my endeavour beginning on page 1. Second, my subtitle – 'ironies, myths and paradoxes' – comes into play beginning with this chapter. Policing is about power and power in my view is in dire need of checks and balances. Power corrupts and absolute power corrupts absolutely. Therefore, in this chapter, I explore again changes in policing but draw attention to the fact that, increasingly 'policing' is being exercised by nonpolice actors. My ironies, myths and paradoxes arguments enter the stage here and will be addressed even more in forthcoming chapters.

Change

One of the most significant developments in modern societies during the past decades has been the transformation of traditional state-based governing mechanisms and the advancement of new arrangements of governance. This has occurred in the private, semiprivate and public spheres and has involved governmental and nongovernmental actors and agencies at various levels (local, regional, national, transnational and global). Typically, these new forms of governance rely less on the state as the institutional form and hierarchical centre of society (www.nwo.nl).

Governance refers to the phenomenon by which many public functions increasingly are assumed and carried out by actors other than the classical government institutions of the nation-state. Public administration is thus becoming more and more 'unbounded', involving in various ways many public, nongovernmental and private actors in the process of determining the public good. The Dutch Netherlands Organisation for Scientific Research (NWO) programme *Shifts in Governance* presents a general discussion of these changes.[7] Below, the NWO framework will be used more specifically to analyse shifts in the governance of security.

Shifts in the governance of security also involve shifts in the location of power and accountability. These shifts are discussed in the section entitled 'Shifts in the governance of security'. I illustrate the necessity of discussing power and accountability in the section entitled 'Principal questions: The location of power and accountability'. Privatisation of security and the increasing interweaving taking place between public and private security has reached – and sometimes even crossed – the lines of legality.

These first few paragraphs aim to introduce, on a theoretical level, notions and concepts for our understanding of changes in shifts in policing and security. Although the principal focus in this chapter lies on local government and local policies, it could be stated that, at a first glance, my argument does not quite seem to fit. I don't agree. My argument here is that we must understand the broader context of shifts in the governance of security to understand localised, small-scale and rather 'innocent' innovations in security (growing private surveillance, increasing outsourcing of surveillance in the public domain and even outsourcing controlling and fining tasks). Therefore, it is necessary not only to describe the 'multiplication of uniforms' in itself, but also as part of the broader context. Local government and local security arrangements are inextricably part of (inter)national changes taking place.

Next, I move from the theoretical level to empirical research into the more mundane subject of 'multiplication of uniforms' at the local level. Two recent Dutch publications on private surveillance in the private and – increasingly often – public domain will be discussed in the section entitled 'Principal questions: The location of power and accountability'. In the section entitled 'Unbounding "public" and "private" on the shop floor', I will argue that issues raised in the theoretical part of my text are applied to the local governance of security. The final section concludes my argument.

Shifts in the governance of security

According to Max Weber, the very essence of the state is the monopoly on violence (military force, taxation, public policing and the criminal justice system). New central theoretical notions in police research and criminology include the current 're-structuring': the 'transformation' or emergence of a 'new security architecture' in which many new actors are involved (Shearing and Wood, 2003). Shifts in the governance of security can be discerned in the proliferation of administrative 'policing' through inspections and authorities for different parts of the economy (Ponsaers and Hoogenboom, 2004; Ponsaers and De Cuyper, 1980; Hoogenboom, 1994). Shifts in the governance of security can also be traced in the involvement of military forces in the war on crime and the war on terror. Traditional boundaries between external and internal national threats have become vague, and military forces in the current, post-9/11 period fulfil vital roles in the new security architecture. Shifts in the governance of security also include the more prominent role of security and intelligence services. After the Cold War, the intelligence communities became involved in the fight against organised crime, and after 9/11, a 'securitisation' trend has been mentioned, drawing attention to the more prominent role of intelligence agencies.

Finally, one of the prominent shifts in the governance of security is the growth and involvement of private security companies in the new security architecture. All functions associated with the state monopoly such as guarding, surveillance, crime analyses, investigation, use of force, intelligence and even 'justice' are being redefined along private (horizontal) lines.[8] In 1979, some 9,000 uniformed private guards were employed in the Netherlands. The private security market consisted of 35,000 guards in 2007. The 'multiplication of uniforms' is also spurred through the introduction – by municipalities and the government – of new surveillance functions. Indeed, a plethora of uniforms and a wealth of (semi-) public and private surveillance technology have been introduced in many parts of society. As Garland (2001) observes, we now live in 'a culture of control'. For the American context, Simon (2007) even argues that Americans have become obsessed with crime. The very notions of risk and fear have spun out of control, fuelling ever more preventive and repressive measures. Within the context of this 'culture of control' and, as Simon argues, the increase in 'governing through crime', an instrumental way of thinking seems to have become deeply rooted in political systems, bureaucracies, law enforcement agencies and in criminology.

Because we are consumed by risks and fears – constantly quoting Ulrich Beck's (1986) *Risikogesellschaft*; using broad and sweeping generalisations of risks and threats, lately also involving Islam and Muslims; lamenting the supposed decline of norms and values; and perceiving risks in the supposed rise of hedonistic individualism (Van den Brink, 2007; Hoogenboom, 2007) – few, if any, questions are being raised about the effects of policies on the fundamental building blocks of our democratic society. The balance between instrumentality and checks and balances on the exercise of power could well be jeopardised in the 'culture of control' we now live in.

Principal questions: The location of power and accountability

With the ongoing transformation of traditional, state-based governing mechanisms and the advancement of new arrangements of governance of security, different questions must be raised with regard to the 'new security architecture'. In the dominant traditional paradigm, power is exercised by law enforcement agencies, and accountability is organised on the local/regional level by the mayor, the public prosecutor and the city council. On the national level, accountability issues come before Parliament. In the 'new security architecture', it is not only operational lines between agencies and corporations that are blurring, but consequently also the precise locations of power ('who makes decisions for whom') and accountability ('who can we ask the questions why, how and to what effect?'). Take, for instance, the complexity of airport security at Schiphol Airport. Formally, it is the mayor of the Haarlemmermeer municipality and the public prosecutor who exercise power. At the same time, Schiphol is an example of 'hybrid' security structures where private security organisations, the military police (Kmar), customs, the national coordinator for terrorism and the intelligence services and finally a large number of in-house security departments (Schiphol, KLM and other international airlines) routinely make security decisions 24/7.

The governance of security beyond the state and even the governance of security without government, therefore, involve important questions concerning the location of power, shared responsibilities, the legitimacy of decisions and decision makers and finally accountability towards citizens and organisations in different national, sub-national and international settings. We inhabit a world of multilevel, multicentred security governance in which states are joined, crisscrossed and contested by an array of transnational organisations and actors – whether in regional and global governmental bodies, commercial security outfits or a burgeoning number of nongovernmental organisations and social movements that compose transnational civil society (www.libertysecurity.org). Sometimes these actors interact, cooperate, share information and combine manpower and means. Sometimes we find 'strategic avoidance' mechanisms when actors wish to retain their autonomy (Hoogenboom, 1994).

A first set of questions related to future research concerns the extent to which the widely held beliefs about the shift to multilevel policing and security governance are actually corroborated by empirical evidence, and how unique or new such shifts may be from a comparative and historical perspective. A clear need exists for conceptual clarification and for a better road map of the ways in which the shifts in governance of policing and security are rendered operational in practice. At the same time, more rigorous empirical and historical analyses as well as tests of observed or presumed trends need to be undertaken.

A second set of questions concerns the consequences of the rise of multilevel security governance for *accountability* arrangements to control the exercise of power and to prevent their abuse or arbitrary application – and, hence, for their overall *legitimacy*. It is indeed striking to notice how underresearched are the areas of regulation, militarisation, privatisation and securitisation. Yet, these shifts in the governance of security involve issues of power and the control of power. Much work still remains to be done in developing new ways of thinking about the meaning of accountability, legitimacy and responsibility in new international or transnational governance of security, and also about how this may be made operational in practice.

Management and operational levels within the new security architecture should not react to these vital matters opportunistically, defensively, blindly or thoughtlessly, but should instead anticipate, think through and even embrace a culture of accountability. This culture should, indeed, be incorporated into the very bloodstream of an organisation. The good news here is that there are in fact people who recognise this: in the United Kingdom, for instance, certain elements are already available for a paradigm shift to institutionalising accountability throughout the police service (Markham and Punch, 2007a). The bad news, however, is that internal accountability is to a degree symbiotic with external accountability, and there are external forces at work that potentially compromise accountability.

In effect, I am saying that the idea of democratic policing and security is effectively synonymous with accountability. The people responsible for policing and security simply cannot be unaccountable: one cannot be held only slightly accountable. In brief, accountability is a broad and diffuse concept related to formal obligations within a democracy. It is also closely related to notions of good governance and of being transparent to the public and other stakeholders as far as policies and conduct are concerned. Finally, it is strongly linked with internally generated norms and standards concerning professional accountability. But, as Bovens aptly notes, accountability also remains something of a 'hurrah' concept, with everyone shouting 'hurrah!' whenever it is mentioned. The same is true for 'ethics' and 'integrity': it is difficult for any institutional leader to say they oppose them. Nevertheless, this attitude in turn also tends to make accountability what Tromp refers to as a 'Sunday' concept in which the noble principle merely forms part of the Sunday rhetoric of good intentions – in the knowledge that, on Monday, it will be "back to business as usual" (Bovens, 1998, 22). Without accountability, an opportunity exists for the arbitrariness of unchecked authority and the unrestrained abuse of power.

Unbounding 'public' and 'private' on the shop floor

Terpstra illustrates the 'unbounding' of public and private elements – among others – by drawing attention to the increased hiring of private security by local municipalities.

Box 1 Some examples of private security officers in public space in the Netherlands, purchased by local governments

On a temporary basis or occasionally:

- Private security officers operating during certain public events (such as annual fairs, summer festivals, etc.)
- Private security officers hired by local government to patrol a residential area at night after this area had been hit by several fires, causing great fear and unrest among residents; the regular police force did not have the capacity for additional patrols; local government funded the private security activities (municipality of Venray, May/June 2006)
- Additional patrol by employees of a private security company in the municipalities of Lemmer and Langweer in the summer of 2000 as a result of summer holiday plans on the part of the regular police force and the large number of tourists staying in the area

On a permanent basis at certain locations:

- By order of some urban district governments in Rotterdam, private security officers maintain surveillance in certain streets with serious disorder problems.
- In the centre of the city of Venray, employees of the private company Q-Park have been given enforcement tasks with regard to certain petty

offences, such as cycling in pedestrian areas. These private security officers are allowed to draw up formal reports for certain offences.

On a permanent basis for the whole community:

For the last few years, the municipality of Enkhuizen has employed private security officers as surveillants in public spaces. Even more far-reaching were proposals made in the municipality of Bloemendaal in 2003 (which, by the way, were not accepted, although this was aggressively debated). The idea here was that round-the-clock private security officers should be used for surveillance in the small (and affluent) villages of Bloemendaal, Overveen and Aerdenhout. The immediate cause underlying these proposals was a serious attack on the house of locally well-known individuals in one of the villages.

According to Terpstra, two major developments dominated the new forms of surveillance and patrol: fragmentation and marketisation. Fragmentation not only refers to an increasing diversity of security patrols, but also to the fact that new security patrol officers – including city wardens – are only *semi-police*, both in the eyes of many citizens and with respect to their powers, professional expertise, social status and authority. One of the consequences of the second development, marketisation, is that the nature of security as a public good is currently and to some extent changing into a 'club good' (Terpstra, 2006). This may result in the social exclusion of certain groups and individuals. Both developments could have unintended side effects.

In *Privatizing Policing*, van Steden analyses the growth, functions and the growing interweaving of public and private security in three local case studies: the Efteling (a fairy-tale recreational park), the Feyenoord football stadium and Hoog Catherijne (shopping mall). At the Efteling, the in-house security team was reduced from 12 employees in 1985 to 9 in 1989 but it expanded again to 15 in 2004. During high-season periods, additional contract guards are hired. The Feyenoord stadium's in-house security team grew from 100 to 500 between 1993 and 1997 and went down to 200 in 2003. Today, the stadium employs 300 (more highly qualified) stewards, excluding the frequently hired security guards who have come and gone in waves of varying strength.

At the Hoog Catherijne, van Steden found a different development. It was not so much the hiring of private security that was of concern here, but rather the appointment of five funded police officers to serve the need for safety and security in the shopping mall. The decision was made on the basis of practical reasons related to authority and democratic accountability, but in general, the municipal council considered public foot patrols to be better equipped than private guards for dealing with security problems. Overall, van Steden describes a tripling of the size of private security over the previous three decades.

Van Steden also concludes that Dutch private security, as elsewhere in the world, has grown progressively. In terms of staff numbers and annual turnovers, private security now occupies 'an important position in the policing landscape'. More and more, the combination of public and private policing represents the 'interpenetrating worlds of organized social control, each with its own appetite for order maintenance and crime-stopping strategies'. Van Steden argues that the police, once the central apparatus of power, are slowly becoming intermingled with privatised uses of compulsion (including arrests), search, seizure and even exclusion.

Conclusions

Within the context of the framework developed in the Dutch NWO Programme *Shifts in Governance*, I discussed the emergence of a new security architecture: a 'hybrid' combination of (semi-) public and private security actors who interact, who sometimes compete and who together share the responsible for security. The old paradigm for the location of power and accountability no longer suffices. Therefore, we have to break away from the dominant public policing framework, raise new questions and come up with new research designs to understand the changing nature of security.

I am convinced that the processes of 'fragmentation' and growing interweaving have only just started and will remain on the agenda for decades to come. I also believe that society is already reaping the benefits today as a result of the ongoing cooperation between the various different security actors – and will benefit even more in the years to come, from a security perspective. I do not fiercely oppose this process, but I do 'fear' some of the simplicity in the use of 'necessity-speak' and the structural lack of attention for some of the darker sides of the new security architecture. And because I am not in the marketing business, but operate as a social scientist, I have raised a series of questions related to accountability and governance within this new landscape that could have profound implications for human rights, privacy and civic society as a whole. The rule of law, due process and accountability are fundamental to the legitimacy of the police and other agencies, but if public policing is becoming part of a new security architecture, do the traditional checks and balances still function? Or formulated differently: are we currently witnessing policing and security arrangements on the brink of crossing accountability boundaries in an increasingly diffuse and even opaque fashion?

We will hardly be able to formulate any useful answers in a political climate that is dominated by fear, stereotyping and one-dimensional arguing, and in which no one can afford to be 'soft' on security. We seem to be caught up in an upward spiralling of security policies of which also the private sector has become an integral part. As van Steden (2007) argues: 'The Netherlands may pay lip service to strict legislation schemes for private security guards, but enforcement is weak and operatives are criticized for proficiency deficits'. Unsound and unsafe practices in the wake of the increasing 'unbounding' are dealt with in an anecdotic way.

Finally, it can be stated here that the prevailing climate is not sufficiently challenged intellectually by academics because we keep feeling predominantly 'safe and secure' with the 'normal science' (Kuhn, 1962) approaches to research and teaching. As a consequence, research remains very much limited to public policing and the public criminal justice system. Shifts in governance and shifts in the governance of security are ignored, neglected, downplayed and, in general, kept well at bay.

6
'Grey Intelligence': The Private and Informal Future

Introduction

At first glance this is an awkward chapter. I will be entering a foglike world of intelligence, espionage and (private) spooks. Intelligence (and espionage) – according to some the second profession after prostitution, and often in conjunction with it – largely falls outside of the realm of police research (and criminology). But again, referring to the political function of policing in Chapters 1 and 2, national security and intelligence have always been, and will always be, closely connected with policing. This world of spooks by nature is underresearched, but what also is neglected is the fact that spooks always intelligence always has, and has even more today, a private equivalent of CIA, MI5 and AIVD. Factual intelligence, as is discussed for factual policing in the first two chapters, is somewhat more complex and diversified than quid pro quo obligatory discussions (let alone scientific work) on what this is all about. This chapter is on the privatisation of what is supposedly a state monopoly, which is a fiction. I need the chapter for two reasons. First, I wish to break away once again from normal science and to break away from commonsense ideas about policing and security. Outside the state apparatus there are private actors performing the same intelligence functions as the state. Second, for my 'ironies, myths and paradoxes' perspective, I need this chapter to draw attention here (and in following chapters) to the drawbacks of interweaving. Also, in this domain of secrecy.

Intelligence: Out-of-the-box thinking

Robert Steele's (2005) answer to Von Clausewitz, Wilensky and other authors who write critically on the quality of intelligence sidesteps the traditional nation-state framework: 'no single nation, and certainly no single intelligence organization, is capable of single-handedly mastering the data acquisition, data entry, and data translation or data conversion challenges associated with 24/7 "global coverage". There clearly has to be room for other organizations, including private ones, who have to work together more closely.'

Intelligence covers 1) information for securing interests – political, economic and otherwise; 2) activities for gathering information and 3) organisations that perform information-collection activities.

I believe that too much focus is placed within intelligence studies on public intelligence services and that too little attention is paid to private information operations for the gradual redefinition of intelligence through public–private means. Next to formal state intelligence, we increasingly often find private – more informal – intelligence. The informal economy is also in dire need of intelligence.

I derive the concept of 'grey intelligence' from scientific police research into the blurring of boundaries between public and private security (Hoogenboom, 1991a and 1994a). 'Blue police services' have started to show shades of grey as the delimitations between public and private surveillance, supervision, enforcement, tracing, upholding order and criminal intelligence processes fade. Now, some 15 years down the line, I also wish to use the word *grey* in terms of political intelligence processes. To indicate the contemporary nature of the issue, I first refer to a number of developments in Iraq regarding PMCs. Next, I discuss the field of intelligence studies and the Netherlands Intelligence Studies Association (NISA).

I shall also address a number of key concepts that are relevant in contemplating the future of intelligence. These include privatisation of security, blurring boundaries, the 'dirty work argument' (or hydraulic principle), and 'grey policing'. I move on to look at a number of historic cases of private and public information operations, and I discuss Robert David Steele's '*seven intelligence tribes*', which he uses to break away from the state-centred framework for intelligence. I put forward a number of explanations for the increasing demand for private intelligence and, finally, include a plea for structurally expanding intelligence studies to include developments in private intelligence – and in particular the evermore blurring boundaries between public and private intelligence.

Private military companies: The Iraq case

In recent years, more and more attention has been devoted to the privatisation of war.[9] A leading book on the subject is *Corporate Warriors.*

The Rise of the Privatized Military Industry (Singer, 2003). In the Gulf War (1991), the ratio of private to military was 1:67. In Iraq it is now 1:10. In his foreword, Singer places PMCs among various scientific disciplines (political studies, international relations, organisation and business studies, political economics and intelligence studies). These highly varied fields occasionally touch on the rapid increase in PMCs, but the issue remains sketchy, superficial, lacking theoretical depth or demonstrating considerable marketing content. PMCs are an enigma. Now this is an interesting issue as they operate, to put it mildly, in controversial environments where secrecy is standard. Today, we find PMCs in Iraq, but in recent years they have been active in the Balkans, in the former Soviet Union, countries in the Middle East, in Asia and Latin America, and certainly in many African nations. War is starting to resemble the times of the Middle Ages: there is absolutely no shortage of mercenaries. But how do military warfare and private warfare relate? Functional relationships exist (contracting out), but can any other issues be distinguished? Singer believes so: 'A number of these firms walk a fine line of legality, with potentially illegitimate clients, business practices, and employees with dark pasts. Some firms are also often at the center of dangerous covert or semi-covert operations that many clients, including the U.S. government, would rather not have discussed'.

In my lectures, I sometimes do Google searches and surf PMC websites. What is important to my story here is that almost all PMCs offer intelligence services.[10] They may not all use the term *intelligence*, and when they do not, they use phrases such as 'risk analyses', 'protective security services' or 'consultancy'.

Intelligence studies

The United States and, to a lesser degree but by no means small extent, countries such as Canada, Australia and New Zealand have a long scientific tradition in intelligence studies. I refer in particular to websites on the history of intelligence, such as the following:

- CIA Center for the Study of Intelligence
- CNN Cold War History
- Department of State Office of the Historian (U.S.)
- Harvard Project On Cold War Studies
- National Archives and Records Administration (U.S.)
- National Cryptologic Museum (NSA)

- National Security Archive (George Washington University)
- Public Records Office (U.K.) (Equivalent to U.S. National Archives)

And not only history is well represented on the web. At www.loyola.edu, thousands of reports, studies, articles and lectures can be found dealing with the international intelligence community. In addition to (historical) websites, a vast body of (semi-) scientific intelligence literature has been published, and the wave of publications continues unabated. The literature contains biographies, case studies, nation studies (much has been written about Israeli intelligence, for example), but also theoretical treatises. An example of the latter is *Silent Warfare. Understanding the World of Intelli*gence (Shulsky and Schmitt, 2002).

In the Netherlands and Belgium, the discussion on intelligence is less open. In the Low Countries, we deal with the world's second oldest profession in a far more hidebound manner. Intelligence here is kept hush-hush. We deal with it like the plague in the Middle Ages – circumspectly – and we would rather avoid the topic altogether, although things are gradually changing. On the other side of the Atlantic, however, the story is very different.

The CIA has its own website (www.cia.gov) where articles from *Studies in Intelligence* (its internal journal) are published. Academia is also involved. A good example in this respect is the Federation of American Scientists (www.fas.org). The FAS runs programmes on strategic safety and publishes on matters such as commando structures, the weapons trade, biological and chemical weapons, government secrecy, intelligence and (nuclear) weapons. Here, I particularly want to point out their intelligence program, which devotes attention to recent news, government reports, reform programmes and threat analyses. The lion's share of these publications relates to public intelligence services. For the last decade or so, a greater focus has been placed on business and corporate intelligence, yet the dominant thought, analysis and discussion frameworks remain limited to traditional services.

Netherlands Intelligence Study Association (NISA)

The NISA is an independent study group that addresses information and intelligence services. Its Daily Board is formed by its members and includes representatives from academia, journalists and (former) staff from the world of intelligence. The foundation's objective is to promote an informed discussion in the Netherlands on all aspects of the work of information and intelligence services, in particular on the enhancement of historical knowledge in the field and opening up archives for research (www.nisa-intelligence.nl). I am a member of the NISA. In recent years, the NISA and/or its members have issued the following publications on (the history of) intelligence:

- *Geschiedenis van de Binnenlandse Veiligheidsdienst* (History of the National Intelligence Services)
- *Spion in de tuin. King Kong voor en na zijn dood* (Spy in the garden. King Kong before and after his death)
- *Gladio der vrije jongens. Een particuliere geheime dienst in Koude Oorlogstijd* (Gladio or the Free Riders. A Private Secret Service in the Cold War Era)
- *Villa Maarheeze* (Villa Maarheeze)

The NISA organises conferences, such as the one organised in 2005, together with the International Intelligence History Association. The majority of its publications relate to public intelligence services. Here, too, the dominant thought, analysis and discussion frameworks are limited to traditional services.

Blurring boundaries revisited

Over the last 15 years, I have become influenced by the American sociologist Gary T. Marx. On his website (web.mit.edu/gtmarx), the reader may find nearly everything he has published on security, policing, surveillance and what it is like to make a career in academia. An interesting chapter in the context of my argumentation is 'Murky Conceptual Waters: The Public and the Private'. Matters are no longer what they seem to be at first sight.

One of Marx's longer observations is particularly relevant here:

> The public/private distinction is often implicitly invoked as a way to structure the discussion and the arguments. In these discussions, the distinction 'public' and 'private' is often treated as a uni-dimensional, rigidly dichotomous and absolute, fixed and universal concept, whose meaning could be determined by the objective content of the behavior. Nevertheless, if we take a closer look at the distinction in diverse empirical contexts we find them to be more subtle, diffused and ambiguous than suggested (...). The public and private (should) be treated as multi-dimensional, continuous and relative, fluid and situational or contextual concepts, whose meaning lies in how they

> are interpreted and framed. Those using the terms public and private would benefit from more clearly specifying which dimensions they have in mind and how they relate. (p. 224)

Marx discusses five interdependencies between public and private: 1) joint investigations, 2) contracting or transferring authority to private organisations, 3) private individuals who contract private organisations, 4) the foundation of organisations in which the boundary between public and private is misty and 5) the circulation of staff.

The hydraulic principle and dirty work 'argument'

An important implication of boundaries blurring is that public and private security organisations become functional alternatives for one another. Despite conflicts of interest, competition and other conflicts, public and private can move towards one another to undertake actions that they cannot or may not do themselves. Marx introduced 'the hydraulic principle', referring to the supposed mechanism that, as the state exerts greater control on the policy and intelligence services, they find private alternatives to ensure, simply speaking, that certain things get done. In other words, they outsource 'the dirty work'.

Grey policing

I have integrated a number of the above concepts in the idea of 'grey policing'. (Hoogenboom, 1991a and 1994a). I later added the informal exchange of classified information via what is known as the old-boy networks. I will illustrate this using a number of empirical cases.

Private intelligence cases

We are currently experiencing a gradual growth of (historical) research into private intelligence. On various intelligence websites, for example, a greater number of contributions can be found on corporate and business intelligence. To a large degree, this is related to the acquisition of competitive intelligence from open sources. There is, however, also a clear increase in the number of case studies on private espionage through infiltration and bribery. In *Het Politiecomplex* (The Police Complex, 1994), I wrote about the 'de-monopolization of political intelligence activities'. The examples I mentioned include the formation in the 1930s of black lists for the registration of employees with 'dubious' thoughts on social relationships ('left-wing agitators'); infiltration in the 1960s of the anti-apartheid movement in the United Kingdom, and the 'formers' (former intelligence agents) from Israel, Britain and the United States who privately collected intelligence in the seventies and eighties. I also used notions developed by such as 'private CIAs and private information boutiques'.

The Netherlands (1905–1950)

Between 1905 and 1966, maintaining the peace within the business setting of the mines in the province of Limburg (in the south of the Netherlands) was in the hands of the Mining Police, a (semi-) public police force that practically and almost exclusively served the corporate interests of the mines (Hoogenboom, 1996). In the early 1920s, a corporate investigator was taken on board, with another three added in 1928 for its new investigations department. The department was charged with investigating the backgrounds of (new) employees in their countries of origin (the Ruhr and Saar area, Silesia, Poland and the Balkans). The emphasis lay on morality issues and political interests. A card system was developed in cooperation with the personnel department and files were created for a total of well over 25,000 miners. On various occasions, the head of the Mining Police was quoted as saying: 'Give me four investigators and I won't need the rest of the Mining Police'. Morality issues at the time related to adultery or absconding and leaving wife and children, financial issues and suicide attempts, to name but a few examples.

Between 1929 and 1937, the average number of investigations per year amounted to 14,305, of which more than half related to background screening. The investigations department had established intelligence relationships with the GSIII, the first national military intelligence service in Belgium, Germany, France and the Netherlands. In addition, information channels were set up with companies such as the Batavian Petroleum Company, Philips, KLM-Fokker and the Rotterdam Shipping Company. These companies also employed internal security officials, through whom contacts were made. Over the years, a number of robberies were thwarted, as were industrial espionage operations and a number of political conspiracies.

Political intelligence at the time related to the detection of people harbouring anarchic, communist and socialist sympathies. In the 1930s, a clear focus was also aimed at rising National Socialism, with the Mining Police preventing what was considered to be aberrant political expression. Parliament questioned the actions of the Mining Police, but no action was taken. An interesting fact to note here is that questions were raised regarding the difference in democratic control with respect to the public police and the (semi-) public – but actually private – mines.

The Philips Company was also actively involved in private information collection in the 1930s. Private intelligence operations flourished during the years following the World War II. A number of former resistance activists found it difficult to adapt and felt bitter about the way in which cleansing activities had taken place – or failed to take place. There was also considerable dissatisfaction about the government's decolonisation policy. According to the private initiatives witnessed at the time should first and foremost be understood within this context and subsequently also within the framework of the Cold War. These private initiatives offered a structure for the expression of social discontent, the continuation of former activities, and for channelling right-wing political notions.

The Stichting Opleiding Arbeidskrachten Nederland (SOAN) (Foundation for Staff Training Netherlands) offers a good illustration of this point. The foundation was financed by a group of preeminent figures from politics, management and business. Within SOAN, a secret group existed that 'collected its information through both group investigations and cooperation with officers at the police, justice and military intelligence services'.

Other publications

Other cases are mentioned in other articles I have written, including the following:

- *Particulier gewroet en ongekanaliseerde waakzaamheiddrang* (Private burrowing and the uncontrolled need for vigilance) (1996)
- *Kwetsbare kennis* (Vulnerable knowledge) (1996, editorial with Marc Cools)
- *Bedrijfsspionage: infiltratie en inlichtingenwerk in de private sector* (Corporate espionage: infiltration and intelligence operations in the private sector) (2001)
- *The Private Eye that Never HSleeps* (2005)

In a number of these articles, I discuss the infiltration by Wackenhut (commissioned by Exxon) in the Alaskan environmental movement. This particular case was investigated by the U.S. House of Representatives and is one of the best-documented cases I have ever seen.[11]

And then: Religious intelligence

Not only political and economic interest groups are active in the espionage market, but also religious and ideological groups. In this respect, the Church of Scientology has been cropping up regularly since the 1970s. Whenever criminal proceedings were instigated regarding members of staff, the Guardian Office (GO) was called in. The GO has since been dismantled, but its activities continue. Allegations primarily focus on the Information Bureau, or Branch I, which has a legal intelligence department (overt data collection) and two illegal intelligence departments: the ODC (Overt Data Collection) and the CDC (Covert Data Collection).[12] Staff members are trained with the help of a 'confidential training programme', in which they are expected to study classic works such as *The Art of War* by Sun Tzu and Von Clausewitz's *On War*. They also cover the 'fundamentals of intelligence operations (Invest Basic), investigative techniques (Investigation Tech), Security and Infiltration, Attacks on Scientology, dealing with governments and public relations as well as the area of law and legal processes'. One chapter in the training programme is devoted to managing private detectives.

More recent work

In his work *Schone Schijn. Smerige streken in de strijd tussen burgers en bedrijven* (Good appearances. Dirty tricks in the battle between civilians and companies), Lubbers discusses more recent cases (2004). With today's ongoing 'acceleration' following the growth of the sector and the increasing attention paid by PMCs to intelligence, private intelligence is adopting a more contemporary look.

Seven intelligence tribes

So, what about the future of intelligence? Steele distinguishes seven intelligence tribes: the government, the military, law enforcement, business, academia, the combination of nongovernmental organisations (NGOs) and the media, and finally religious groups. In doing so, he sidesteps the traditional intelligence framework that is limited to the state. He also advocates extensive cooperation between the seven tribes and argues that a standardised concept apparatus for preventing misunderstandings (www.oss.net) represents the basis for cooperation.

Steele is highly critical of the oldest tribe. He talks and writes about intelligence failures in intelligence collection, processing and analysis. This is topped by a leadership failure, which altogether demands a redefinition of intelligence (new craft of intelligence). To achieve this, the tribes must work together systematically.

Reasons for the increasing demand for private intelligence

A number of reasons may be given for the increasing privatisation of security, including private intelligence. Below, I cover each of them briefly.

Declining public trust in government

It is frequently seen that people and parts of the market no longer trust governments. Public trust is declining because people feel that procedural rules have (too) many limitations to fight crime effectively. Trust may also decline as a result of perceived corruption on the part of the political-governance and official apparatus.

State withdrawal

An increasing cost consciousness within government is currently leading to governmental cutbacks and the disposal of public duties. Internationally, government has now become the largest client, also on the security market.

Increasing crime and subjective insecurity

Over the last 40 years, crime statistics around the world have risen, as have objective and subjective feelings of insecurity. Crime is especially violent in third-world countries. The free market principle has led to the rise of commercial (nongovernment-controlled) media. Negative news collection – and therefore crime – simply sells. The media blow up sensational crime incidents and thereby enhance feelings of insecurity. Also, competition within and between the public and private services sector is leading to an 'exaggeration' of threat analyses. We are increasingly often confronted by new annual reports and surveys that point to (new) forms of criminality (cyber crime, Internet fraud). These reports partly reflect reality, but they are also prompted by political, political-positional and commercial interests. This generates a self-perpetuating dynamic, which in turn leads to an even greater demand for security. Supply is creating demand: the more civilians and companies protect themselves, the more the feeling of insecurity grows. At the same time, the present belief that public policing cannot (any longer) meet expectations is also stronger than ever before. Ergo: a demand has risen for private security.

Changes in the economic system

Today, we are witness to an immense shift in scale in the private domain. Residential areas, shopping malls, recreational and production sites are all increasing in size. In these large-scale private domains, the need for security equals the security needs felt in the public domain. Thus, we see a demand for private security as well as a demand for intelligence. And as stated earlier, those with economic interests (the new authorities) therefore increasingly often organise their own security measures.

Changes in the political system

The privatisation of transport, telecommunications, utility sectors, education and so forth makes these institutions more vulnerable. Privatisation also generates a demand for private security.

Other explanations

Other explanations include the growing transfer of authority regarding police services and their execution by supranational organisations. This holds for both public and private policing. Authority (power and control) is increasingly often exercised by international public bodies such as the United Nations (peacekeeping operations), the EU (Europol, Eurojust) and transnational police organisations (FBI, U.S. Customs, DEA), but also by multinational private security operations.

'Seven tribes': Opportunities and threats

On the basis of the issues mentioned above, I would favour a structural expansion of the intelligence studies arena to include private intelligence developments, with a particular focus on the ever-blurring boundaries demarcating the field. To dust off an old but relevant cliché: a changing world demands new theoretical and empirical insights.

From a social perspective, there is a clear need to organise intelligence more quickly and more effectively. I am convinced that the private security sector can and must play an important role in this development. As always, however, there are two sides to this coin. On the one hand, we can distinguish instrumental objectives ('war on drugs', 'war on terror' and so on). On the other, we see objectives that focus on the protection of human rights.

Singer is diametrically opposed to Steele regarding the use and necessity of extensively blurred boundaries. We are witness to a new phenomenon that no longer fits in with existing scientific frameworks and that is not only controversial but also occurring in secret. The PMCs – and their associated intelligence operations – demand far greater transparency. Who is doing what and for whom? And who is monitoring it all?

Steele opposes Marx. The latter writes that 'new technologies for collecting personal information (intelligence, BH) which transcend the physical, liberty enhancing limitations of the old means are constantly appearing. They probe more deeply, widely and softly than traditional methods, transcending barriers (whether walls, distance, darkness, skin or time) that historically made personal information inaccessible. The boundaries which have defined and given integrity to social systems, groups and the self are increasingly permeable. The power of governmental and private organizations to compel disclosure (whether based on law or circumstance) and to aggregate, analyze and distribute personal information is growing rapidly'.[13]

Any self-respecting scientist has to reply by saying that more research is required to answer the question how instrumentality and the protection of human rights are related. Or rather: how they can be harmonised? This is no run-of-the-mill problem concerning your every-day garden variety of crime in the streets. However, in the worlds of private tracking and tracing, private warfare and private intelligence, harmonisation would seem to be virtually impossible. This is logical and at the same time disappointing, because it is precisely here that developments take place the fastest and in the most drastic fashion. It is also here that they are being researched the least.

7
The Sopranos: Narrative Knowledge to Disrupt Academic Language

Introduction

This chapter is somewhat strange, somewhat out of place and somewhat nonsciencelike. Of course all of this is somewhat 'not true'. For almost a quarter of a century, I moved in and out of social sciences to understand a little of policing and security. Throughout the years from time to time, my dissatisfaction with theory, concepts, methodology and other scientific rules and regulations popped up. As Goffman states, 'Life is too complicated for theories'. Along the line I developed an interest in 'narrative knowledge'. Telling stories goes right back to the dawn of civilisation. Ancient myths are still today strong and powerful ways for us to understand life and death. I trained as a historian in the 1980s and remember the often-heated academic debates on whether or not history is an academic discipline or merely an art of telling (convincing) stories. Narrative need not involve language only; 'it often gains impact through enactment or the emotional focusing that music offers in dance, theater, opera or film, or the visual focus in stage lighting, comics or film'.

In this chapter, I bring in Tony Soprano because I love the guy and the series, but also because the series in my view is a perfect example of the way we – as social scientists – are sometimes lost in macro, abstract and nonemotional exposés on crime, policing and security. I believe series like these are useful in understanding social reality and useful in formulating new research questions. Of course 'normal science' hates the very idea. The original Dutch version was part of a thematic issue of *Justitiele Verkenningen* (Judicial Explorations) from the Ministry of Justice titled 'Imagination and Crime'. People from different backgrounds wrote about computer war games, crime and literature, crime and the movies and crime in television series. One of the editors flatly denied cooperation up front ('this is not science'). It turned out that the Ministry of Justice received more hits for that issue than for any other policy or scientific report it had previously published. Sometimes satisfaction lies in little stories. Therefore, I created a play with Tony Soprano acting as a guide for the social sciences. There are many more ways to satisfy our academic curiosity than abstract language only.

Tony Soprano is instrumental for me also in terms of the factual interweaving of under and upper world. I always have found the distinction between good and bad guys, bona-fide corporations and organised crime and the like somewhat lacking in imagination and ignorant of factual sociological knowledge. In this way, this chapter is a sort of introduction to Chapter 10 in which I argue that the boundaries between (organised) crime, white-collar crime, state crime and terrorism are not that clear. I need this chapter also to pinpoint 'ironies, myths and paradoxes' in policing and security: the interweaving of crime, organised crime, white-collar crime and state crime is interesting in itself, but at the same times offers perhaps a glimpse into our understanding of why the state (and therefore the police) is pursuing a policy of integration of different policing and security actors: only in the combination of fragmented information can pictures of the whole criminological spectrum be understood.

Setting the stage

The stage is a nightclub called the Bada Bing ('where all the drinks are on the house'). Naked women are dancing in the background. Tony Soprano is sitting at a table full of Italian food and is discussing organised crime. Among his guests are a few famous criminologists. The topics they are about to discuss include the fear and anxiety felt by organised crime figures (Tony is on Prozac), their irrational behaviour, the fact that chance, luck and improvisation are constant factors in 'organised' crime, that those involved in organised crime constantly imitate Hollywood gangster movies (as Marlon Brando 'wannabes') and finally the structural nature of corruption in all social processes. This is offset against theories and stereotypes dealing with 'organised' crime in terms of 'alien conspiracies'.

The idea for the play stems from the concept of narrative knowledge (storytelling), which states that, for empathic reasons and for developing new ideas and hypotheses, rational thinking can and must be complemented by art and literature.

My all-star cast features

- Tony Soprano, one of the main characters in the television series *The Sopranos*;
- William J. Chambliss, the criminologist who wrote *On the Take; from Petty Crooks to Presidents* (1988). His analysis of criminal networks in Seattle is a true classic. The networks he describes consist of alternating coalitions of entrepreneurs, politicians, law-and-order professionals and criminals. Nobody has absolute power. Again and again, new choices have to be made regarding the next strategy;
- Patrick Van Calster, the Flemish criminologist who obtained his PhD degree in 2005 for a book in which he supplements the various classic hierarchical, economic and network approaches to organised crime with anthropology and notions from chaos theory. He discusses coincidental interactions and conversations that, on occasion, generate criminal projects. In practice, these are held together through irrationalities, coincidences, insecurities and improvisations (Van Calster, 2005);
- Serge Gutwirth, Van Calster's professor and author of *Dostoevsky: A Criminologist?* (Gutwirth, 1985). Gutwirth, pleading for narrative knowledge, is interested in 'underground characters' who are dissatisfied with the wall of scientific and moral values by which the 'mediocre' surround themselves;
- Gary Marx, who believes that many scientific professionals are 'unduly timid, antiseptic, laundered, formal, and scholastic'. He recommends movies, books and TV series to understand the reality of crime and punishment;
- Maurice Punch, the very first police researcher in the Netherlands. Punch wrote *Fout is fout; gesprekken met de politie in de binnenstad van Amsterdam* (Wrong is wrong; discussions with the police in the heart of Amsterdam, 1976) as well as *Grievous Business Harm; Exploring Corporate Violence* (1995);
- Dr Melfi ('I've always had a charm for sociopaths'), Tony's psychiatrist; and
- Edwin Sutherland, the criminologist who analyses the structural character of crime in corporate life in his *White Collar Crime* (first published in 1949).

Everyone is sitting at a round table filled with plates of spaghetti marinara, bolognese, pomodori, carbonara and bottles of Barolo. They are about to discuss 'organised' crime, albeit from a completely new and original perspective. Stress and fear, irrational behaviour, coincidental meetings and imitating Mafia bosses form the central themes. The assembled group will also touch on corruption as a structural aspect of social processes, and end with a plea for *storytelling* (narrative knowledge) to address the plain fears concerning all these events – everything that is discontinuous, argumentative, violent, pugnacious, disorderly and precarious – in short, all those issues that do not or should not fit in with standard scientific thought and analysis systems (Foucault, 1976).

Scenes from *The Sopranos* are interlaced with scientific insights into organised crime. I find inspiration in *Instrumentaliteit en rechtsbescherming* (Instrumentality and legal protection) by Foqué and 't Hart (1990). In Chapter 10b, *Narrativiteit als ontregeling* (Narrative as a form of disruption), they put in a plea for creating space for stories alongside the rational scientific ideal.[14] Literary stories transgress the political and the scientific – often abstract and thereby simplified – representations of reality by pointing out inherent contradictions, indistinctness and the diversity of all that is possible in reality. Literary stories can highlight hidden meanings and paradoxes. They also have the ability to touch readers on an emotional level.

Stress and fear

Chambliss: Do you remember me writing about Frank? Frank who is always playing with his keys, sitting in the *Starfire Room Cabaret*? Naked women dancing on three different stages. Waitresses serving diluted drinks to the customers. Every now and then, one of them heads upstairs with one of the dancers. Frank is bored to death. The money, the women, the discussions about business and his involvement. None of it really touches him any more.' (Chambliss, 1988, 75).

Soprano: That's my Bada Bing.

Dr Melfi: You're Frank, Tony.

Sutherland: Who's going to tell the audience about *The Sopranos*?

Marx: Tony Soprano is the main character in the American TV show *The Sopranos*, which went on air in 1999 and ended in 2007. Year in, year out, the show received the highest awards. In the series, Tony Soprano is trying to run two families: his own and a Mafia family in New Jersey – with varying degrees of success. He regularly loses control of both families and of himself. In the first episode of the first series, hounded by stress and fears that lead to panic attacks, Tony ends up on the couch of female psychiatrist Dr Melfi, whom he visits in almost every subsequent episode. As a true macho man and Mafioso, Tony finds it extremely difficult to share his inner conflicts – especially with a woman. He conquers the issue. Dr Melfi prescribes Prozac for him.

Gutwirth: David Chase, the creator of *The Sopranos*, makes the absurd joke that life in America is now so selfish that even gangsters, the epitome of selfishness, can no longer endure it and therefore need therapy.

Sutherland: 'Throughout the series, traditional Mafia scenes (murder and manslaughter, criminal acts and blatant violence) are interlaced with scenes from the daily lives of the various characters. Violence is offset by tenderness. Machos are machos, but from time to time also highly vulnerable and sensitive. Tony has difficult and troublesome relationships with his mother, his wife, his two growing children, all his confidants, and all of his business partners, whether legal or illegal. On the one hand, Tony Soprano is an extremely violent Mafioso confirming all the stereotypes. On the other hand, each episode highlights his fears. He has plenty of reasons to be on Prozac. This variation and the humour with which it is presented throughout the series are a combination that has proven to be irresistible to million of viewers around the world.

Van Calster: Mattijs van de Port points out the importance of emotions and living in fear in the world of crime. Both impact the creative processes in criminal organisations. He is surprised that so little attention has in fact been paid to the matter in the various studies available. He refers to Bourgeois (1995) who described the horrifying existence of crack dealers. Katz (1988) also writes about criminals' 'emotional housekeeping'. Van de Port calls for a greater focus on fear, paranoia and mistrust.

Irrational behaviour

Sutherland: Much has been written about the Mafia, Mr. Soprano. Scientists have filled book after book with theories on 'organised' crime: about its hierarchical structures, the (threat of) violence, the corporate planning and the distribution of markets.

Soprano: I have never heard so much crap in my life. Look at episode 1.9 (*Boca*) and Uncle Junior, my very own uncle with whom I'm always fighting about family power. Of course he cares about money, networks and contacts, but he gets really mad and motivated when someone gossips (*chiacchierone: chatterbox*) about his cunnilingus skills. That touches his manhood ('it's a sign of weakness – at least if you give. Taking is something else').[15] He first directs his anger at his mistress. She gossiped about Uncle Junior's talent with his business partners' women, including Carmela, my wife. Carmela told me. And I play the card during a round of golf with Uncle Junior. It's a repeating factor in my life. Hints are rife: 'going down', 'whistling in the wheat field', and so forth. Emotions, in this case about manhood and associated slurs, often dominate over hierarchy or corporate interests. In episode 1.8 (*Legend of Tennessee Moltisanti*), Christopher Moltisanti, one of Tony's lieutenants, is treated disrespectfully by a baker and asks him: 'Do I look like a pussy to you?' He's shot on the spot. Entirely irrational, but understandable in our macho world. It's like the fact that it took me a great deal of effort throughout the series to admit to others that I am undergoing treatment with Dr Melfi.

There's an even better example in episode 4.2 (*No Show*). Johnny 'Sack', one of the boHsses, turns against the family because he heard through the grapevine that Ralphie told a joke about his corpulent wife: 'I heard she had a 95-pound mole removed from her body'. The bosses are in the middle of a lucrative real estate scam, but the deal starts to fall apart. Johnny 'Sack' wants to have Ralphie killed and some of Ralphie's friends want to prevent it by having Johnny 'Sack' knocked off. Johnny's honour is at stake, but so are the Family's mores. For three full episodes, the entire family finds itself on a knife's edge– an emotional battlefield – and threatened to be cut in half. It's only about feelings, about respect and the lack of it, yielding or not yielding, and lying or not lying. Irrationalities, to use your scientific jargon, but on a different level – our level – highly rational.

Coincidental meetings

Sutherland: Mr. Soprano, can you tell us anything about your middle-term to long-term planning and the setup and maintenance of your organisation?

Soprano: Jesus Christ, cut all the rational shit. Things just happen. It's like George Michael sings: 'Turn a different corner and we never would have met'. I meet someone. We get into a discussion. Somewhere in the middle a business opportunity pops up amongst all the other stuff. Sometimes it's a criminal plan.

Punch: Hasn't this sort of thing been said about Schiphol Airport near Amsterdam? Sixty thousand people working in full-on jobs where they are randomly approached by illegal immigrants and drug smugglers to help them out to facilitate criminality for three to five thousand euros?

Van Calster: Frank Bovenkerk, the Dutch criminologist, says that close criminal ventures are created by linking pins looking for new contacts and transactions.

Dr Melfi: And anyone could be that pin. And they can meet anyone at any time of day.

Marx: Linking pins can be compared to movie producers who also act as a pivot in temporary cooperative ventures (Van Calster, 2005; DeFilippi and Arthur, 1998). Producers link financers, scriptwriters, actors, movie companies and directors. They in turn create other networks, although they organise these themselves. They are also personally responsible for the relationship and for making contacts. There is no central leadership, not one single *Capo di Tutti Capi*, and no tight schedule. Again and again, they are asked to improvise. When the project's over, everyone goes home. Sometimes they'll meet again, often they won't.

Soprano: And this happens all day every day: in the Bada Bing, at the town hall, within the attorney general's office, in newspaper editorials, and certainly in boardroom meetings at Enron, Ahold and Shell.

I meet these people all day long. Often here in the Bada Bing.

Punch: This suddenly reminds me of Yab Yum, the luxury brothel in Amsterdam that was mentioned in the parliamentary inquiry into the building industry in relation to 'the culture of bribery and lavish behaviour' witnessed in the construction industry.

Soprano: The Bada Bing and the Starfire Room Cabaret and Yab Yum are all the sance. Do you guys ever get out?

Van Calster: If you look at the autobiographies written by criminals such as Howard Marks and Sammy Gravano, you will notice the large number of changing interactions and meetings (Morselli, 2000). Marks, like we do in 'normal' life, meets thousands and thousands of people and during some of those meetings and discussions – generally coincidental – the individuals influence one another and devise (criminal) projects.

Dr Melfi: My ideas for articles, lectures or books also stem from discussions with Joe Sixpack. Sometimes the conversations are planned: semistructured interviews in the context of an investigation. At other times, however, they're coincidental discussions. Or maybe based on a book that I've read, a movie I've seen, or a commercial on TV.

Van Calster: Howard Marks got involved in pot smuggling without a grand plan. He smokes pot himself. As a student, he came to know Graham Plinston and after a while they lost track of one another. Marks pursued an academic career and still smokes pot. Years later, they meet again and Plinston occasionally supplies Marks with hashish. Sometimes Marks buys more than the recreational amount and involves himself in small-scale drug dealing.

In his biography, Howard Marks describes how Plinston met 'Lebanese Joe' in Morocco. Joe knows Sam Hiraoui, who works for the Lebanese airlines and runs a textile company in Dubai. According to Marks, Dubai is the largest smugglers' port in the Middle East – not only for drug trafficking, but also for the smuggling of gold and silver. Sam's partner in Dubai is an Afghan called Mohammed Duranni. Plinston gets involved in discussions with all these people and the idea is formed to smuggle pot on a larger scale. Howard Marks, however, is completely unaware of this.

At a certain point, Plinston disappears from the scene. His wife asks Howard Marks to help her look for his old friend. She last heard of Plinston having an appointment in Germany. Howard Marks finds the trail and starts investigating. Plinston has been arrested and is locked up jail in Basel. Howard organises a lawyer. Mohammed Durani is impressed by Marks's actions. He offers him Plinston's place. Initially he refuses, but finally agrees. In his biography, he explains how he had no idea how to handle the meeting with Durani. He also did not know how that he was going to sell the batch of hash. He moves to London, where he frequents parties and initiates conversations with strangers in search of turnover.

Soprano: There's a constant throughout the episodes: many of the scenes take place in the Bada Bing, in restaurants, in the kitchen at my home, and at outdoor cafés where we drink espresso. I'm talking constantly. The majority of the conversations are just a load of hot air. Common or garden texts about each other, about sports, about politics. Suddenly, in the middle of one of these conversations, we come up with an idea.

Gutwirth: On a more analytical level, one of the most important patterns you discern in Howard Marks's criminal career is that each new criminal project arises from more or less coincidental meetings. You can't pinpoint a particular time or place. There is no prior rational planning. The same is true for the localisation of a director, the *Capo di Tutti Capi*. Criminal careers are formed by years and years of brief discussions. These discussions in turn lead to new ideas and actions by those involved.

Sutherland: So this means that we can discard much of our criminological explanations. It's generally coincidence combined with a natural aptitude to learning.

Van Calster: I usually call them transformations: discussions create ideas. Discussion partners exert a mutual influence and improvisation is rife in both the planning and the execution stages. Through ongoing interactions, adjustments are continually being made to the plans as well as their implementation.[16] There's really no beginning or end to criminal projects. Discussions often arise from coincidence. There's no fixed pool of participants, and it's certainly not planned. The speakers are constantly improvising and there's huge insecurity (Zaitch, 2002). Everyone has his or her own personal objectives and interests that don't necessarily serve the venture (Kleemans et al., 1998).

Sutherland: So it's not about individuals' rational qualities? It sounds as if success is determined by the ability to improvise. By pragmatic qualities.

Van Calster: Yes, those with a pragmatic attitude can deal with the unpredictability of a given situation. At the same time, they can influence matters. But again, there's also simple coincidence. Part of my inspiration came from research into the way the unemployed look for jobs. The majority don't find employment through advertisements or headhunters and the like, but rather through personal contacts (Granovetter, 1973). And even then, these people are often chance acquaintances and not people they know well: the so-called friends of friends (Boissevain, 1974; Granovetter, 1973).

Punch: I like 'organised' crime's messy character. It's seems to me that it's no more than improvised acting. The actors come together and one simply starts talking. The other reacts and gets an answer. Nobody actually knows where the play is heading, and people are constantly dependent on the words spoken in response to someone reacting to someone else.

Sutherland: Crime's microstructure is logical. In science, we look for major theoretical words on meso and macro levels. This kills the micro world. It eradicates the contradictions, coincidences, fears and idiocies. The love. The melancholy. Aniskiewicz (1994) – Patrick Van Calster quotes him – says that the formation of theory on organised crime can only be understood when researchers concentrate on 'an existential understanding of the microstructure (that) would concentrate on identity, danger, violence, risk, and excitement within the criminal lifestyle'. Peter Klerks (2000, 353) notes that criminology is not up to that yet. It doesn't have the frame of thought to fully realise such an ambition.

Van Calster: No, because we're looking for patterns and regularity. Laws and universal principles. However, there's an immense amount of insecurity. Howard Marks often has no idea how to use his relations. Ideas are only formed during conversations. In 1980, Marks was convicted for drug smuggling. He was in jail for almost two years and was released in May 1982. Marks promised his wife never to get involved in crime again. To celebrate his release, they go to Corfu. Their neighbours are esteemed bigwigs on the island and introduce the couple to the British consul. At various receptions, they meet government officials, international business people, journalists and a gun smuggler. The latter was on the island because of the Falklands war. Over a drink, Marks talks about his smuggling history. The weapons dealer hands him his business card and before you know it another criminal project is underway.

Imitative behaviour

Punch: Mr. Soprano, does the Mafia actually exist?

Soprano: Words, words, and more words. Do you know the only person who knows what the Mafia is? Marlon Brando. Mafia, Mafia! There's corruption in politics, in bureaucracy, on Wall Street and in business. In between, there are a couple of clever guys, often of Italian origin, who bring together supply and demand when it comes to illegal goods and services. The rational concept of 'organised' crime is an invention by Hollywood, the press and boring scientists. Marlon Brando was the right man at the right place at the right time. In the sixties and early seventies, the importance of the Mafia, led by a number of Italian Americans, quickly dwindled. At the same time, the grip of organised crime on the collective imagination started an irrepressible rise to the top.[17] In his book *Underboss*, convicted assassin Sammy 'The Bull' Gravano describes how members of the Gambino family were obsessed by the Godfather movies. This was indeed so much so that the habits and the language displayed – and even titles such as 'consigliore' – were adopted.

Van Calster: Winlow says that not only publications on organised crime, but also movies, newspaper articles and (auto) biographies provide a wide range of ideas to (potential) criminals. He describes how criminals try to imitate Robert de Niro in *Goodfellas*. They take on his use of language, the violence and the gestures. Interaction processes between art and reality. Who imitates whom? Who influences whom? In interviews, criminals have said that the way in which they held up a truck was directly taken from *Goodfellas*. Remick speaks of criminals who have imitated de Niro's chuckle in *Mean Streets*. One criminal has stated that he learned much of his trade from *Once Upon a Time in America* and *Goodfellas*. And in his work *Misdaadprofielen* (Crime profiles), Bovenkerk describes how Klaas Bruinsma was known to be influenced by books on gangsters. This is what Taussig calls 'social mimesis: a space (...) in which it is far from easy to say who is the imitator and who is imitated, which is the copy and which is the original'.

Sutherland: But what are scientists and research journalists then actually researching?

Soprano: At the moment, *The Sopranos* is by far the best illustration of the meshes formed by fiction and reality. I don't know exactly what 'mimesis' means, but it sounds like mimic. I like that.

Dr Melfi: You know, I talked to Bob Hoogenboom recently. He's writing an article on the *ring tones* on the mobile phones of those he meets in the police force, in the private investigation sector and the intelligence community. There's a pattern: *The Godfather, Mission Impossible, the A-Team, The Persuaders* and *Blackadder* ('I have a cunning plan'). His point is that a number of them can no longer distinguish reality from fiction. They live in the real world, but have boyish fantasies that date back to the days when they were teenagers and teamed up in their own secret little 'Black Hand Gang'. Boys will be boys. Hoogenboom has a *Sopranos* ring tone. Pauli says: 'This phone's bugged. Don't say nuttin' about the place. Or the other place either. Or the guy from the other place. Now pick it up!

Soprano: Pauli's horn plays *The Godfather* music. The whole series is a tribute to *The Godfather*. We all want to be Marlon Brando.

Corruption everywhere

Chambliss: An interesting feature of Patrick Van Calster's story, and of that in *The Sopranos*, is the interweaving of legal and illegal activities. The hash smuggling takes place within a legal corporate context. Howard Marks has a regular job, Sam Hiraoui and Duranni own a textile company and Hiraoui works for the Lebanese airlines. The legal context is instrumental for the criminal activities, but wasn't set up as such.

Soprano: In each episode, the boundaries between the underworld and the straight world blur. I talk and do business with hotel owners, waste disposal companies, transporters, board members, bureaucrats, car dealers, priests, shop owners, university managers and the police. The majority of my dealings with them are legal, but in the middle of it all, I hand out loans to decent people for their gambling debts. And if they don't pay, I get violent. Politicians, bureaucrats and police officers approach me, and I approach them. We do some business and everyone gains. I deal with politicians, civil servants and police officers who generally work within the framework of the law. But these politicians, civil servants, project developers and I benefit from investments through inside knowledge. Policemen provide information. I give them an envelope and for the rest of the day they go back fighting crime. And I don't mean the latter cynically.

Chambliss: Nobody is completely pure and innocent.

Marx: My hero Irving Goffman said it all: 'Life is too complicated for theories'. People function on 10 or 12 levels. In the morning, scientists-cum-consultants may be giving wonderful lectures on integrity and ethics in public administration, and later in the day circumvent the tender regulations for scientific research for the common good. Rational scientific thought is one-dimensional. Life – and therefore life in crime – is multi-faceted.

Chambliss: The group of financiers includes jewellers, project developers, lawyers, businessmen and industrialists. The financiers meet the organisers. The organisers consist of three categories. First, there's the businessmen. They own restaurants and gambling halls, they're cabaret and hotel proprietors, pawnbrokers and club owners. Decent people like you and me. Second, there's the politicians. They're on various boards (mayors, aldermen, members of the Provincial States and national politicians), in organisations that dispense permits, and they're in supervisory bodies. Finally, there's the supers. Heads of police, public prosecutors, policemen responsible for controlling the nightlife, youth and the vice squad, and policemen in the upper and lower ranks of surveillance. The criminals are the fourth category. The underworld. The gamblers, the pimps, the hookers, drug dealers, bouncers and the bookies.

Punch: I came across this sort of setup in the mid-70s in the Amsterdam Warmoesstraat. In *Conduct Unbecoming* (1985), I describe police corruption. The Stones sympathise with the devil and sing: 'Just as every cop is a criminal, and all you sinners' saints'.

Dr Melfi: The first three categories are formed by people with whom we engage in professional and social interaction, and when you come to think about it the fourth is too, actually. There's no real difference. No separate category for criminals with their own bus lanes. They're with us in our cars, in the trains, we have meetings with them, and we do business with them.

Chambliss: That's exactly why I describe Richard Nixon in his Watergate period. The presidency is not set up for it, but it certainly offers the necessary opportunities for a few criminal activities in between. That's why I chose *From Petty Crooks to Presidents* as the book's subtitle.

Punch: The same is true for Philip Morris and British and American tobacco. CEOs from these multinationals decided to sell a quarter of their production via criminal networks. They were ducking duties on a major scale. The EU recently handed out fines to the tune of 1.3 billion euros.

Soprano: I should give these guys a call sometime.

Chambliss: To fine-tune the picture even further, I called my last chapter *The Enemy Is Us*. Corruption is embedded in a large number of social processes. People react to the opportunities they're presented with, often as a result of the positions they hold.

Sutherland: I thought you spent a lot of time and energy on organised crime in Holland?

Punch: Sure, on paper. And a lot of that time and energy goes to the bowels of Antillean drug swallowers.

Sutherland: Surely they can't fit that much in there?

Punch: The other 99 per cent of the smuggling takes place by means of containers, but it costs a lot of money – and therefore trade – to devote too much time to that (Zoomer, Nieuwkamp et al., 2004).

Chambliss: One of the reasons we don't manage to understand crime is that we define crime as a separate set of activities. Entirely separate from – and intrinsically different from – legal business. But much of crime is not easy to categorise. It's just business, or politics, or running a city. The fact that from time to time the activities are illegal is an historic slipup over which those who are involved in the activities have no control (Chambliss, 1998, 53).

Punch: It's true for customs officials at Schiphol, and also in part for the other 60,000 people who work there. It's true for the CEOs of multinationals, too. And in between, there's the government functionaries with supervisory roles or charged with enforcement and tracing. A number of them devise creative opportunities for self-enrichment within the positions they hold.

Van Calster: Many of Howard Marks's legal business ventures are instrumental in solving practical and important problems in his illegal trading. The same is true the other way round. Both business activities make Marks who he is and contribute to his success.

Sutherland: My definition of *white-collar crime*: people who make use of their position and status to enrich themselves.

Soprano: I do everything within a legal context. The Bada Bing has a permit. I have a registered consultancy in 'waste management'.

Dr Melfi: 'I first thought it was because of his depression. That's why I prescribed Prozac. Later I realised that many social processes are characterised by structural incidental corruption. Mayors have discussions at home with contractors, fly to football matches, do their management part, and somewhere in between there are criminal activities.

Chambliss: That's exactly the way the criminal network in Seattle works. I started with participative observations. As a taxi driver, as a barkeeper. I witnessed the fourth category. The stereotypes from the underworld. Not until later did I notice the meetings between the other three categories: the financiers, the organisers, and those who uphold the law.

Punch: Violence is always seen as an important criterion in defining 'organised' crime and in distinguishing it from other social occurrences. That's rubbish. Violence occurs in a wide range of settings, and especially in a legal context (Punch, 1995). In the sixties and seventies, the automotive industry produced unsafe cars in the full knowledge that they were unsafe; for decades, the tobacco industry has manipulated scientific research in its attempts to show that (passive) smoking doesn't cause cancer; huge disasters such as Chernobyl, Three Mile Island, Seveso, Sandos, the Amoco Cadiz, the Torrey Canyon, the Exxon Valdez and Bhopal were (in part) caused by a conscious failure to invest – or by investing too little – in safe working conditions. As a result of the Bhopal disaster alone, an estimated two to five thousand people have died. Every year, the pharmaceutical industry dumps out-of-date medicines on third-world markets with fatal consequences for the patients. The latest discussions concern the manipulation of scientific research by the pharmaceutical industry sector in bribing professors and having them conduct scientific fraud to make sure they show the positive effects of medicines we don't actually need.

Soprano: I like the Prozac.

Sutherland: I recently read something about physical and psychological violence, neglect and sexual abuse. In the Netherlands, it is estimated that between 50,000 and 80,000 children are mistreated by their parents each year. It would seem that this Mafia-like behaviour is not limited to the lower social classes but in effect occurs in all layers of society. About 50 children die each year as a result of it.[18] That's one a week. How many liquidations take place in criminal circles? How many Theo van Gogh's have their throats cut?

Soprano: That's criminal. A child a week! If I got my hands on one of those fucking people I'd kill them with my own bare hands. Where the fuck have all the standards and values gone in this society?

Punch: Each year, thousands of people die from medical blunders, and nobody knows just how many there are. This has to change, says the health-care inspectorate.[19] Okay, we have to be careful not to compare apples and oranges. But many more people die as a result of negligence, carelessness, and pure and simple intent than through 'organised' crime or terrorism. Is it not hypocritical to blow up the violence on the streets – be it or be it not through organised crime – and to play down the daily violence in the safe environment of our families, our hospitals or on the roads?

Marx: Why should it be considered naive to invest more money to comply with health and safety regulations, to fight illegal economic activities or violence against children and women behind closed doors or to improve traffic safety compared with fighting crime in the streets?

Sutherland: My *White Collar Crime* of 1984 is a report based on almost 25 years of research into legal cases in which 70 major American companies were convicted for a total of 980 offenses and crimes. Some companies were in fact convicted several times for one and the same crime. I also closely examine the illegal dealings of 15 governmental organisations and analyse the diaries of 12 powerful entrepreneurs. I compare their diaries with the CVs of criminals. And would you believe it: they contain a remarkable number of similarities! The 'failed' (convicted) criminals and those who 'succeed' as businessmen are both prepared to take major risks in life, to suddenly and totally change their course; both categories have underdeveloped social feelings and can be hard as nails if need be. Another similarity is that criminals as well as managers are great judges of character. They use this talent to manipulate people, to set them up against each other and to divide and rule.

Dr Melfi: That brings us back to where we started: the psychopathic character of the Tonys in this world'.

Soprano: So I'm like the CEOs of Worldcom, Enron, Shell, Ahold, Ballast Nedam, and all the others.

Marx: Yes and no. Yes because you mix legal as well as illegal activities. No, because you are far easier to criminalise. Just take your sentence constructions and your use of short and simple words.

We need fucking people like you

Soprano: So those *mainstream* scientists don't have a clue what's going on? But why then all these blown-up pictures of the Mafia?

Chambliss: According to Durkheim, societies need 'criminals'. It strengthens social cohesion. Us against them. There's good reason for 'organised' crime being seen in terms of an 'alien conspiracy'. The system is threatened by 'enemies' from the outside. Durkheim says that this is why criminals – and therefore certainly the blown-up version in terms of 'organised' crime – fulfil an important social function. Social solidarity is supported through the fact that 'they' are defined as morally repugnant. This makes 'us' morally superior and leaves our self-awareness intact (Vold and Bernard, 1986).

Marx: Societies need fear. Benjamin Barber, a former Clinton advisor, describes the phenomenon in *Fear's Empire: War, Terrorism and Democracy* (2003). We simplify security into bite-size pieces. Colleague Vincenzo Ruggiero dedicated a superb chapter to it in *Crime and Literature*.

Soprano: Fuck, you guys read a lot. Do you have a life? But seriously, so you need people like me?

Gutwirth: Mr. Soprano, why do you have that poster of Slavoj ŽiŽek hanging on your wall?

Soprano: Who?

Gutwirth: That poster over there of the Slovenian philosopher ŽiŽek.

Soprano: Well, let me tell you. I'd been on the road for a few days and had run out of Prozac. I was driving myself mad and was at my wit's end. I saw the poster somewhere and liked the text for some reason: 'Welcome to the desert of the real.

Marx: ŽiŽek uses pop, movies and television series to substantiate his philosophical arguments.

Soprano: Isn't that what this play is about?

Marx: ŽiŽek discusses horror movies like the zombie movies about the living dead. He draws various parallels between zombies to express the laziness and tedium of these times. He talks about 'a lifeless universe full of pseudo-events'. You could use the same description for the easy and dull scientific images of 'organised' crime.[20]

Punch: That sounds somewhat dramatic and bombastic.

Van Calster: It's the essence of telling stories.

Gutwirth: That's why we need artists and literary writers. It's because of their freedom, epistemological buccaneering and lack of intuition that they understand so much more of crime than the meticulous cerebrals in their antiseptic lab coats with their wages covered by the Ministry of Justice (Gutwirth, 1989).[21] Only those who mix with the underground, such as Dostoevsky, can express reality properly, but only in terms of literature or, more broadly, of art. Here there is no control or disciplinary mechanism. There are no enforced frames of thought, methodological accounting or prescribed forms. Writers have the scope to escape the stifling 'truth' of science: the 'weapon' of the contented who find their satisfaction in a wall of regularity and that drives them into tepid civil servant lives. Those in the underground dismiss reality with a wry smile (Gutwirth, 1989). In literature, movie scripts and TV series, anarchy, chaos, inconsistencies and madness can rant and rave so that we gain knowledge on 'issues' that cannot be discussed (Hoogenboom, 1994).

Dr Melfi: 'So the language of science is the problem. The abstractions, the generalisations have a "crushing" impact because language is manipulated. Language dulls and penetrates individual autonomy with semi- and whole truths (...) individuals don't have to believe all the mystifications, but they must behave as if they do, or at least silently put up with them or interact with those who work with them. As a consequence, though, they have to live a lie (...) they are the system' (Havel, 1990).

Soprano: You guys are fuckin' mortadellas. Get the fuck out of here! I've had enough of your pseudoscientific bullshit. Give me History Channel and old *film noirs* any day.[22] At least then I learn something. Pauli, Christopher, kick them out.

8
Ironies, Paradoxes and the Seven Plagues of Policing and Security

Introduction

As the subtitle indicates, I'm interested in 'ironies, myths and paradoxes' in the unfolding stories of policing and security. For this reason, I will now discuss the seven plagues. Unlike the plagues in the biblical book of Revelations, the plagues that I am concerned with in this chapter affect the regulation, supervision and law enforcement activities of the many dozens of inspectorates, supervisors, special tracing services, regular police services and various new supervisors or authorities such as the Dutch Competition Authority (NMA), Telecom Authority (OPTA) and the Authority for Financial Markets (AFM) (authorities to enforce fair competition in the Dutch commercial markets, compliance with regulation in the post and telecommunications sector, and honesty and transparency in the financial markets).

Here I discuss seven plagues to demonstrate that the entire rapidly and massively expanding 'policing and security complex' brings with it a large number of (un)intended side effects. Some of the ironies, inconsistencies and irrationalities of the new security architecture are addressed in this chapter.

Plague 1: Institutional spaghetti

Amsterdam alderman Mark van der Horst recently called for any 'institutional spaghetti' found in the Netherlands to be comprehensively slashed. He feels he can no longer handle the effects of what he sees as a viscous consultative culture. The alderman is highly eager to tackle bureaucracy and, in particular, the omnipresent conference culture in the Netherlands. Institutional spaghetti is a perfect metaphor here, not only to illustrate the character of public administration as a whole but certainly also for the supervision and control arena. Anybody Googling the terms *supervision* and *control* is inundated by links to institutions, organisations, reports, training programmes ('how to write a supervision and control memo'), conference reports and tools – lots of tools – ranging from risk matrices to checklists.

We, as civilians and ordinary mortals, are being flooded by massive waves of regulation, supervision and control. Existing regulatory agencies are currently being presented with more and more tasks. A new generation of supervisors is born, and as far as budgets, task expansion and job positions are concerned, their numbers are flourishing. The foundation and rapid expansion of supervisory bodies such as the NMA (for price fixing), OPTA (for the regulation of the telecom market), the Dutch Food Authority and certainly the AFM are particularly striking. In today's neoliberal climate ruled by market forces, the state is harbouring a certain amount of distrust regarding the degree of social responsibility demonstrated by Dutch (and international) businessmen. Developments can be referred to as 'controlitus'. The control virus is burrowing uncontrollably into institutions and primary operational processes. Supervision and control are in vogue. After each new scandal, urgent appeals can be heard for improved supervision, more control, and – ideally – a new authority.

Supervision has not only come under pressure itself, but has at the same time also become a *cause* of pressure: pressure on organisations, people, compliance as well as policy, and pressure for the creation of new rules. These pressures are often considered politically and socially desirable. The supervisory spaghetti thus created is an inextricable tangle of controls, information obligations and audits. Even in the Netherlands, a speck of a country in global terms, inspections and authorities are competing for space and attention in carrying out their jobs. Still, nobody is wondering whether there may in fact not be too much supervision. Recently, AFM's former chairman Arthur Docters van Leeuwen cynically remarked that he still hopes to maintain at least some supervision-free zones in his lifetime. And this is exactly the point. There hardly are any 'free zones' left.

The regulatory complex has an unstoppable internal dynamic. Not only are previously supervision-free zones being subsumed, but even supervision and controls themselves are being stacked on top of each other. The average businessman increasingly finds himself welcoming the next supervisory body right after the first has left, often for comparable checks.

And the end is nowhere in sight. In early April 2006, the Consumer Protection Organization called for a new authority for consumer affairs. In *De Raad in de staat* (Council in the State), the 2003 annual report of the Netherlands' Council of State, Vice-President Tjeenk Willink stated that 'the functionality of the public sector is limited by an unmanageable "middle layer" of controllers, supervisors, advisors and managers in the public, semi-public and private sectors'.

Plague 2: Bloated policy

Institutional spaghetti is supported, secured and legitimised by armies of new captains – not at sea, but steering from high-rise office buildings. They have completely lost touch with reality. They meet in conference rooms and discuss matters in abstract jargon only understandable to close insiders who play the same game. These civil servants talk and write about supervision and control but lack any grounded knowledge on the subject. Nevertheless, they are important, very important. At least this is how they feel about themselves. There is a growing imbalance between the number of policy positions and operational positions. Bureaucracies invest in a) 'general policy functions', and b) 'supervision and control monitoring policy functions of primary processes'. So, in fact, controllers are controlled and supervised to check whether enough control takes place. This bureaucratic madness can only be analysed and truly appreciated when it is featured in one of the famous Dilbert cartoons.

The general policy functions have become entrenched in a bureaucratic swamp with days spent in meetings for which minutes are compiled that in turn are followed by reports on supervision and control. The reports are getting bigger and heavier. In recent years, the policy circus surrounding issues such as nodal security, integral safety or public private cooperation has truly ballooned – and the relationship with the daily practice of supervision and control is often sketchy at best.

The policy function of 'supervision and control monitoring' is a new phenomenon. Distrust in the level of professionalism displayed by the police, inspections, special tracing services and (financial) supervisory bodies is such that battalions of civil servants have thrown themselves at monitoring. In sum, the ancient position of national police inspector-general has resurfaced, and the checklists wielded by the supervision and control monitors are keeping the professionals off the streets.

The result is an operational drain. More people are active in secondary supervision and control processes than in their primary equivalents.

Policy terrains are becoming bloated. More time is devoted to talking and writing about supervision and control than to influencing the behaviour of companies and citizens that are supposed to be addressed. Bloated policy can be found in departments, but also in operational services and organisations.

Plague 3: Short-term memory loss

In the film *Finding Nemo*, Dory, an adorable little fish, has an irritating affliction: a short-term memory problem. The same applies to the current generation of policy makers in supervision and control. Emerging problems lead to reflex responses that are completely in line with Pavlov's theories. The knowledge basis used in making decisions is getting narrower and narrower. Research entitled *Met het oog op de toekomst* (With an eye to the future) carried out by the Dutch Science and Technology Advisory Committee states that the knowledge infrastructure related to crime and crime prevention is characterised as ad hoc – with a strong focus on policy – fragmented and focused on short-term interests.

The civil apparatus would seem to be primarily concerned with 'keeping the minister out of the limelight' instead of being focused on content. Consultants and scientists provide bite-size knowledge fragments. No reflexive thought is devoted to the philosophical fundament of the constitutional state or that of democracy. And thus the question may well be asked what law enforcement strategy follows from this. People act just for the sake of acting. Action shows 'power'. Action shows 'determination'. Montesquieu is cast aside by Clint Eastwood lookalikes who think and act along action-reaction lines. Reflection or any indication of nuance or dissenting opinion, sometimes also called democracy, is regarded as a sign of weakness. The 'regulatory system' is all about action. Strategic questions on the use of and the reasoning behind the creation of a new supervisory body are no longer asked. Also, and perhaps equally importantly, the question is ignored as to what the envisioned combination of supervision and control is going to look like and what exactly we intend to achieve with it. Get on with it! Make your targets!

A parallel can be drawn with the discussion currently being held in the United States on the role and responsibility of business schools. The position is that, over the last ten years, study programmes and curricula have been 'dumbed down'. Study materials have become increasingly 'easier' and simplified. Students are given mere fragments on small-scale subjects that are thought to do well in business practice. Instantaneous, cheap and superficial knowledge is all around. And all of this is done in the name of applicable knowledge and offered as abstract management concepts, handy checklists and other simple techniques. The accusation vented here is that 'major questions' and 'major themes' are no longer addressed: individual responsibility, ethics and integrity, the position of companies in society, derailments in the market economy placed in a historic context – and there are many more. An indirect link is laid between this 'dumbing down' and major financial scandals such as those that took place at Enron and Worldcom, both of which were peanuts compared with the unfolding credit crises and – in their wake – fraud cases involving amounts of money that remain incomprehensible to us as scientists, newspaper readers and voters.

The short-term memories of the current generation of policy makers involved in regulation, control and law enforcement have also been affected. The most clear-cut example is the increasing appeal for criminal repression, particularly in relation to police operations. There is a lack of enforcement. There is too much tolerance. Subsequently, repression follows and thus, performance contracts. Major questions are no longer asked in this context. What, for example, is the added value of the police? What is the effect of criminal law? Which other enforcement strategies – ranging from information, discussion and stimulation to administrative law or civil law modalities – can be applied?

These major questions were in fact answered for the police a long time ago, namely, in police literature and criminology classics. But who still remembers Ericson's *Making Crime. A Study of Detective Work*? Who still opens Skolnick's *Justice without Trial*? Is *Patterns of Policing* by Bayley no longer as relevant now as it was then in settling the discussion of 'prevention versus repression'? Who still quotes *Overheidsgeweld* (Governmental violence) by Van Reenen or his essay *Het ijzeren politiebestel* (The iron police system) on the dynamics within the police system? Which civil servant uses *Politiële Misdaadbestrijding* (police crime prevention) by Fijnaut? This regrettable lack of sound short-term memory capacity makes most people forget the following insights:

- Police work is endlessly varied and is characterised by the input of a large number of intervention strategies;
- Criminal law enforcement is part of the overriding body of intervention strategies. Simple criminal justice repression has in itself a limited influence on criminality levels in societies. It leads to no more than the stabilisation of a certain crime level, but it is also

more likely to lead to the displacement of crime (geographical and crime markets). Additionally, (organised) crime gets tougher (goes underground, for example) and may negatively affect (parts of) the integrity of the maintenance of law and order (corruption or breaking rules such as witnessed in the Dutch International Detective Team (IRT) affair on the abuse of investigative methods);

- Criminality and open disturbances of the peace are complex social phenomena. The police have little or no influence on their deeper causes;
- Criminal law enforcement is socially overestimated as a solution to criminality, as a promoter of feelings of safety or as an effective answer to a lack of these feelings;
- Criminal law enforcement is an important link in the entire chain of organisations that are in some way or other involved in supervision, enforcement and/or tracing activities. However, as mentioned above and by definition, its influence is limited;
- Too great an emphasis on criminal law enforcement by the police results from – and illustrates – the above limitations. They also burden the police with too great a responsibility when it comes to solving complex social issues;
- Criminal law enforcement is an important, yet limited, part of the entire structure in which the personal responsibility of administrations, citizens, businesses and civil-society organisations – also called the 'social midfield' – are essential. This responsibility should be enhanced;
- By definition, the added value of the police (in a criminal law sense) is limited. It is thus disproportionately valued in the political/social debate (and in policies);
- The added value of the police lies in its sheer presence in society (symbolic value). This is realised by means of surveillance in the public arena. The police's added value is especially large in the exertion of soft force and hard power (sword power function; government monopoly on physical violence) in correcting or limiting unwanted behaviour;
- The police's added value lies in the backing it offers to administration authorities and social actors, by its ability to intervene in protecting the integrity of the whole – and primarily the citizens within that whole.
- Interventions are closely linked to capacity and availability. By definition, the number of these interventions is limited. Any incident room can only respond in accordance with the number of staff and

resources available: the national Criminal Investigation Department (CID) can only carry out criminal investigations to the extent allowed by its capacity. The same is true for regional and district criminal investigation teams.

- The police's added value (from the perspectives of criminal law and public order and given its limited capacity) mainly lies in the timing of the actions and its professional nature.

Regulation and control are not carried out exclusively by the regular police. A large number of inspectorates, special tracing services and (financial) supervisory bodies are charged with this supervision and control. Other classics covering the operations of these services, and in particular their control strategies, are no longer read either.

Australian criminologist Braithwaite has investigated the tasks, authorities, and scope of negotiation of 108 Australian government services. He has developed a typology of services with a great degree of freedom of movement (the mediators, the genial bone breakers): services that can stick to 'the book' to a greater or lesser degree, services with a large or little small amount of freedom of policy and services that must always fully abide by the regulations and cannot negotiate with other parties involved. Hawkins and Thomas also describe differences in control strategies between inspection agents ('regulatory agencies') and the regular police. They distinguish between a *deterrence strategy* and a *compliance strategy*. Van de Bunt and Huisman form another duo that wrote about different control strategies. Nobody quotes them.

These days, Malcom Sparrow is making some waves in the Netherlands with his book *The Regulatory Craft. Controlling Risks, Solving Problems and Managing Compliance*. Sparrow discusses a large number of control strategies. He is explicitly critical of a reactive, criminal control strategy. He mentions six points of critique to underline its ineffective character:

1. Reactive strategies are almost exclusively repressive in nature and are therefore (too) unilaterally based on the exercising of power. This differs from prior behavioural manipulation that is not only less confrontational but also less costly. Reactive strategies are considered inappropriate tools.
2. Sparrow also feels that reactive strategies focus mainly on less smart individuals (generally criminal 'failures') such as drug addicts, repeat criminals and drug couriers who are caught, often time and time again. The criminal system hunts and tracks down this limited clientele one-by-one. The process, however, leaves no time for the system

to address broader social problem groups more creatively and at a higher level of abstraction.

3. By definition, responses in this type of reactive strategy are always too late: the crime has already been committed. In the case of reactive strategies, people fail to make the most of experiences and insights in their inability to adopt preventive strategies, let alone use them.
4. An emphasis lies on incidents that automatically manifest themselves externally. Work pressure is therefore determined by external factors, and it is these that determine what is to be done. The preoccupation with what is forced upon those who deal with the issues is too great, while other problems go unnoticed and are certainly not tackled.
5. These days, success is more and more measured on the basis of performance contracts and statistically measurable variables. This leads to an internal fixation on certain problems. Control statistics alone say nothing of the nature and scope of the problems that have been solved, but only about the amount of time that has been devoted to the issue. Nowadays, it would seem that the quality of work done is subordinate to quantity. In other words, Sparrow emphasises that the wrong results are being measured.
6. Sparrow also argues that reactive, criminal interventions can only be maintained fleetingly. Rules and regulations are increasing, so that the demands, wishes and needs expressed by the public and the authorities are becoming endless. At the same time, however, neither the capacity nor the resources available to organisations are being expanded substantially. Furthermore, reactive strategies lead to bottlenecks and hindrances in the judicial chain. As a result, the criminal system is losing part of its legitimacy: the administration of justice can no longer meet the demands of meticulousness (with an added risk of bureaucratic errors) and, for example, rapid adjudication.

Plague 4: Fear

It may seem odd to use the word *fear* in the present time of policing, security, supervision and control. Nevertheless, the term is not too far off the mark. We can distinguish certain gradations of fear in the 'supervision complex'. There is a fear of certain 'targets' such as trailer inhabitants (seen as occupying tax-free mini-states beyond the reach of law), but also of initiating criminal proceedings against companies. There is a fear of the 'opposition', such as lawyers who initiate proceedings for their clients (organised crime or white collar criminals) and threaten with civil proceedings. There is a fear of negative publicity (image loss). People fear creativity and innovation in supervision and control as a result of the findings laid down in the Dutch Van Traa report on the (il)legality of investigative police methods. And there is a fear – or at least extended mistrust – among the political and administrative elite of what happens on the shop floor – or doesn't happen. Ergo: increased supervision of the supervision instruments.

It can safely be stated that the fear factor leads to risk avoidance. There is insecurity and fear reduction on every possible level. In the public sector, officials receive a virtual bonus for risk-avoiding behaviour. Ergo: a flight into bureaucracy and increasingly fat and bloated policies. As a result, the 'supervisory system', in addition to supervision and the maintenance of law and order, wastes a significant amount of time on itself.

Plague 5: Organisational guerrilla warfare

In *Post-Fort. Evaluatie van strafrechtelijk onderzoek* (Post-Fort. Evaluation of criminal investigation) by Van de Bunt, Nelen and Fijnaut, the authors conclude that there is 'a lack of etiquette in the handling of information'. It is, of course, a euphemistic description of the deep-seated competition witnessed within and among law enforcement agencies and, in this case, particularly within the regular police. The lack of 'etiquette' is not restricted to the period described by Fijnaut and his fellow authors, and it is not limited to the police. It is a structural issue. Under the surface of the 'cooperation within the criminal justice system', 'integral security' and, for example, 'public–private cooperation', large and small 'Rambos' are at war with one single objective in mind: expediency. Their weapon: information. Ongoing information wars are waged from the highest to the lowest levels, harming the general interest. The *public good*, for the advancement of which civil servants were appointed in the first place, has become subordinate to small and large egos and office-political interests that manifest themselves in the need to score. Turf wars are endemic.

Supervisors and control authorities operate in organisations that, like all organisations, have two realities: *front stage* and *backstage*. The *front stage* reality is the world of the glossy annual reports, policy plans, conferences and formal operating structures. There is a completely different story going on *backstage*. This play has an entirely different dynamic, with its own rules. Alongside friendships and blind loyalty, it is also rife with intense hatred, envy, irritations and slumbering quarrels. Condoleezza Rice, when she testified before the 9/11 investigation committee, stated that good and effective cooperation took place between the FBI and the CIA. This led to an immensely irritated reaction from one of the senators, who interrupted her and said that everyone who comes to work in Washington knows within 24 hours that these services cannot stand one another. This intense competition in supervision and control is structural.

In his thesis *Opdat de macht een toevlucht zij?* (So that power be a refuge?) Fijnaut analyses the institutional battleground from a historical perspective. Two centuries of police history demonstrate a constant pattern of 'guerres des flic'. Police services are sometimes 'at war' with one another. The result then is a far-reaching disintegration and splintering of information. There is too little *intelligence* in *intelligence* during these turf wars. It is nevertheless fascinating to note that, since 1985, the Netherlands' General Auditor's Office in particular has been pointing out Gordian knots in the hardware and software of information systems and, in particular, in the police force. With the Netherlands measuring the small number of square miles that it does, in the police force alone there are many hundreds of different information systems that cannot communicate with each another – and in some cases do not even wish to.

Plague 6: A slow yet constant strangulation of independence

Tjeenk Willink questions what he calls the 'unmanageable 'middle layer' of controllers, supervisors, advisors and managers in the public, semi-public and private sectors'. Let us take a closer look at the advisors and controllers in this layer.

In the land of supervision and control, (prior) evaluations are performed by consultants and scientists. They form part of the 'middle layer'. Not only through prior evaluations (feasibility studies and so forth) or evaluation studies, but also particularly through the increasing intertwining of advice on the one hand and more traditional research on the other. This is currently leading to increasingly large conflicts of interest that (in)directly erode objectivity. The 'middle layer' is characterised by 'assignment dependencies' that harm the objectivity of research, including that in the land of supervision and control.

A virtually invisible network exists of mutual dependencies between clients and formerly independent professional groups. Those who pay have the say. And this happens with a vengeance in major infrastructural projects such as the Netherlands cross-country Betuwe railway line, the construction of high-speed rail links or the expansion of Schiphol Airport, where time and time again we hear about incidental strangulation attempts – and not in the last part in the land of supervision and control. Each year, ministries, provinces and municipalities spend billions of euros on the recommendations of experts. These recommendations have to ensure that politics and bureaucracies make good decisions: decisions that are in the interest of our country.

Professor Berkhout, geophysicist and former chairman of the Schiphol noise standards committee, brings things to a head in an article published in the Dutch newspaper NRC: 'But thanks to major political or economic interests, the conclusions of these recommendations are generally predetermined. The "independent" advisors are expected to give recommendations that support the desired conclusions. Regardless how they manage it, they have to work towards the desired results. The experts often break. The pressure is too high. Those who nevertheless stand their ground are, to put it mildly, in for a hard time. Whatever the case, they can certainly forget about any follow-up assignment. The question concerned is whether or not in the Netherlands any independent expertise can still be found'. Berkhout resigned as chairman: 'the committee was supposed to be independent – and it was independent in name – but we were actually seen as a scientific façade for predetermined political policies that were highly controversial. When it turned out that the committee's findings were not to the taste of the political establishment, they were not only ignored but they were manipulated.'

It is not only scientific objectivity that is at risk, however. Objectivity on the part of controllers and accountants also hangs in the balance. There are countless (inter)national examples of controllers listening somewhat too closely to the wishes of their clients. Accountants may have a responsibility to guard in social traffic, but the responsibility towards the continuity of their own sector is equally large, if not larger. Accountants have job responsibilities with respect to the future. The results are new regulations and new supervision of 'independent' accountants.

Plague 7: Political symbolism: the terror of empty words

In accountancy and business administration, the term *in control* is used for situations in which management has a grip on the primary work processes and in which internal controls (as offered by a company's supervisory board, management board and shareholders) are actually implemented. The previously described complexity in the land of supervision and control is smothered by the enormous supply – and frequent repetition – of empty words. The security issue leads to the development of a number of policy concepts that, to a greater or lesser degree, have created the illusion that we, as a society, are actually 'in control': integral security, public-private cooperation and nodal governance. This has triggered the rise of bloated policies.

A small but highly penetrating scientific work by American political expert Edelman springs to mind in this respect: *Constructing the Political Spectacle*. Here we find a well-considered analysis of the political character of policy processes – and therefore also processes in the land of supervision and control – in which 'success' is measured by well-constructed sentences without any tangible content instead of being measured by tangible results in terms of behavioural influencing, success degrees, declines in feelings of insecurity and so on. According to Edelman, we should distinguish between words and actions: 'words that succeed, and policies that fail'. The irony is that those involved are not actually interested. It is image that counts: organising a press conference at the right time, putting in an appearance with a prime-time talk show or writing a positive newspaper article. And onwards we go, on with the show!

Today's risk society has become obsessed with making plans and developing 'arrangements' intended to give citizens a sense of safety and security. One after the other, supervisors are helped aboard in order to implement policies. This process is reinforced by the fact that 'security' has been politicised. And since 'security' has been politicised, it is possible to 'score' with new supervision. With increased control. With powerful language and 'politics' interfering with individual cases. 'Politics' sets objectives: 'security' – preferably integral – a 25 per cent crime reduction within a period of four years, performance contracts.

In the field of 'politics', major policy plans are issued, but do they have any effect, or are they actually of no importance? According to Garland (*The Culture of Control*, 2001), a structural ambivalence can be seen between the political system and the executors. He refers to this as 'policy schizophrenia'. This phenomenon creates a paradoxical situation: 'steerability' and 'makeability' are concepts that have either become outdated in almost all policy areas or are used only with the greatest caution. Nevertheless, the idea of a 'makeable society' has persisted in large-scale policy programmes surrounding criminality and safety policies since the 1980s and 1990s. Aftereffects are long-term.

The makeability idea finds its roots in the report *'Samenleving en criminaliteit'* (Society and criminality, 1985), which appeals to the various civil-society organisations, citizens and businesses to work personally and jointly towards a safe society. The policies spearheaded administrative prevention and personal responsibility.

These echoes of the 'makeable society' are particularly strong in the idea of integrating prevention and repression, police/judiciary and administration, government and business, civil servants and civilians. The dominant ideology is expressed through concepts such as 'integral safety' and public-private cooperation. The term *win-win situation* has become uncommonly popular. Could we not employ a supervisor to eradicate the use of this empty sloganeering?

'Integral' stands for comprehensive, all encompassing, taking all factors into account. It also stands for asking too much. Current programmes are far too pretentious and evoke associations with the planned economies of a bygone political system. The heterogeneity of the concept of security is gradually becoming clearer. Security is a 'container concept'. Security is a 'stretched concept'. Everything and everyone is binned under the 'security' denominator so that the concept has become meaningless: it includes great danger, risks, calamities and catastrophes up to and including criminality and terrorism. Nobody discusses causality and coherence anymore: disruption is mentioned as a 'safety risk' alongside noise, stench and degeneration, but it actually concerns livability. Traffic safety (parking issues) and 'graffiti' are mentioned alongside criminality and depicted as a 'lack of security'. Worries about increasing crime often go hand-in-hand with worries about other risks that threaten safety. Ergo: new rules and regulations, new supervisors and an expansion of supervisory tasks.

Integral safety and security policies and public-private cooperation presuppose a communal objective, while what we find in practice is bureaucratisation, conflicts of interest, office politics, policy competition, passing the buck, and citizens' and business' decreased preparedness to report (strategic avoidance). Integral safety therefore remains 'virtually unmentioned': words that succeed, policies that fail. It is remarkable how this concept is based on the 'ideology of social harmony' and on overextended expectations regarding the government's steering capacity and the effects of new policies: 15 years of policy reports, 15 years of committees, 15 years of integral safety, 15 years of conferences, 15 years of well-structured sentences without tangible content. In other words and with hindsight, safety and security policy has produced relatively little effect. Safety, like other social processes, is far less 'makeable' than the ideology presupposes.

The 'empty words argument' becomes stronger if we realise that there is virtually no empirical knowledge on the basis of which valid statements can be made concerning the effectiveness of all those dozens of inspectorates, supervisory bodies and control authorities, not to mention the greatly expanded security market. This is because the knowledge infrastructure of crime and punishment is almost entirely intertwined with the regular police it focuses on and, accordingly, with registered crime. What do these people do all day and what effect does what they do have on civilians and companies? The major accounting scandals in the United States and Western Europe were not discovered through proactive supervision and control behaviour, but rather through investigative journalism. Supervisors read what is happening in the newspapers and then spring into action. Of course, this is a bit of a caricature, but are all those supervisors truly professional? Effective? Do we need them?

In conclusion

'In recent decades, as a result of privatization and the disposal of government tasks, a middle layer of semi-public and private bureaucracy has arisen that frustrates the political primate, inhibits the executors and limits citizens in their public responsibility', says Tjeenk Willink, vice-president of the Council of State, in the council's recently published annual report. In order to break through the ports of this 'close covenant', Tjeenk Willink is calling on Chamber members to go back to their core business: closely following the results of policy. It should also be recognised that the executors (doctors, teachers and policemen) are the true experts when it comes to solving problems. In addition, private initiative should be given a wider berth.

In this chapter, I have distinguished seven regulatory and control plagues. Based on these discussions, I am strongly in favour of rethinking some of the backgrounds, objectives, operations and organisational principles that form the foundation of the 'supervision complex'. In our country, a clear lack of vision can be discerned concerning the very fundaments of the system of supervision and control. The usual Pavlov responses (more people, more resources, new authorities and so forth) can all be typified as 'structural incidentals'. Below, I will formulate six propositions for the future of supervision and control.

Simplification

The 'regulatory complex' is unnecessarily complicated. Simplification may be achieved on various levels. On a local level, integrating supervisors into a single joint service could end the institutional spaghetti we are witnessing today. This would shorten the lines, allow the integration of information systems within the service, and solve the laborious planning activities and actions undertaken in the framework of an 'integral safety policy'. Bloated policy would also be countered.

Luckily, the integration of (financial) supervisors that has been set in motion is continuing. Following Great Britain's lead, supervision is to be housed in a single organisation. The main new authorities in the economic domain (the Dutch Food Authority, OPTA, NMA and others) could be integrated into one single economic authority. A national police force could be formed.

Modesty

We must redefine the culture of fear and the imminent political 'misuse' of security issues for direct political gains. Governing through fear could very well be detrimental to the quality of our lives and the democratic nature of our societies. We should implement far more intelligent control strategies: communication, the provision of information, discussions, mediation, administrative sanctions and publicity ('naming and shaming').

Expertise

Instead of focusing on automatic expansion, mainly in terms of personnel, high-quality and effective investments are to be made far more frequently and far earlier. This concerns the quality of prior education and the quality of supplementary training. A system of life-long learning should be introduced throughout the 'supervisory system'.

De-bureaucratisation

Bloated policies should be brought to a halt. The imbalance between policy processes and operational processes must be corrected.

Trust, responsibility and friendship

It is essential that attention be devoted to the restoration of trust within the 'supervisory complex': that individual responsibility is returned to where it belongs and that new friendships are created. Weber writes about the three qualities of a true politician, but why not include a special supervisory civil servant or a law enforcer, namely, one with passion, a sense of responsibility and insight. At a first glance, these would seem to be ancient and outmoded concepts, yet they are of critical importance.

Nowadays, we talk of human resource management for which we have balanced scorecards. The crucial factor, however, lies in leaders having faith in their administrations and administrations having faith in their (political) leaders. It is all about ensuring motivation and involvement. In an introduction to Woldring's political philosophy, I was recently struck by a chapter on friendship in which he addresses friendship in Greek and Roman antiquity. In those days, friendship was seen not only as a relationship that exclusively belonged to the private arena, but also as one that extended into public relationships and public responsibilities. The public case – now as it was then – should be served by an involved and motivated public 'regulatory complex'.

Reflection

The fragmented knowledge infrastructure on crime and punishment laid bare by the advisory council for science and technology policy is of course disquieting. The 'wheezy' ad-hoc knowledge on which actions are based is irresponsible. In addition to control and supervision issues, the 'supervisory complex' touches on democratic principles: who is guarding the guards? There is a great need for more reflection, and not only by flicking through a number of 'classics'. That, in itself, is inadequate. One alternative would be to set up a state committee for the creation of supervision and control structures.

9
Technopoly

Introduction

Joseph Fouché, the architect of high policing in revolutionary France around 1800, is supposed to have said to the emperor Napoleon that if at that very moment three people were having a conversation somewhere in Paris, probably one of them would be working for him. His report would be on Fouché's desk the next morning. It is doubtful whether Fouché's system ever reached this level of sophistication, but the story touches the very essence of (high) policing: obtaining information. In the days of Joseph Fouché and in many ways until this very day, obtaining information was and is done in the physical world (observation, interrogation, dossier analyses, informant handling and so on).

This chapter traces the blurring boundaries between the physical world and digital realities. More and more, technology in the broadest sense of the term finds its way into many facets of policing and security. One particular story from Iraq and Afghanistan will illustrate the point. In these areas, coalition forces are faced with 'faceless, nameless terrorists, and we don't know who they are'. In cooperation with CSC, a U.S.-based R&D and consultancy company, identification management processes and techniques have been developed to protect U.S. facilities against inside attacks. When a foreign national requests access to a U.S. military facility, he or she must report to an enrolment station to provide biographical information, an iris image and fingerprints, and to be photographed. This information is packaged and sent via satellite to a U.S. facility, where CSC runs the information against the Department of Defense's (DoD) Automated Biometric Identification System (ABIS) and the FBI's Integrated Automated Fingerprint Identification System (IAFIS) databases. The databases house biometric data taken from detainees, enemy combatants and other persons of interest. ABIS information is combined with other relevant data to determine whether to grant access. Once the DoD has verification of identity and a complete, approved background check, the applicant is given a smart-card-enabled ID card, with fingerprint and photo, to access the facility. This provides an extra layer of protection against infiltration, says Daniel Munyan, chief scientist with CSC, who helped develop ABIS. Joseph Fouché would have been delighted.

Changing context: Technopoly

According to Postman (1993), we live in a *Technopoly*, 'a self-justifying, self-perpetuating system wherein technology of every kind is cheerfully granted sovereignty over social institutions and national life (...) a transformation is taking place from a society that uses technology to one that is shaped by it'.[23] This technopoly argument cuts straight through the militarisation, securitisation and privatisation of policing and security, yet it is not part of many systematic academic studies.

Three factors act as technology multipliers: general scientific revolutions (especially in computing) from the end of the Cold War onwards to the spread of military technology to law enforcement, the intelligence community and private security, and finally the acceleration that took place following 9/11 and other terrorist incidents around the world. First, I will define relevant concepts that are useful in understanding the relationship between policing/security and technology. Next, I will draw attention to the large-scale investments made in security technology, especially in the United States and the European Union.

In the following paragraphs, I will list a number of topical examples of technology in policing and security, mainly derived from the 1996 Council of Europe Report *Technologies of Political Control*. My principal objective here is to make you aware of the varieties of security technopoly already at work. Then I will take you along to the United Kingdom to discuss the changing nature of public policing by drawing attention to investments in technology and to the various different ways in which new technologies are being integrated into different aspects of policing. Finally, I will discuss two software programmes developed in and for the private sector (financial institutions) for the detection of fraud, insider trading and money laundering. These are presented here not only to illustrate the sophistication of electronic monitoring and analyses of money transactions in the private sector, but also to raise the question whether or not an 'unbridgeable gap' has come to exist between the public and private sectors.

I also bring into this discussion the fact that the public sector increasingly often integrates these sophisticated information systems (taken from marketing, financial institutions and retail) into policing and security. Predictive marketing tools and advanced technologies to monitor commercial goods around the world on their way from manufacturer to consumer are today being used for the monitoring of potential criminals and terrorists. We have come a long way from Joseph Fouché's informants and are finding ourselves in the midst of a process of blurring boundaries between the physical and digital worlds. Fouché could not have understood this new security language with terms like 'commercial, off-the-shelf applications' as taken from retail and introduced into national security procedures. For that matter, he would not have understood 'interfaces' and 'connectors' linking computers in money laundering cases or the concept of computer interoperability used for social network analyses and profiling. And last but not least, Fouché would not have been able to grasp the military concept of network-centric warfare for the combination and integration of data or sensors, images, sound and 3-D imaging techniques applied with the help of computers or satellites, glass-fibre networks and nanotechnology.

Relevant concepts

Policing is information work. The most important aspect of police work is 'information work' (Nogala, 1993). Police are 'knowledge workers', and information is the 'central input and basis for action in policing' (Manning, 1992a).

Conceptually, police work can be regarded as an endless cycle of information collection and processing – penetration, surveillance, information, registration, knowledge, administration – for social control. My argument here is that the very essence of policing – being information work – is and will be 'revolutionised' through the increased application of different technologies ranging from the use of computers to artificial intelligence and from DNA to biometrics.

Methods. Fouché's primary source of information was an extensive network of informants (human intelligence). Little did he know then that over the next two centuries human intelligence was to become supplemented with signal intelligence, technical intelligence and open-source intelligence.

The technopoly argument in itself is not new and 'revolutionary'. During the Cold War, spy satellites were introduced and the interception of telephone and fax followed by e-mail became integrated in policing and (national) security processes. The National Security Agency (NSA) has been with us since the 1940s. My argument here is that human intelligence, which will remain essential in many ways, is becoming more and more supplemented with technology.

Data, information and intelligence. Data can be found relatively easily. In the modern world, everything we do leaves behind a data trail. Considered alone, 'data' have no meaning. Every flight, bank withdrawal, e-mail message, border crossing and telephone conversation as such produces meaningless data. Technology is used and developed for a first level of filtering, fusion and aggregation, done as closely as possible to the source of information. Data come from different sources, sensors and organisations. Volumetrics is the principal issue. Too much data kills information.

Information. Filtering, fusion and aggregation is a first step in capturing 'the bigger picture'. As the U.S. 9/11 Commission concluded, the greatest challenge is 'to connect the dots'. Data become more meaningful if useless data are filtered out and relationships have been established between persons, organisations and events. However, this is still a long way from intelligence.

Intelligence. To change information into intelligence, information needs to be correlated to find nonobvious links between facts, people, objects and events. To this end, technology tools are being developed and integrated into policing, security and the intelligence community.

Public and private intelligence. Intelligence is mostly associated with the public sector and often refers to intelligence and security organisations (such as MI5, for example). As was discussed earlier, the concept of intelligence can also be found in the private sector. Business and corporate intelligence refers to a set of strategies, functions, methods and techniques used to gather data concerning relevant market developments. Intelligent software developed for marketing or business efficiency in retail, for instance, is gradually being introduced in policing and security. Consumer behaviour and the shipment of consumer goods or, for instance, containers are monitored on an unprecedented scale. The same technology is – and will be – increasingly often introduced in policing and security.

Converging technologies. Many different technologies have been – and will continue to be – integrated into different phases of data gathering, information and intelligence, both in the public and the private sectors. Trends include miniaturisation (from the large mainframe computers in the 1960s to today's PDAs) and especially the increased convergence of different technologies (data, audio, video, biological/chemical).

Money pouring in

The U.S. Center for Public Integrity (2004) chronicles investments in security technology. Following the extraordinary success of the Washington-based Carlyle Group, which has built a private equity empire that has earned billions of dollars for its investors, a number of firms have lined up rosters of former government officials and high-ranking military officers as they pursue companies that are in the national security business.

Carlyle, which ranked as the ninth largest Pentagon contractor from 1998 to 2003, has made billions of dollars by investing in the defence sector. More than a half dozen other companies signed up former high-ranking government and military officials in pursuit of contracts from the Pentagon and the Homeland Security Department.

These private equity firms have hired five of the past nine defence secretaries, two secretaries of state, two national security chiefs, two CIA directors and dozens of distinguished retired military officials. Venture partnerships have been formed, with hundreds of millions in funds, to invest in the national security market.

According to the Center for Public Integrity, the homeland security industry is currently the fastest growing sector of the U.S. economy, predicted to grow from a $5 billion industry in 2000 to $130 billion in 2010, according to the Homeland Security Research Corporation, a private California think tank.

In August 2004, former U.S. Defense Secretary William Cohen disclosed his plan to form a merchant banking firm, TCG Financial Partners, to invest in defence companies. Cohen, who heads The Cohen Group, a consultancy firm in Washington D.C., hired a top investment banker from Bank of America to head the new private equity firm, which aims to raise $300 million. In September 2004, Bear Stearns Merchant Banking, the private equity arm of investment banking and securities trader Bear Stearns, entered into an alliance with GlobeSecNine, a little-known private equity group headquartered just a few miles from the Pentagon in Arlington, Virginia.

Bear Stearns Merchant Banking, which manages $1.5 billion, has earmarked $300 million to invest in national security-related companies, while GlobeSecNine has connections to the country's defence and national security establishment. David C. Miller Jr., one of GlobeSecNine's founders, was a special assistant to President George H. W. Bush for counterterrorism and counternarcotics. Gregory S. Newbold, another founding member of the firm, served as director of operations for the Joint Chiefs of Staff before he retired in 2002.

'The war on terrorism and possible confrontation with Iraq have focused investors' attention on defence and homeland defence,' Bob Grady and Jay Koh, members of Carlyle Venture Partners, wrote in a February 2003 article in the *Venture Capital Journal*. 'The events of Sept. 11 have drawn many new investors into the sector, spawned a host of new companies and redefined some old companies.'

Paladin created a Homeland Security Fund immediately after 9/11 to invest in homeland security firms. Boeing Co., the second largest Pentagon contractor, was an early investor in the firm. Paladin has made at least three investments in companies that do business with the Department of Homeland Security. It invested more than $10 million in AgION Technologies Inc., a Wakefield, Massachusetts-based company that makes antibioterrorism products. Paladin also bought stakes in ClearCube Technology Inc., which developed a computer-security system, and SafeView Inc., a Santa Clara, California-based firm that provides personnel screening technology.

Arlington Capital Partners, a $450 million private equity, acquired two top federal contractors, ITS Services in April 2003 and Science & Engineering Associates Inc. in January 2004. The firm combined the two and named the new company Apogen Technologies, which provides 'technology solutions' to the departments of Defense and the Homeland Security, as well as other branches of the government. Apogen ranks among the top ten Department of Homeland Security contractors.

Another major investor in the national security market is Behrman Capital, which acquired two defence and homeland security contractors in the past two years. The New York and San Francisco-based firm bought Hunter Defense Technologies, Inc., It acquired majority stakes in ILC Industries, Inc., a defence, aerospace and industrial products provider. The firm owned Condor Systems, Inc., a defence electronic firm, in the late 1990s.[24]

Cumulative private and public sector security spending in the United States is forecast to exceed $1 trillion over the coming decade. The technopoly market is clearly visible in exhibits and trade fairs. More than 800 companies attended the American Society for

Industrial Security exhibition in Dallas in 2008. A few weeks later, many of the same companies were at the annual Army tech expo in Washington, D.C.

Money flowing into military and homeland infrastructure security will leverage revolutionary technologies and materials of the new digital age. This will fuel entrepreneurs and capitalists to combat terrorist threats, collaterally spurring a new round of basic innovation. The enabling technologies for terror-sensing tools will rapidly migrate to applications in medicine, industry, transportation, telecom and even entertainment, driving a tech boom. Examples are sensors to sniff potential chemical weapons that will improve industrial processes and environmental monitoring. Scanners to see through packages will advance medical imaging. Infrared vision to keep a 24/7 all-weather eye out will land in automotive dashboards. Radar to monitor perimeters and borders will be seen in safety enhancements in trucks.[25]

The Pentagon is spending $100 million a year just to help coordinate civilian technology transfer for security. Plus, the Department of Defense is spending $60 billion a year for new technologies – $15 billion for advanced research and development – with security-related technology an important part of the total. Much of the R&D money is flowing to university researchers and start-ups. Venture capital is targeting this sector, too. Many defence companies, like L-3, GE and Northrop Grumman, have security divisions to advance these technologies.

Technology traders

Software titans like Oracle and Sun are promoting the creation of a national identity-card system. Defence contractors like Raytheon and Northrop Grumman are reinventing themselves as security providers, hiring 'homeland security directors' and pitching their technologies to shield nuclear plants or the Coast Guard's patrol boats. Small start-up companies are developing fake-document detectors, anthrax-handling robots, and dubious 'brain finger-printers'. InVision, a California-based maker of explosives detection systems, was forced to lay off 6 per cent of its workforce. But the company hit the jackpot in March 2003 when the newly created Transportation Security Administration placed a $170 million order for its detectors. A few weeks later, InVision raised more than $90 million by selling a raft of shares for $36.50 a piece; on September 10, the stock had traded for just $3.10. Shortly afterward, the company's CEO announced that thanks to the federal action, its order backlog was 'by far the largest in the company's history'.

Meanwhile in Europe

A report by Statewatch and the Transnational Institute, *Arming Big Brother: The EU's Security Research Programme*, discusses the emergence of a security-industrial complex in Europe and the development of the EU Security Research Programme (ESRP). In a bid to compete with U.S. rivals, the European Union is committing at least 65 billion euros to security research to ensure a 'level playing field' for European multinational companies. Some examples of research projects are listed below:

- **SOBCAH** (Surveillance of Borders, Coastlines and Harbours), renamed 'Safer European Borders' by the commission and led by the Italian company Galileo Avionica (Finmeccanica), will 'tackle the European border surveillance problem and the 6,000 km of land borders and 85,000 km of coastlines, with possibilities for access for illegal migrants, drug smugglers and terrorists'.
- The **TERASEC** project will improve 'homeland security' by delivering a new technology 'to detect threats, explosives, pathogens and chemicals hidden by a person or inside an object such as letters or luggage'.
- The **PROBANT** project, led by French aerospace and defence contractor Satimo, concerns the 'visualization and tracking of people inside buildings and the development of a powerful tool to guide security forces in surveillance and crisis management'.
- The **ISCAPS** project (Integrated Surveillance of Crowded Areas and Public Spaces), run by Sagem along with BAE systems, will produce surveillance technology for 'restricted areas in which strict controls and full biometric identification can be performed at entry points'.

Security technology

A rich source for security technology is *Jane's online*. In Jane's Police and Homeland Security Equipment, we find a comprehensive information source featuring more than 1,600 items of law enforcement equipment, including firearms, armour and personal protection, along with riot and crowd control equipment, communications, security equipment and more. Key contents include the following:

- Operational equipment, including vehicles and motor cycles, surveillance and search equipment, rapid entry devices and EOD equipment;
- Biometrics;
- Police uniform and duty gear;

- Personal protection equipment;
- Riot and crowd control equipment;
- Firearms and weapons;
- Communications and security equipment;
- Computerised systems and data management;
- Access control, perimeter protection and structural armour.

Automatic number plate recognition

Automatic number plate recognition (ANPR) is an already well-established technology that allows vehicles observed by camera to have their vehicle registration mark 'read' using pattern recognition software. It is operated as a proactive tool, with the primary objective of targeting terrorism, serious and organised crime and volume crime (for example, as part of the City of London's 'ring of steel') as well as antisocial behaviour. ANPR can also detect vehicle documentation offences such as uninsured driving and road tax evasion. Many of those who are stopped by the police for committing routine road traffic offences are, in fact, likely to have been involved in more serious offending.

ANPR technology has enabled police officers to produce an arrest rate equating to more than nine times that of the nationally accepted average and to achieve three times the number of Offences Brought to Justice (from arrest through to being sentenced at court) compared to conventional policing methods. The Home Office in the United Kingdom has made £32.5 million available to the police service in the years from 2005 to 2007 for the provision of ANPR technological development. A significant proportion of this funding has been allocated to the development of the National ANPR Data Centre (NADC), a facility that will enhance the police's postincident investigation capability.

Surveillance technologies: A quick glance[26]

The field of surveillance technologies covers a vast range of products and devices, but the overall trend is towards miniaturisation, more precise resolution through the adoption of digital technology and increasing automation so that the technology can be more effectively targeted.

Automatic fingerprint readers are now commonplace, and many European companies make them. But any unique attribute of anatomy or personal style can also be used to create a **human identity recognition system**. For example, Cellmark Diagnostics (United Kingdom) can **recognise genes**; Mastiff Security Systems (United Kingdom) can **recognise odour**, Hagen Cy-Com (United Kingdom) and Eyedentify

Inc. (United States) can recognise the pattern of capillaries at the back of the retina, while AEA Technology (United Kingdom) is capable of **signature verification**. More than 109 companies in Europe are known to be supplying such **biometric systems**.

The leading-edge companies are racing towards developing **face recognition systems**, which they see as being able to revolutionise crime customs and intruder detection as well as service access control. Although fully reliable systems are perhaps five years off, prototype systems have been developed in France, Germany, the United Kingdom and the United States.

Night vision technology developed as a result of the Vietnam War has now been adapted for police usage. Particularly successful are **heli-tele surveillance** versions, which allow cameras to track human heat signatures in total darkness. The art of **bugging** has been made significantly easier by a rapidly advancing technology, and there is a burgeoning European market. Many systems do not require physical entry into the home or office. For those who can secure access to their target room, there is a plethora of devices, many of which can be prepackaged to fit into phones or look like cigarette packets or light fittings. And some can even be tuned into from a suitable radio. However, the next generation of covert audio bugs are remotely operated. For example, the multiroom monitoring system of Lorraine Electronics called DIAL (Direct Intelligent Access Listening) allows an operator to monitor several rooms from anywhere in the world without effecting an illegal entry. Up to four concealed microphones are connected to the subscribers' line, and these can be remotely activated by simply making a coded telephone call to the target building.

Neural network bugs are built like a small cockroach. As soon as the lights go out, they can crawl to the best location for surveillance. Japanese researchers have taken this idea one step further, controlling and manipulating real cockroaches by implanting microprocessors and electrodes in their bodies. The insects can be fitted with micro-cameras and sensors to reach the places other bugs cannot reach.

Passive millimeter wave imaging developed by the U.S. company Millitech Corporation can scan people from up to 12 feet away and see through clothing to detect concealed items such as weapons, packages and other contraband. Variations of this through-clothing human screening under development (by companies such as the Raytheon Company in the United States) include systems that illuminate an individual with a low-intensity electromagnetic pulse. A three-side very-low X-ray system for human usage, envisioned for use in fixed sites such as prisons, is being developed by Nicolet Imaging Systems of San Diego.

Electronic monitoring of offenders or '**tagging**', with the subject wearing an electronic bracelet that can detect if they have relocated from their home after certain hours, entered into use in the 1990s after being developed to regulate prison populations in the United States. Finally, **satellite tracking** of VIPs, vehicles and other objects is facilitated by global positioning system (GPS) equipment – once reserved for the military, but now available for commercial uses.

An immense range of surveillance technologies has evolved, including the night vision goggles and parabolic microphones to detect conversations a mile away. Laser versions marketed by the German company PK Electronic can pick up any conversation from a closed window in line of sight; the Danish Jai stroboscopic camera can take hundreds of pictures in a matter of seconds and individually photograph all the participants in a demonstration or march. The automatic vehicle recognition systems can identify a car number plate and then track the car around a city with the help of a computerised geographic information system.

Such systems are now commercially available. One example is the Talon system introduced in 1994 by U.K. company Racal at a price of £2000 per unit. The system is trained to recognise number plates and is based on neural network technology developed by Cambridge Neurodynamics. The system can 'see' at night as well as during the day. Initially, it was used for traffic monitoring but its function has been adapted in recent years to cover security surveillance, and it has been incorporated into the ring of steel around London. The system can record all the vehicles entering or leaving the cordon on any particular day.

The art of visual surveillance has dramatically changed over recent years. Police and intelligence officers still photograph demonstrations and individuals of interest, but such images can be stored and searched increasingly easily. The current revolution in urban surveillance is expected to generate the next generation of control tools once reliable face recognition comes in.

Bugging and tapping. A wide range of bugging and tapping devices has evolved to record conversations and to intercept telecommunications traffic. In recent years, the widespread practice of illegal and legal interception of communications and the planting of 'bugs' has been an issue in many European states (see http://cryptome.org/stoa-atpc.htm#52#52).

Modern snoopers can buy especially adapted laptop computers and simply tune in on all the mobile phones active in the area by cursoring down to their number. The machine will even search for numbers 'of interest' to see if they are active.

Area denial replaces personnel guarding either areas or perimeters. It has involved deploying technology that can either create punishment when its limits are infringed or systems with built-in intelligence that can both locate the point of infringement and activate a corrective response. Sophisticated varieties incorporate punishment mechanisms that vary from pain induced by electroshock to kill fences and fragmentation mines.

Neural networks with semi-intelligence are being introduced to protect sensitive control zones. Systems allow pattern recognition and have an ability to learn. Neural systems will play an increasing role in sentinel duties as robot technology improves. Already, prototypes for inexpensive devices known as insectoids are being evolved to replace personnel on routine guard duties that require 24-hour cover. These insectoids can be programmed to track the fence and carry either lethal or sublethal weapons.

Interception. Within Europe, all e-mail, telephone and fax communications are routinely intercepted by the U.S. NSA, transferring all target information from the European mainland via the strategic hub of London and then by satellite to Fort Meade in Maryland or via the crucial hub at Menwith Hill in the North Yorkshire Moors of the United Kingdom. Other work on what is now known as **signals intelligence** was undertaken by researchers such as James Bamford, who uncovered a billion-dollar worldwide interceptions network he nicknamed 'Puzzle Palace'.

A more recent work by Nicky Hager, *Secret Power* (1996), provides the most comprehensive details to date of a project known as ECHELON (http://jya.com/echelon.htm). Hager interviewed more than 50 people concerned with intelligence to document a global surveillance system that stretches around the world to form a targeting system on all of the key Intelsat satellites used to convey most of the world's satellite phone calls, internet, e-mail, faxes and telexes. These sites are based at Sugar Grove and Yakima in the United States, Waihopai in New Zealand, Geraldton in Australia, in Hong Kong, and also in Morwenstow in the United Kingdom.

The ECHELON system forms part of the UKUSA system, but unlike many of the electronic spy systems developed during the Cold War, ECHELON is designed for primarily nonmilitary targets: governments, organisations and businesses in virtually every country. The ECHELON system works by indiscriminately intercepting very large quantities of communications and then siphoning out what is valuable using artificial intelligence aids like Memex to find key words. Five nations share the results, with the United States as the senior partner, under the UKUSA agreement of 1948. Britain, Canada, New Zealand and Australia are very much acting as subordinate information servicers.

Intelligence and security informatics. Intelligence and security informatics (ISI) is an emerging field of study aimed at developing advanced information technologies, systems, algorithms and databases for national and homeland security-related applications through an integrated technological, organisational and policy-based approach. Several key ISI research areas include cross-jurisdiction information sharing, terrorism information collection, analysis and visualisation, and finally 'smart-border' and bioterrorism applications (Chen[27]).

Trends in the United Kingdom

In his preface to *Police Science Technology Strategy Report 2003–2008*, John Denham, minister of state for policing in Great Britain, comes straight to the point: 'I want to ensure that the police is equipped with the best means and technology available, so that it is capable of achieving maximum effectiveness and efficiency'. The primary objective is to integrate science and technology in maintaining law and order. This integration is seen as essential. Science and technology would be capable of making an important contribution to the achievement of prime prevention objectives as formulated in the national criminality policy plans. These objectives are listed below:

- The identification and neutralisation of public disturbances of the peace, whereby increasing attention is devoted to terrorist threats;
- The effective deployment of intelligence-gathering technology;
- The exchange of information between forces and other relevant partners in the maintenance of safety;
- The introduction of mobile data systems;
- Maximising the probative value;
- Effective management of the investigation process, including management of crime scenes (forensic evidence);
- The introduction of automated management-support systems;
- The monitoring of potential perpetrators;
- The integration of technology in surveillance strategies;
- Effective localisation and securing of traces, and therefore evidence; and
- The protection of police functionaries and vulnerable citizens.

In addition, a distinction is made between four categories: operations, deployment, development and research. The integration of science and technology in operations relates to the creation of the possibility for the police to have direct insight into national criminal systems in its daily work, access to local, regional and national support services, the national DNA databank and automated fingerprint systems.

The integration of science and technology in deployment relates to the further development and introduction of new digital information systems that link forces, facilitate wireless communication, expand the automated number plate registration system, expand the video identification parade electronic recording system for the identification of individuals in large groups, and the further introduction of portable drug-testing equipment allowing the police to perform analyses on the spot.

As far as development is concerned, the integration of science and technology concerns middle-term to long-term investments for the (outsourced) development of automated and portable equipment for DNA analysis and other trace investigations (including fingerprints and explosives) on a PD ('lab-on-a-chip'), the development of national trace databanks, the application of technology in surveillance (night vision, movement detectors), and the improvement of video surveillance to generate images that can be used as evidence.

The integration of science and technology is also strongly driven by investments in scientific research areas such as biometrics, DNA, chemical tracing and more advanced detection systems for drugs and explosives (for example, in entrances or on the road).

Home Office Scientific Development Branch (HOSDB)

HOSDB is based at two sites in the United Kingdom: at Sandridge, Hertfordshire, and Langhurst, West Sussex. The R&D is conducted both in-house and through extensive links with industry and academia. With 23 technical programmes and more than 125 current projects, the organisation is serving almost every branch of policing. HOSDB employs more than 200 scientists. HOSDB holds a central stock of the latest search and surveillance equipment that is provided to police forces on request. This avoids all forces having to keep complex and expensive equipment. Over £1 million of equipment was deployed at the last Commonwealth Games, comprising more than 100 different technologies. Technologies mentioned are the very latest explosives detection, X-ray screening and weapons detection technologies, an innovative X-ray scanner that reveals items hidden below clothing without the need for an intrusive hands-on body search, state-of-the-art thermal imaging equipment can detect people at long range by their body heat, even if they are unconscious, and closed-circuit television (CCTV) for crowd safety.

Unbridgeable gap or interweaving?

Much of the broader knowledge about crime is produced by and for institutions other than the criminal justice system. Within the private sector, parallel 'policing' systems operate that are based on preventive security arrangements and administrative compliance: 'these systems for policing risks are much more elaborate and have greater technological and personnel resources than the public police Hoogenboom, 1987, 1994. To illustrate the point, I will discuss two different fraud and money-laundering detection systems developed by two different companies.

FraudVision

Building upon traditional fraud-detection tools, such as signature verification and data analysis, FraudVision takes a holistic view of the check, rather than focusing on one single factor. It analyses such characteristics as check stock, signature, payee name and handwriting, extending intelligent character recognition to include both machine and cursive handwriting. FraudVision maintains a profile of these characteristics, so when an image of a check is presented, the system automatically determines if the check characteristics match.

Using a combined analysis rules engine (CARE), FraudVision combines the results of this image analysis with results from external data analysis systems, resulting in better quality and more accurate results. For example, if the bank's data analysis system flags a check because of a suspect dollar amount, FraudVision can quickly verify the check characteristics to rule out fraud. Likewise, if the data analysis system misses a fraudulent check because the payment pattern matches the user's profile exactly, FraudVision can detect that it is indeed fraudulent because the check stock is irregular. This image and data analysis is combined and presented to the user at a single, easy-to-use Fraud Analyst Workstation. With a high volume of checks to analyse daily, it is important to banks that only the most suspect checks are referred to investigators for analysis. 'A bank that processes a million checks a day doesn't have time to have someone look at every check. They want to exclude 99 percent of incoming checks as assumed good,' Engan says.

Norkom Technology Platform

Norkom's technology platform consists of a data model and repository that captures and maintains information, a profiling, detection scenario and analytics engine that pinpoints suspicious behaviour, a configuration engine that allows the end users to tailor its products to their needs, an alerts engine and case management function that provides the information that investigative teams need and a workflow engine that streamlines the investigative and other business process. This comprehensive and configurable platform is what makes Norkom different and enables them to deliver, at speed, sector-specific products that keep pace with evolving criminal activity and the ever-changing regulatory framework.

Norkom's financial crime platform provides user security, audit tracking, administration and single sign-on capabilities. It provides the ability to access data from any source system coupled with prepackaged data models designed specifically for the needs of the different financial services sectors. The firm's configurator enables partners and other validated third parties to configure elements of its products to suit their unique business needs – for example, screen layout, workflow, user access, permission rights, detection scenarios and profiles.

Norkom's profiling engine creates profiles based on peer group analysis, behavioural analysis and risk analysis to perfect the art of detection. Its detection scenario engine provides predefined and configurable detection scenarios that are specific to particular sectors and crime types. The workflow engine enables workflows surrounding the financial crime and compliance business processes to be configured into Norkom's platform, ensuring the correct processes are followed right across the organisation. The company's alert engine and case management service delivers prioritised alerts directly to investigators' desktops that are prepopulated with all the information necessary for investigation and end-to-end management of cases.

Norkom claims that its products and services have been proven to deliver 98 per cent improvement in investigation efficiency; 200 per cent improvement in the accuracy of detection; 70 per cent decrease in fraud levels; reduced business risk of exposure to sanctions and reduced cost of ownership, capital expenditure and support costs. Balance sheet impact is immense in terms of reduced operational overheads and decreased financial losses.

Norkom's fraud screening detection scenarios utilising advanced analytical techniques enable accurate profiling and risk rating of claim details. These can be extended and reconfigured as business requirements evolve. Fuzzy matching is used to match claims data against internal and external data and sophisticated link analysis works to uncover hidden relationships and spot organised and opportunistic fraud attempts.

Public–private security ICT–architecture: Pushing back the fog of the unknown

No Place to Hide illustrates the U.S. government's effort to break down the walls between commercial and public data in its wish to compile detailed files on virtually every adult American. O'Harrow works as a reporter for *The Washington Post* and is an associate of the Center for Investigative Reporting. He was shortlisted for the Pulitzer Prize with his articles on privacy and technology. In 2003, he received the Carnegie Mellon Cyber Security Reporting Award (NoPlaceToHide.net).

For nearly a decade, marketers have been collecting the electronic footprints we leave behind as we consume our way through the modern world; they know what politicians we give money to, what prescriptions we file, and what sex toys we buy from mail-order catalogues. Now the government knows, too. But it insists it can use this information to ferret out terrorists. A large number of digital sources can now be tapped, cross-linked and subsequently used for security purposes. The marketing world is the prime example of this process. 'Welcome to the realm of predictive intelligence, consisting of a new generation of analytical applications for quickly analysing large amounts of data.[28] This highly inviting slogan is used for a data-mining system 'to help enterprises push back the fog of the unknown'. There is a trend, particularly in the United States, to apply such techniques in intelligence services' analytical work.

O'Harrow explores how the government is teaming up with private companies to collect massive amounts of data on citizens and how, he writes, 'More than ever before, the details about our lives are no longer our own. They belong to the companies that collect them, and the government agencies that buy or demand them in the name of keeping us safe'. O'Harrow uses companies like *Choicepoint, Seisint, Seismic Intelligence, Verint* and Verifiable Intelligence to illustrate his point. The portrait that emerges is that of an industry of finding links between people, establishing patterns, showing trends and conducting risk assessments. Choicepoint, based outside of Atlanta, has bought 58 companies since 1997. These include a genetic repository and companies specialising in biometrics and fingerprints. In fact, the company is becoming a fingerprint specialist. Choicepoint has something like 19 billion records, and it has become the nation's largest background screener. In *No Place to Hide*, O'Harrow concludes that Choicepoint is operating as a private intelligence service.

The ultimate goal of 'predictive intelligence' is to organise this analytical process in such a way that terrorist incidents can be predicted and thereby prevented. In the United States, this has led to the development of computer systems and programmes such as the Total Information Awareness Program, the Multistate Anti-Terrorism Information Exchange and the Computer Assisted Passenger Profiling System.

The Total Information Awareness Program (TIP)

The TIP programme is intended to collate as much information as possible, from as many databases as possible, in order to identify potential terrorists. It remains unknown exactly how many databases TIP covers, but it is assumed that it includes medical and financial data, (historical) travel information, political convictions, consumer behaviour, education and training data, personal and family relationships, and information on communication (phone, e-mail and Internet surfing).

Multistate Anti-Terrorism Information Exchange (Matrix)

The Matrix system composes files on civilians through data mining in a number of public and private databases. The Matrix analyses millions of files and seeks out 'anomalies' that may point to terrorist or criminal intentions and/or activities. On the basis of scarce open sources, it is assumed that the data mining relates to systems in which information is stored on loans, photographs from driving licenses, marriages and divorces, social security numbers, dates of birth and the names and addresses of family members, neighbours and business relations.[29]

Computer Assisted Passenger Profiling System (CAPPS II)

The CAPPS II system focuses on performing background checks of American aircraft passengers. Using this information, the system develops 'risk scores'. A large number of European airlines have been providing their passenger data to the United States for a number of years.

National security will increasingly depend on private sector involvement

Because every aspect of civilian life could be affected – from food distribution, financial transactions, gas and electricity to public transit – a wide range of industries will become increasingly involved in national security one way or the other. 'The private sector is going to play a much more important role in homeland security than it did in national security in the past', says retired Air Force Colonel Randy Larsen, director of the Anser Institute for Homeland Security, a think tank created by the Rand Corporation.

It is not only through combining information on citizens that the public and private sectors have become intertwined. Because of the interlocking interests and mutual dependencies in what is called 'critical infrastructures', public and private spheres can no longer be looked upon as separate entities. Recent developments in the Netherlands illustrate the point.

Security-Industrial Security Complex

In his 1961 farewell address, President Dwight D. Eisenhower famously warned that the government agencies and defence contractors tasked with keeping America safe from communism could themselves become a threat to the American way of life. 'We must never,' he urged, 'let the weight of this combination endanger our liberties or democratic process....Only an alert and knowledgeable citizenry can compel the proper meshing of the huge industrial and military machinery of defense with our peaceful methods and goals, so that security and liberty may prosper together.' Eisenhower spoke of a 'military industrial complex'. Nowadays, we can speak of the existence of a 'security-industrial complex'. We find ourselves at the very beginning of mapping out trends here, and the first seeds of understanding any possible (un)intended consequences of technopoly on a conceptual level have only just been sown.

10

Blinded by the Light: The Interweaving of (Organised) Crime, White Collar Crime, State Crime and Terrorism

Introduction

From the 'Technopoly', I now return to more mundane matters: rule breaking, crime and other assorted forms of deviance. The governance of policing and security is all about national security, public order and the prevention and repression of crime. My argument in this chapter is my criticism of the 'one-sided' analyses of crime by the multitude of different actors – both operational actors and certainly those in criminology. Only by combining crime analyses from the public police, regulators, intelligence and security services and private security can the hundreds of crime pieces from the big jigsaw puzzle make some sense.

Although it is not really substantiated, I think the idea is gradually gaining ground within the different silos in the policing and security communities that only through sharing information, analyses and intelligence can some understanding be gained about the complex nature of crime in our societies. What I try to do in this chapter – in line with my 'unbounding' argument or 'interweaving' argument – is that if we look at the undertows of crime, many of the 'borders' between organised crime and organisational or state crime are not that clear. I'm interested here again in 'blurring of boundaries' between all sorts of crime. Also, I need this chapter to help people understand in a rudimentary way why the state (and therefore the police) is increasingly creating forms of cooperation between the police, regulators and private security. Probably the simple reason is for one to understand the limitations of 'vertical' or 'silolike' intelligence. This traditional (criminal) intelligence reflects priorities, dominant conceptual lenses and day-to-day operations of all the different actors in all the complex policing and security networks. On the ground, things aren't as easy as this. On the ground, money launderers operate with banking officials; on the ground, intelligence officials operate with organised crime figures; and on the ground, politicians operate with entrepreneurs and criminals for all sorts of reasons. Crime is sanitised in crime statistics, but on the ground, all sorts of interweaving takes places between the state and organised crime and between the intelligence community and policing. This chapter introduces concepts like *symbiotic* and *functional* perspectives on 'organised crime', which are neglected in normal science. As Springsteen sang, 'We're blinded by the light.'

Blinded by the light

It may be stated that police research and most of the criminological research is 'blinded by the light'. It is predominantly focused on street crime and 'organised' crime. The theoretical and empirical light mostly shines on precincts, community policing and high-profile 'mob cases'.

The light shines on street violence, drug-related crime and theft and burglaries. The two major works on policing, *Handbook of Policing* (Newburn, 2003a) and *Policing. Key Readings* (Newburn, 2005), do not – or only sparingly – touch upon state crime, organisational crime, white-collar crime or fraud. The index of the latter book does not even mention these criminological concepts. In *Handbook of Policing*, fraud and white-collar crime are mentioned on pages 445 and 446 only. The other concepts remain undiscussed. Both police research and mainstream criminology almost exclusively focus on crime that the criminal justice system deals with on a day-to-day basis. The prison systems around the world are filled with young, working-class offenders, ethnic minorities and people convicted for drug-related offences.

Public policing, regulation, military involvement in crime fighting and terrorism, security and intelligence operations differ very much when it comes to academic interest. Public policing has a very strong theoretical and empirical basis – as is illustrated by the handbooks mentioned. The other 'pillars' of the emerging new security architecture are relatively under-researched. We should also bear in mind that these 'pillars' in fact operate in different or 'multiple realities' (Hoogenboom, 1994).

Whereas public policing mainly deals with reproducing order and with street and organised crime, regulation is primarily directed at economic irregularities that, in their most manifest forms, could be labelled organisational crime or white-collar crime. Nevertheless, this type of crime is rarely addressed by the police. The principal explanation is that economic irregularities are not regulated by criminal law but by administrative law. Public policing and regulation operate in different realities. As was discussed earlier, overlapping activities can be found, and they are on the rise, but this should not blind us to the fact that primary processes to a large extent remain separate.

The 'multiple reality' argument also holds for the private security market. Admittedly, the state has become the largest demand factor, and yes, hybrid security structures can be found in airport and seaport security. However, on another level, between 50 and 80 per cent of internal fraud cases investigated are not handed over to the criminal justice system. Next to the criminal justice system, an elaborate administrative and civil law (and private justice) system exists. 'Thus, white collar criminals are segregated administratively from other criminals and, largely as a result of this, are not regarded as *real* criminals: not by themselves, not by the general public nor by criminologists' (Sutherland, 1948).

In the intellectual debate on crime, deviancy, law and rule breaking or irregularities, state crime is dismissed even further because a state may engage in state terror and terrorism, torture, war crimes and genocide. Nationally as well as internationally, there may be corruption, state-corporate crime and organised crime. More usually, the state is directly involved in excessive secrecy and cover-ups, disinformation and unaccountability (including tax evasion by officials), which often reflect upper-class and nonpluralistic interests and infringements on human rights.

My arguments – that we are 'blinded by the light' and are facing 'multiple realities' – can be extended not only to military involvement in the war on crime, but also to the intelligence communities themselves. It cannot be denied that increasing interweaving is taking place today, but primary processes generally remain separated as a result of different (noncriminal justice, nonadministrative and noncommercial) functions that revolve around the use of force and/or national security interests.

Why do I need this introduction and why do I have to bring up this 'unsolvable problem' in criminology in defining crime and – again – touching upon the useless intellectual energy going into these 'wars between the academic schools of thought'? It is not because I am interested in these 'normal science' debates so much, and it is not because I want to use the valuable and pristine pages of this book to repeat all these ancient arguments, but simply because I wish to draw attention to the undertows in crime: the interweaving of (organised) crime, white-collar crime, state crime and terrorism. I am interested in concepts like *interoperability, interconnectivity* and *functional* or *symbiotic* relationships between state agencies, bureaucracies, corporations, 'criminals' and terrorists. The line 'just as every cop is a criminal, and all you sinners saints (Rolling Stones, 1971) does not cover reality. Yet, as we all know, truth in some cases may be stranger than (rock-and-roll) fiction.

In the weeks before 800,000 Tutsis were killed in Rwanda in 1994, large shipments of small arms were brought into the country. Initially – and as a result of researchers being blinded by the light – criminal networks were mentioned as perpetrators. Next, the United Nations, Jane's and NGOs like Amnesty International peeled away the various outer layers of the initial explanations concerning the issue and drew attention to the involvement of legitimate arms corporations in Belgium, Israel and the United Kingdom as well as to the economic interests these corporations have for their own countries. These ironies and paradoxes are the subject of this chapter: not only to illustrate a certain degree of superficiality in crime discussions, but mainly because I am convinced that within the intellectual (academic) and operational silos, the fundamental insight is gaining ground that the various different crime manifestations are in fact interlocked. Money laundering cannot be understood if it is detached from the context in which it takes place: in certain offshore constructions, for instance, normative crime and financial integrity arguments increasingly often make way for commercial interests held by legitimate financial conglomerates operating from Frankfurt, London and Amsterdam.

The financing of terrorism cannot be detached from the street crime context in which terrorists are involved in robberies, extortion and fraud – as case studies targeting the Euskadi Ta Askatasuna (ETA), Irish Republican Army (IRA) or today's Afghan opium trade shows. Distinctions between under and upper worlds, state bureaucracies and war lords, (local) officials and drug criminals as well as law enforcers and law breakers are not as distinct as 'normal science', the mass media, politicians and nine-to-five criminologists so tenaciously believe them to be.

A greater sensitivity to today's blurring crime boundaries, I argue, is a fundamental driving force for the trends (of which interweaving is one example) discussed in the preceding chapters. If national security interests are more clearly defined in terms of financial dimensions (money laundering, terrorism financing), the intelligence community has an interest to cooperate with regulators and financial institutions. If financial crimes (Enron, Worldcom and the credit crises, for instance) are increasingly often perceived as criminal (white-collar crime) cases, it is only logical that law enforcement agencies increasingly often cooperate with regulators. To understand these undertows in crime (and crime control), I will discuss certain crime dynamics while stressing the symbiotic or functional relationships between the 'good' and 'bad' guys. Just to illustrate this point, a description is given below of two scenes from the Al Pacino movie *Scarface*.

Scene 1

Pacino portrays a Cuban refugee who becomes a prominent drug dealer in Miami. In one scene, the bank manager wants a bigger piece of the action. He wants to raise his fee for money laundering. Pacino feels cornered and wonders who the 'bad' guy in this scene actually is. Pacino turns to his criminal associate and says 'watch carefully, you can learn a lot from this guy'. Pacino is left with no choice but to close the deal. To me, this is a quintessential scene for raising questions about who is who in crime – and crime analyses. For the better part of almost 25 years of professional life, I have been reading, talking, lecturing and writing on crime and criminology. Increasingly, discomfort kept slipping in about the stereotyped way that society, as well as the social sciences, deals with (organised) crime issues. The good and bad guy routine and other associated languages of the under and upper world increasingly to me are in some way fairy tales – fairy tales from the imagination of ivory tower academics trying to grasp the complexities of social life who, in the process, keep clinging to cardboard concepts. Of course *Scarface* is taken from popular culture, but do the plot, the story lines and the characters really differ from the writings on white-collar crime?

Scene 2

In another scene, Pacino has dinner in a high-class restaurant. He is drunk and stoned and argues with his girlfriend and partner. He stumbles out of the restaurant and turns back to face the offended clientele, saying: 'Where you all looking at? You're all a bunch of fucking assholes. You know why? Because you don't have the guts to be what you wanna be. You need fucking people like me. So you can point your fucking fingers. So you can say that's the bad guy. So does that make you feel good? You're not so good. You just know how to hide a lie. Me, I don't lie. Me, I always tell the truth, even when I lie. So, say goodnight to the bad guy'. Scarface here touches, in my interpretation of the scene, on the hypocrisy and superficiality of mainstream images of crime. In real life, distinctions between 'good and bad', law enforcement and crime, under and upper world aren't that clear. It is this I want to deal with in this chapter. I will use historical examples from around the world and will slowly work my way to current examples and cases. Crime is not only a problem for many in society, it is also beneficial for many others. Crime can be functional for the political system, the business community, law enforcement and the intelligence communities.

Functional perspectives on crime

In the following paragraphs, I will take you on a historical journey around the world to sensitise you somewhat to the social (and criminal) interactions between different public and private actors operating simultaneously both in legal and illegal contexts. There are all sorts of 'grey' areas between politicians, law enforcers, intelligence operatives, criminal and political assets and informants, businessmen and organised crime figures. Like Alice, we descend into a sort of criminological Wonderland. We start with the Mafia in the nineteenth century.

One study into the Mafia, particularly in Sicily and Calabria between 1861 and 1914, shows that the Mafia gained a quasipolitical and economic power that threatened the authority of the state. At the same time, however, the Mafia fulfilled a functional role for the political elite as it assisted in maintaining public order: 'It was paradoxical that some parts of the government were fighting to destroy the Mafia, while others sought to collaborate with it'. Another Italian study suggests that organised crime can only flourish where overlap exists between the formal and informal economy. In the grey areas, legal and illegal players are repeatedly granted favours.

After the World War II, studies refer to the mixture of this formal and informal economy that allowed the Mafia to expand its position. Despite the economic growth, the south trailed behind: 'This, however, has strengthened the state bourgeoisie, who administrated state funds, and the Mafia, who benefited from manipulation in jobs, insurance and pension funds'. A parliamentary enquiry investigated why the Italian government failed to come to grips structurally with the Mafia. The answer was found in the fact that the weave between political, administrative, social and economic structures and the Mafia was and still is close. There are mutually facilitating relationships between official functionaries and criminal entrepreneurs.

In one Italian research project, corruption is defined as 'the provision of privileges to third parties by government officials in exchange for money or goods'. This investigation points to the 'intermediaries' who affect relationships between bureaucratic and criminal networks[30] Klerks (2000) uses this functionalistic perspective for the period 1890 to 1940 in the United States.[31] Various researchers such as Trasher and Landesco have focused on 'the influence of social conditions under which crime developed and on the functionality of extra-legal activities and the organisation of gambling and the liquor trade'. Between 1929 and 1931, the presidential Wickersham Commission investigated fraud, extortion and protection. The commission concluded that businessmen and gangsters were working hand-in-hand.

According to Mastrofski and Potter, the U.S. government did not succeed in stopping organised crime because it was always defined as an 'alien conspiracy': the danger was thought to come from outside, threatening the respectable civil society. The authors nevertheless point to corruption within the civil society and to the fact that 'these loosely structured enterprises successfully exploit symbiotic relationships with public officials and professionals (...) In fact, organized criminals do not corrupt public officials so much as they provide ways for them to willingly partake of illicit markets.' By placing the 'hazy ghost' of organised crime outside society, and thereby implicitly assuming that fraud, violence, crime and corruption are 'alien to the American life', they lose touch with reality. Crime is an 'entrepreneurial challenge, not simply a criminal phenomenon'.

An investigation into 'organised crime' in the ports of New York over a 50-year period concludes that public supervisors, professional criminals and politicians not only promoted and exploited the scope and nature of crime in the ports, but actually managed for a considerable period of time to safeguard it from any form of external interference because everyone was benefiting from the situation. The same symbiotic relationships appear in research into arson in Boston. Small-time hoodlums are involved in the arson as executors, but they are only front men in a corrupt network of policemen, firemen, insurance officials and project developers. Banks and project developers enjoyed the greatest profits by commissioning arson through 'the grapevine' to facilitate newly planned projects. The official path would have taken too long and would have been too costly.

Chambliss investigated the nature and social composition of crime in Seattle and argues that the 'hidden hand' of organised crime in the United States is not the Mafia, but much rather prominent, respectable men who are part of the establishment. Chambliss finds links between front men and the establishment who at first sight are beyond suspicion yet who, in the end, control the criminal networks: policemen, lawyers, businessmen, local government officials and officers of justice.[32] Initiatives, control and cover–up processes related to criminal activity are carried out by respectable pillars of society. According to Chambliss, crime is an integral part of political-administrative and economic processes. He uses the term *political economy*: business income is earned through illegal actions that are interlaced with legal activities. This does not occur on an ad hoc basis or incidentally as the opportunities happen to arise, but instead as a structural phenomenon.

From the end of the 1950s to the 1980s, a group of entrepreneurs had their operational base in the Bahamas and were involved in a wide range of organised fraud. The entrepreneurs did not, however, have the characteristics of the traditional underworld figures, nor were they allied with traditional organised crime groups. This 'Serious Crime Community', as Block calls them, consisted of respectable lawyers from the United States who had originally moved to the Bahamas to set up banks and offshore organisations. The Serious Crime Community grew through the business ties that evolved between these lawyers and finance and development companies, offshore film companies, insurance companies and a number of savings and loan organisations. These primarily legal financial services offered a broad range of illegal financial services. The Serious Crime Community played a role in large-scale bank, tax and (re)insurance fraud, insider trading through anonymous accounts and fraudulent share transactions.[33]

The Bahamas also became the playground of lawyers, financiers and (project) developers from Europe who in principle were up to the same things as their American colleagues: large-scale fraud. The victims were European banks and companies. The business network expanded to include the Cayman Islands, Panama, Monte Carlo, Luxemburg, the Dutch Antilles and the Channel Islands, among others. The Serious Crime Community also provided illegal financial services to important American and European underworld characters and financed the illegal campaigns of a number of intelligence services. The community was also involved in financing oil transport from South Africa that was boycotted by the international community at that time.

In the 1970s, we saw organised crime in the Rotterdam harbour: (illegal) labour subcontractors. Creative entrepreneurs recruited workers who were paid in black-market money. The subcontractors had been able to enter the stage as a result of the demand for flexible labour from renowned harbour companies that were perfectly happy to pay black-market wages. The labour subcontractors not only provided them with flexible and good staff, but they were also relatively cheap. The black-market money was deposited in accounts with the Slavenburg Bank. A network of people with a wide range of interests benefited from the system's status quo. It was beneficial for all participants – who thus came to work for perfectly legal companies.

A similar analysis is possible for the so-called illegal sewing workshops in the Netherlands in the 1980s. Commissioned by renowned department stores, these cheap workers produced tailored clothes. Here, too, mutual advantages for legal and illegal entrepreneurs existed in setting up and maintaining illegal trade. Another striking example is the fence world. In our society, many stolen goods find their way to other respectable citizens through intermediaries such as café owners, taxi drivers, shopkeepers, car salesmen and the arts and antique trade. Thieves and fences offer each other their facilitating services and are together embroiled in the informal economy.

In Canada, functional or symbiotic relationships have been documented within the port infrastructure of Vancouver, Montreal and Halifax, which shield the import, forwarding and export of highly criminal products. This happens through the development and cultivation of a network of corrupt relationships with functionaries in business (ship brokers, lumpers, insurance companies and assessors, port security firms, transport companies, and so forth) and supervision and control organisations, including customs. These networks provide valuable information on the import, port and customs procedures and intelligence activities. The networks also allow the facilitation of illegal import, forwarding and export. These illegal networks have a major influence on container processing.[34] According to the Canadian criminal investigation service (CISC), criminal organisations are 'entrenched within the infrastructure of Canada's maritime ports'. There is extensive cooperation between companies and the underworld. As a result, criminal networks have access to strategic information and are therefore capable of shielding illegal import, forwarding and export activities.

In 1997, U.S. President Clinton installed the Graham Commission on Seaport Security. The reason: a discrepancy between the level of security in airports and the 361 seaports where monitoring and security was described as 'poorly coordinated'. The basis of this commission's work was that, in the past decades, the United States had invested greatly in the security of airports, but that this one-sided focus led to the neglect of security in the many ports.[35] The Graham Commission focused on the analysis of the nature and scope of fraud, corruption and criminality in a number of areas:

- Terrorism
- Car theft
- Load theft
- Drug smuggling
- Currency smuggling
- Food quality
- Illegal alien smuggling

The Dutch entrepreneur organisation EVO estimates that, in 1999, some €60 million worth of theft and fraud took place in the transport of goods. Crime analyses by the Rotterdam police report the existence of organised crime in the business community. This type of crime goes hand-in-hand with increasing corruption and the interweaving of legal and illegal markets, says the Rotterdam seaport police. The study entitled *Kwetsbaarheden in de logistieke keten* (Vulnerabilities in the logistics chain) concludes that 'service provision, such as providing information to criminals, is a serious problem'. In addition to the active involvement of staff in fraud, smuggling and resource criminality, staff may also be bribed. Furthermore, businesses pay out kickbacks to ensure that the monitoring activities run 'smoothly', whereby government officials aid in criminal activities.

Another functional perspective is found in the analysis of Russian organised crime, which on the one hand is described traditionally in terms of criminals who corrupt business and government, while on the other it is increasingly often explained in terms of widespread corruption within the government and the business community. Russian law enforcement agencies, security organs and intelligence services, far from being reliable instruments in the fight against organised crime and corruption, form an institutional part of the problem, due not only to their co-optation and penetration by criminal elements, but to their own absence of a legal bureaucratic culture and their use of crime as an instrument of state policy, according to Waller and Yasmann.[36]

Russian society is not threatened so much by external forces such as organised crime, but parts of the legal system (politics, finance, police as well as justice and intelligence services) are themselves fraught with corruption. A myth is being unveiled. In the early 1990s, the myth was that Russia would make the transition to a liberal democracy with the help of the West. As Brent Scowcroft, National Security Advisor to President George H. W. Bush said: 'We probably have been deluding ourselves that reform has taken hold'. Russia could, in time, still make the transition to a democratic market economy, but as things stand, the country seems to be in a transitional phase that has been described as a 'gangster state'.[37]

The term *organised crime* generally suggests that threats enter society (politics, bureaucracy or business) 'from the outside'. Michael Waller and Victor J. Yasmann suggest that 'it becomes apparent that Russia's political, economic, security and law enforcement elites fundamentally are part of the problem.' What is mostly seen as a 'spontaneous development' (the growth of organised crime) is in many cases a directed process in which KGB criminals pass on institutional and organisational experiences as well as information, techniques and (inter)national contacts.[38]

Symbiotic relationships were also exposed in the 1998 Dutch research project into organised crime sponsored by the Ministry of Justice, which concluded that there is much common ground between the various types of organised crime and their social environment. 'On the one hand, the environment is threatening to criminal cooperatives (...) while on the other, it is not only a risk factor but also an ally. Conscious or unconscious cooperation by the environment is critical for the production of illegal goods and for those who purchase them. Sometimes, the environment is even prepared to support the operation or to protect the crime. Few types of organised crime have only a negative effect for others: often, in addition to the damage, symbiotic relationships are created with parts of the social environment.[39]

The above study also distances itself from the organisational model that has become so popular in analysing organised crime. It often discusses cooperative ventures that frequently change composition and in which the task distribution between the members has no sustainable character. These characteristics deviate strongly from the image of criminal cooperation, which have a pyramid structure and in which task distribution and task execution run according to fixed patterns that are maintained through codes of conduct and internal sanctions. These cooperative ventures are characterised by all manner of social relationships that 'deviate from the analytical distinction between the legal environment and the illegal environment'. In other words, here, too, a great deal of common ground exists between organised crime and the legal environment. The presence and the support of the legal environment are a vital condition for many types of organized crime. This holds, for example, for the necessary cooperation of the legal environment in the production of illegal goods (for example, raw materials for synthetic drugs) and the sales of goods. Many types of organized crime would have no hope of survival if the legal environment were not a consumer of their services or products. The traffic in women and the sale of illegal goods such as drugs and illegal CDs are the most clear-cut examples.

The legal environment also appears to make a facilitating contribution to organised crime. The benefits of the standard social infrastructure (transport, housing, service provision) are also used by criminal forms of cooperation. The report concludes that this use can occur without any conscious cooperation by the legal environment. Nevertheless, situations were also discovered (in transport and the service industry) that point to a culpable involvement of individuals or organisations in organised crime.

We also find entanglement of the social structures in illegal practices in another source. In an analysis of 149 criminal investigations into Dutch organised crime, the trade sector is mentioned 249 times in relation to the organisation of criminal cooperative systems. The automobile trade (39), hotel and catering business (37), import/export industry (32) and transport (26) were most frequently mentioned for the Netherlands.

In Jamaica, drug trafficking and drug-related crime are deeply rooted in its social, cultural and political life. The Jamaican Constabulary Force, media and academics analyse organised crime in terms of gangs (within Jamaica) and posses (within Jamaican communities in Canada, the United States and Great Britain). The gangs, of which there are many, are loosely organised: constantly interchanging social networks of youngsters operating mainly in downtown Kingston. Like similar gangs around the world, they are the product of social alienation, inner city poverty, disintegrating family and community life and a lack of employment. In Jamaica, however, there is a difference in the functional relationships between the gangs and the political system. Professor Carl Stone writes, "The gangs have been emboldened and empowered over the years by their connections with top political organizations, and run the country'.

Jamaica's political landscape is dominated by two parties. Members of Parliament (MPs) are chosen in local constituencies or garrisons.

Within these local constituencies, informal power is exercised by so-called Dons or Bosses. These Dons control their neighbourhoods on a legal and an illegal level, and MPs – or potential MPs – have to build relationships of trust with them. There have been political affiliations between the Dons, the gangs and political parties since the 1960s. In exchange for votes, the Dons receive money and protection for their illegal operations. In return for election-incited violence exercised by the gangs, the gangs receive guns.

A vital common factor between the Dons, the gangs and political figures is the control over parts of Jamaica's port system. A free passage of guns is ensured through political contacts in and around the wharves along the southern part of Kingston. Political influence extends throughout the police and customs. From the 1970s onwards, the guns were supplemented with drugs. Illegal money earned through the drug trade was used increasingly to buy guns, political power, corrupt officials, for investment in new trafficking, and was brought into the country for conspicuous consumption and investment (with or without money laundering).

We come across similar patterns in the preparations for the Bay of Pigs invasion. The CIA and other American police and intelligence services were involved in recruiting and training Cuban refugees. This so-called Operation Mongoose, involving American services, Cuban refugees and the Mafia, generated all manners of functional relationships. It led, among other things, to various (failed) joint efforts to assassinate Fidel Castro. Since the 1960s, the American-trained Cuban refugees have appeared regularly in association with organised crime in narcotics.

Bovenkerk and Yesilgöz describe the history of symbiotic or functional relationships between the government and organised crime in Turkey. In 1792, Sultan Selim III founded an 'illegal committee' to operate alongside the police and the army. Since the early twentieth century, the government has been setting up specific units to perform 'special assignments'. Their staff was and is recruited from the criminal underworld. Bovenkerk and Yesilgöz have traced variants of this 'illegal committee' and the special units through the centuries, and they continue today to analyse the operation of this informal shadow organisation.[40] A structural characteristic is the interchange between (parts of) the state (police, justice, the army and intelligence services), political (terror) movements and the illegal organised trade in drugs and weapons. The existence of cooperative ventures between (parts of) the state and the underworld are not incidental, but are part of a larger (historical) pattern.

In the 1970s, the underworld smuggled weapons into and drugs out of Turkey for both left-wing and right-wing organisations. The profits of the narcotics trade were subsequently used to purchase weapons. 'It is no longer easy to distinguish between crime and politics in Turkey', say Bovenkerk and Yesilgöz. Examples include the accusations about the involvement in the narcotics trade, extortion and the murder campaigns between the Turkish government and the Kurdish PKK.

Bovenkerk and Yesilgöz have devised a model to analyse the relationship between politics and crime. In the first phase, illegal entrepreneurs adopt avoidance tactics. Illegal operations are organised out of the sight of the government. As the smuggling operation grows, increasing numbers of people become involved. Actors on the grey and black markets find out about the activities and also join in: transporters, lawyers, brokers and others cover the project's logistics and financing. In the second phase, individuals are bribed or blackmailed. Subsequently, this corruption spreads to entire departments of police or customs stations: 'a symbiosis is formed by the police on the one hand and the underworld on the other'. In the third phase, parts of the government take over the initiative and assume an 'organisational role'. Finally, if the project has become sufficiently large-scale, the entire state may become involved in organised crime.

In a report by the Turkish intelligence service (1987), further references are made to the relationship between political parties and the underworld. It provides examples of politicians and government officials who maintain contacts with the underworld and who facilitate the latter in providing licences or organising storage space for smugglers in the ports. In 1992, the Turkish parliament set up a commission to investigate the 'many murders by unknown culprits'. The commission concluded that these murders were of a political nature and were committed by government gangs. Another conclusion relates to the involvement of a spy department of the gendarmerie in smuggling weapons and narcotics. A national newspaper spoke about 'a state in the state'. Turkish correspondents working for the Dutch national newspaper *NRC* have written about the involvement of soldiers in the narcotics trade, extortion and other grim affairs, and talk about 'gangsters in uniform'.

In an analysis of the involvement of government services and business in the weapons trade in Europe, the activities of these legal actors are compared to those of illegal actors (organised criminals). In addition to the question of the ethical and legal dimensions of the international weapons trade, and the inequality in prosecution between legal (almost none) and illegal actors (some), it also points to the presence of civil servants and businessmen on the grey weapons market, where the boundaries between legal and illegal are far from clear. Whenever and wherever illegal transactions occur, a link is laid with organised crime. Again, the boundaries between the legal world and the underworld blur. And, of course, there is the mutual benefit for the actors involved.[41] There is 'a surplus of evidence that the international weapons market is characterized by broken regulations and corruption. It is estimated that 10–12% of the annual turnover of USD 15–20 billion is illegal'.[42]

The *International Organisation for Migration* estimates that there are some 100 million immigrants in the world today. It is assumed that 30 million immigrants do not have legal documents. Four million immigrants are transported or 'traded' through illegal circuits. This trade is thought to be worth some USD 7 billion. The organisation of this illegal trade is enmeshed with purely functional, relevant third parties: customs officials, legal authorities, transport companies, printers and so on.[43]

The dynamics between the legal environment and organised crime can also be found in the history of Japan. In the nineteenth century, relationships were formed between the Yakuza and various politicians and civil servants. Both parties benefited: it meant freedom for illegal trading and (violent) support for the ultra-nationalistic party. Various secret societies were set up to this effect. The terror of the ultra-nationalistic lasted into the thirties of the twentieth century. The Yakuza supplied the 'muscle men' for politics and was involved in assaults, coercion, blackmail and extortion.[44] There was a relatively high level of tolerance with respect to the Yakuza in Japan until well into the twentieth century. As long as it did not disturb the peace, the police left it alone. On occasion, this 'ignoring' was also related to the functions that gangsters fulfilled in various parts of politics, the legal system or the 'regulation' of social relationships: the underworld as lubricant for the formal system or informal social service provision. People also benefited from the Yakuza's 'disciplined' activities towards street criminals. Alongside the police, the underworld took care of a certain amount of public peacekeeping.

Symbiotic relationships also exist between the Yakuza and business. Businessmen use the Yakuza to control their workforce problems. These relationships are particularly prevalent in construction and shipping. As a result of the scarcity of workers on the job market, there is a need for illegal employees who are apparently provided by the Yakuza. Project developers use the Yakuza to pressure stubborn house owners or tenants. This involves a certain amount of 'mental harassment'.[45] The Yakuza is also used by entrepreneurs to ensure silence for tricky questions in shareholder meetings or for extorting companies under the threat of violence. There are even symbiotic relationships between the Yakuza and financial organisations.[46] Until the 1980s, there was no legal apparatus in Japan for strengthening consumptive credits. Nevertheless, there was of course a demand for them. A number of financial institutions used the Yakuza to set up an informal credit system. The banks provided the capital and collection was left up to the Yakuza, which introduced 'operating costs' in addition to the bank's interest.

In the American discussion on the war on drugs, many references are made to symbiotic relationships between government services or functionaries and the organised trade in drugs. *Cocaine Politics. Drugs, Armies and the CIA in Central America* analyses the increasing militarisation of the war on drugs, and in particular its political dimensions. The latter suggests a direct involvement of the CIA in the production, trade and distribution of drugs. The underlying political logic is that the CIA supports or has supported opposition parties in the drug trade in various parts of the world. This is tolerated – or even actively supported – because the drug trade generates resources for financing political parties. Various examples are given in the publications mentioned. During the Vietnam War (1960s), the CIA supported governments and resistance groups in South-East Asia; during the Afghan War (1980s), the CIA supported resistance groups fighting against the Russians. The same pattern was adopted during the various conflicts in Central and South America and the Caribbean (1980/1990s).

The financing for these foreign (illegal) political activities is supposedly run via the drug trade. This would not only mean that an American government organisation was (partly) responsible for the renascence of the drug trade (creating preconditions), but it also points to the existence of a schizophrenic situation in which the CIA is throwing a spanner in the works of American investigation services such as the DEA and Customs. The CIA not only looks the other way, but also is getting its own hands dirty.

The Politics of Heroin in Southeast Asia by McCoy discusses the tenfold increase in opium production by resistance groups financed by the CIA. Blumenthal draws the same conclusion with respect to the heroin trade. In an article in the *New York Times* (1988), a senior State Department analyst is quoted as saying: 'We won't let a small issue like drugs get in the way of the political situation (in Afghanistan).' In the investigation by the American Senate in the 1980s, the Kerry Subcommittee on Terrorism and Narcotics (1989) stated: 'On the basis of this evidence, it is clear that individuals who provided support for the Contras were involved in drug trafficking, that the supply network of the Contras was used by drug trafficking organisations, and that elements of the Contras themselves knowingly received financial and material assistance from drug traffickers. In each case, one or another agency of the U.S. government had information regarding the involvement either while it was occurring, or immediately thereafter.'[47] The Kerry report declares that 'the subcommittee heard abundant testimony by drugs dealers and pilots about CIA connections to cocaine smuggling'. The report concluded that the United States allowed foreign policy objectives to interfere with the war on drugs.

One member of the Kerry Commission, Jonathan Winer, writes on the cover of *Cocaine Politics* by Marshall and Scott: 'tells the sordid story of how elements of our own government went to work with narcotics traffickers, and then fought to suppress the truth about what they had done. The ways and means by which U.S. government officials joined forces with cocaine criminals, and then engaged in a largely-successful cover-up to hide the truth, are meticulously documented by Marshall and Scott, making *Cocaine Politics* essential reading for anyone interested in understanding the real Iran/Contra story.'

In the Bank of Credit and Commerce International (BCCI) affair, the CIA's use of the bank laundering of (drug) money, financing political movements, undermining political regimes as well as other clandestine operations and attempts by the CIA to thwart (criminal) investigations came to light.[48] Dayle, a former chief of a DEA unit wrote, 'In my thirteen-year career at the DEA and similar services, almost all the most important *targets* of my investigations worked for the CIA.'[49] Celerino Castillo III, a clean DEA agent who worked in New York, Peru, Guatemala, El Salvador and San Francisco, was ordered not to investigate U.S.-sponsored drug transports led by Oliver North. He resigned, 'amazed that the U.S. government could get away with drug trafficking for so long'. He wrote about his experiences in *Powderburns: Cocaine, Contras, and the Drug War* in which he reveals in detail the role of the United States in the drugs and weapons trade. He not only writes about the illegal trade, but also about laundering, torture and the training of death squads in El Salvador and Guatemala by the DEA. The *Subcommittee Staff Report* of October 28, 1992, by the House Judiciary Committee's Subcommittee on Crime and Criminal Justice on the Bekaa Valley in Syria states that 'heroin traffickers have close ties to the Syrian government and Army, and that President Bush ignored this problem in his policy towards Syria'. The involvement of the CIA is supposedly deeply rooted in its history and explains why the service will never entirely support those fighting in the war on drugs. This would entail a compromise of its sources, the loss of political support and endanger the indirect financing of its operations.[50]

A letter from the State Department Advisory Committee on Historical Diplomatic Documentation (Historical Advisory Committee) to U.S. Secretary of State Albright (March 6, 1998) refers to a 'feeling of crisis on the future of the *Foreign Relations* publication series.' The reason: the continued refusal by the CIA to declassify 30-year-old sources relating to covert operations in support of foreign politics. The letter also says that 'if sufficient documentation cannot be declassified to provide the broad outlines of those covert activities, then any U.S. government documentary compilation about our foreign policy in situations where such activities took place will be so incomplete and misleading as to constitute an official lie'.

Alice in Wonderland

Criminal statistics, the basis of most criminological research, only touches the surface of the above-mentioned complex interactions between officials, businessmen and the criminal element who seem to move in and out of official roles and illegal activities. In the Lewis Carroll classic story of *Alice's Adventures in Wonderland,* Alice follows the White Rabbit down the rabbit hole and into a series of extraordinary adventures in Wonderland, a country of crazy logic where the absurd and surreal are the norm.

'Crazy logic' and 'surreal' seem to be adequate labels to describe functional and symbiotic perspectives on (organised) crime. Gradually, authors are looking into these undertows. A fine example is the work of Loretta Napoleoni (2004). She uses an economic framework to analyse the emergence and growth of different actors operating in ever-changing criminal networks for the financing of terrorism. There is no clear distinction between governments, state bureaucracies, financial institutions and criminal and terrorist organisations. In all the recent and current international conflicts – from the war in Indo-China in the fifties, the Vietnam War in the sixties, the conflicts in Central and South America in the seventies and eighties, the Afghan conflict in which the Soviet Union moved into the country in the eighties, right up to the Balkan conflicts in the nineties – a number of manifestations of crime never found their way into criminological statistics or a number of textbook introductions into crime and crime control.

In a recent thematic issue of *Justitiele Verkenningen* (2009) of the Dutch Ministry of Justice, a number of authors address the 'surreal' writing on the dynamics between the political system and organised crime in Italy, Russia, Belgium and Bulgaria.

Aalberts (2009) uses the concept of 'blurring boundaries' to address the nexus between transnational terrorism and organised crime, which grew in importance after the terrorist attacks of September 11, 2001. The author scrutinises this so-called black-hole thesis and its relationship to the crime-terror nexus by addressing the political significance of such conceptual blurring within an international context that is increasingly characterised by uncertainty and uncontrollable risks. In 'The political-criminal nexus in Italy: 150 years of relationships between mafia and politics', Paoli (2009) analyses the so-called political-criminal nexus in Italy, that is, the relationships of exchange and collusion between politicians and civil servants, on the one hand, and members of organised crime – and specifically Southern Italian Mafia – groups on the other. His main thesis is that today, the political-criminal nexus in Italy finds no parallel in any other Western, developed nation, with the possible exception of Japan. In 'André Cools and Agusta; A Belgian Affair', Cools (2009) (no relation) describes the relationship between the murder of the Walloon Social-Democratic politician André Cools on July 18, 1991, at Liege and the corruption case Agusta – dealing with the purchase of army helicopters – in order to reflect on typical Belgian criminological issues in this political organised crime topic. The murder committed by Tunisian hitmen was ordered through the influence of the personal cabinet of Van der Biest, a former minister. During the murder investigation, a link with the Agusta corruption case was discovered and would bring down several ministers as well as the former NATO Secretary-General Willy Claes. Due to the use of primarily journalistic sources and a lack of scientific criminological material, the conclusions of this article are strictly personal, according to Cools, although the murder and the corruption prove the fact that political organised crime at that point in time was a reality in Belgium, the author claims. Siegel (2009), in her 'Crime and Politics in Russia', analyses the link between politics and crime in the Soviet and post-Soviet Russia. The same is being done by Gounev and Bezlov in their 'Organized crime, corruption and politics in Bulgaria'. They zoom into a specific type of criminal structures: the ones controlled by former security officers. The way they use the instrument of corruption changes though the years when they evolve from relatively unimportant racketeers into powerful local oligarchs.

Certainly not everybody is 'blinded by the light' as many of the (historical) studies and the recent excellent thematic issue of *Justitiele Verkenningen* indicate. Under-researched as the topic of this chapter may seem to be, theoretical and empirical research indeed seem to be gaining in importance.

11
Unsafe and Unsound Practices

Introduction

In this chapter, I change perspective again.[51] Like the ancient Trojans, we hail the strange horses with names like privatisation, technology, increasing cooperation between public policing with regulators and the intelligence community. We say praise to cooperation in security networks and want to combine 'nodes' and govern security to safeguard society from the evil of crime, fraud and terrorism. But the new security architecture – designed for public order, crime control and national security – could very well foster unsafe and unsound practices. In essence, what I am saying here is that policing and security are, in some ways, at the individual or collective levels, a hazardous, unpredictable and risky enterprise and that this needs to be recognised. At the institutional and operational levels, organisations have to anticipate and institutionalise responses to critical incidents. This is because policing and 'trouble' go hand in hand in the sense of controversy, adversarial disputes, legal actions and media-led affairs (Newburn, 1999). The organisation's response to dealing with 'trouble' and its repercussions are often crucial to determining the legitimacy and credibility of the executives in the eyes of the public.

Yet another factor is that, in organisations, those in charge have, to some extent, to be able to 'trust' the people with whom they work; no institution can fully control everyone who functions within it, and this is particularly true of policing and security where many officers enjoy high autonomy and exercise considerable discretion.

It must be remembered that policing and security as institutions in Western, democratic society – and some other jurisdictions – are formally based on respect for the rule of law, adherence to due process and, above all, **accountability**. Given the unique powers of the new security architecture and its far-reaching responsibilities for a wide and diffuse range of tasks, it has to be held accountable for its actions. It is debatable whether or not the architect was so mesmerised by structure that accountability was left out.

There is, however, considerable evidence that police forces, in common with government agencies and private corporations in times of stressful turbulence, have at times endeavoured to avoid responsibility and evade accountability. This leads to the sombre conclusion that people in organisations from time to time tend to avoid responsibility and evade accountability (Ermann and Lundman, 1996).

There are many examples of organisations in trouble resorting to cover-up and denial through noncooperation with authorities, threats of legal action against critics, destruction of incriminating data, false propaganda, counter-condemnation, intimidating and manipulating the media, scapegoating, making personnel unavailable for interviews, buying off potentially hostile witnesses and, in business, offering 'sacrificial lambs' in the form of the 'Vice-President for Going to Jail'.

In fact, it is often the deception and cover-up that does more to undermine institutional credibility than the original incident itself. And especially if evasion is exposed in policing or other parts of the criminal justice system, then it is seen as highly damaging and as a serious abuse of public trust (Reiss, 1987). As O'Neill (2002) observes, trust is 'hard earned and easily dissipated. It is valuable social capital and not to be squandered.'

The message here is then to argue that the new security architecture should not react opportunistically, defensively, blindly or thoughtlessly to these vital matters but should instead anticipate, think through and even embrace a **culture of accountability**. This culture should, indeed, be in the very bloodstream of the organisation. The good news is that there are in fact people who recognise this: in the United Kingdom, for instance, elements are already available for a paradigm shift to institutionalising accountability throughout the police service.

The bad news is that internal accountability is to a degree symbiotic with external accountability and that there are external forces at work that potentially compromise accountability. In effect, I am saying that the idea of democratic policing and security is effectively synonymous with accountability. Policing and security simply cannot be unaccountable: one cannot be held only slightly accountable.

Accountability is a broad and diffuse concept related to formal obligations within a democracy, notions of good governance and of being transparent on policies and conduct to the public and other stakeholders, and of internally generated norms and standards of professional accountability. But, as Bovens notes, it remains something of a 'hurrah' concept – because everyone shouts 'hurrah!' whenever accountability is mentioned. Rather like 'ethics' and 'integrity', it is difficult for any institutional leader to say they oppose them. But this, in turn, also tends to make it what Tromp refers to as a 'Sunday' concept, where accountability is part of the Sunday rhetoric of good intentions in the knowledge that on Monday life will be back to 'business as usual' (in Bovens, 1998, 22).

Accountability, in addition to being diffuse, is also a slippery concept. Many different forms may be distinguished. In general, we formulate the following:

- Democratic and political accountability
- Legal accountability
- Internal accountability
- Managerial accountability
- Community accountability (Bowling and Foster, 2002; Neyroud, 2005).

Without accountability, the opportunity arises for the arbitrariness of unchecked authority and the unrestrained abuse of power – as witnessed in totalitarian societies and countries where the police force is violent, corrupt and effectively uncontrollable (Hinton, 2005).

In the current chapter, I wish to address this complex and often misunderstood area and discuss the arbitrariness of unchecked authority and unrestrained abuses of power in some parts of the new security architecture. I will draw attention to the constant tension between formal rules and what participants see as the 'unavoidable' practical necessities that justify their rule breaking: sometimes 'good' people engage in 'dirty work' and seek rationalisations and justifications for this.

Unsafe and unsound practices

I want to introduce the concept of 'unsafe and unsound practices' to draw attention to yet another undertow in policing and security: the possibilities of unchecked power in performing crime control. The new security architecture is and can be **criminogenic** in that it provides the context, means, opportunity and motives for crime to those who are its members, workers, operational managers or senior executives. The new security architecture, in fact, provides the (un-)holy trinity of standard criminal inquiry – **motive, opportunity and means**.

There is ample evidence from the literature of organisational deviance, corporate crime and police corruption that some forms of deviance may be systemic, that people routinely lie and dissemble and that leading figures in organisations attempt elaborately to conceal their misdeeds from external scrutiny (Ermann and Lundman, 1996; Punch, 1996). In this chapter, I will briefly discuss some unsafe and unsound practices within public policing, private security and the intelligence community. My aim here is not to question the legality of all that is being done by public officials and private entrepreneurs but to draw attention to some of the undertows in the new security architecture that deserve our attention from a rule of law perspective.

Police corruption

Some forms of 'corruption', in its wider sense of abuse of power rather than in the narrower sense of bribery, crop up at some time in almost **every police force** (Newburn, 1999). Indeed, policing has often been associated with other grave forms of deviance such as excessive violence and systemic racial discrimination. There does, then, appear to be something in the nature of police work and the institutional context of policing that fosters deviance from internal rules, and even from the law, in the people who join the police across time and in many cultures and many societies (Sherman, 1978).

This cannot just be a few 'bad apples' – a few corrupt individuals, as is so often maintained by officialdom – because often large numbers of officers and even entire units are involved on a long-term, systemic basis. In New York, for example, there has been a corruption scandal roughly every 20 years since the founding of the city's police force (NYPD). This implies that **deviance is cyclical** and cannot be individual because the personnel have changed substantially since the previous cycle. And when Serpico started plain-clothes work in the NYPD everyone was 'on the take', including the supervisory officers. Because he would not accept bribes, Serpico became the deviant and subject to sanctions (Maas, 1974). This was clearly no case of bad apples, but of a bad barrel – or even a bad orchard (Punch, 2003).

From the above, it follows that the working environment was effectively 'crime coercive', and that the individual was forced into deviance as a requisite of occupational membership, otherwise he or she faced exclusion and even intimidation. Indeed, some areas of police work are associated with a predictably high risk of corruption – as in drugs enforcement, 'vice' (gambling and prostitution), undercover work, licensing of premises and businesses and running informants. Individuals entering these areas run an enhanced risk of becoming part of a system of corruption.

Then some units employ excessive force across time, meaning that it is not incidental but repetitive and institutionalised. The Mollen Report (1994) on the NYPD, for instance, detailed that some officers routinely beat up suspects and sometimes assaulted people at random just to display their control of the streets: they even used violence consciously as a rite of passage into deeper corruption for newcomers. Their young buddies were carefully manipulated and coached onto the 'slippery slope' of deviance. In the Louima case in New York, the victim was exposed to gross violence: he incurred serious internal injuries as a result of being sodomised with a broom handle. This happened within a police station in sight of other officers who did not intervene (Skolnick, 2002). In the Selmouni case in France, the severe and degrading abuse of a suspect also took place inside a station over several days and with a number of officers observing it. In fact, several of them urinated on the suspect when he was tied naked to a staircase, but again no one intervened.[52]

The sociological conclusion is that people were prepared to enter a collective entity where they ceased behaving as individuals and were prepared to accept the systematic breaking of rules – and even of the law – in latent or overt concert with others. The result is that officers in the police organisation, who are meant to enforce the law, end up not only breaking the law but also becoming criminals. They display contempt for the law and find creative ways to get around it. They lie in court, manipulate or destroy evidence, take or extort bribes, steal drugs and sell them, beat up the defenceless, ensure that the guilty go unpunished and the innocent go to prison, cooperate with criminals and even commit murder. And somehow they can justify this to themselves.

The conclusion must be that the organisational context and occupational culture of policing can be so powerful that they in some way sponsor and even encourage deviance, which can be no less than a perversion of the expressed aims of the organisation, and induce individuals to take deviant and even criminal paths. These recurring patterns, which are extensively documented, simply cannot be viewed as an individual phenomenon: rather I refer to **organisational deviance** (Ermann and Lundman, 1996).

Private justice

Unsafe and unsound practices are not only relevant in the context of public policing. Because policing as a process nowadays includes the private security sector, the concept is also relevant – and perhaps even more relevant – in the context of private security, private investigations, private justice and private intelligence.

Inherent to the idea of a nation-state is the notion that the state is the prime public authority and that all other authorities operating within its territory are subordinate to it (Shearing and Stenning, 1987a). Within this context, the empirical evidence that **private** security is engaged in a great deal of contemporary policing comes, then, as a bit of a shock. The conceptual consequences of this shock are minimised, however, if this evidence is absorbed into the traditional national state frame (Shearing and Stenning, 1987a). I will argue indeed the 'conceptual consequences' are 'minimised' and private security includes all sorts of 'justice arrangements' that harbour unsound/unsafe practices.

Shearing and Stenning, starting as early as the early 1980s, have used Thomas Kuhn's work on scientific revolutions and the intrinsic 'normal science' character of (social) sciences to analyse the persistence of paradigms in policing. Kuhn (1962) describes how increasingly often anomalies can no longer be fitted into the dominant paradigm but, for (longer) periods of time, are neglected and absorbed into the existing thinking modes. When more and more anomalies surface, an academic community at a certain moment reaches a point where the old paradigm makes way for new frameworks, theoretical notions and definitions.

Anomalies

The growing and diversified private investigation activities, both in-house and contract, are intrinsically linked to what we call 'private justice' arrangements. In the Netherlands, for example, between 500 and 1000 private organisations conduct a wide range of investigations into irregularities within the business community – from background checks to employee crime, from due diligence research to fraud committed by third parties (and this in a relatively small society with a population of 16 million).

Many of these investigations have a preventive character and are primarily aimed at minimising risks. However, a large number of investigations are also directed at employees, consumers and corporations that have all the characteristics of a public policing investigation. A recurrent feature in empirical research in the Netherlands – and elsewhere – is the relatively small number of 'criminal' cases handed over to the public prosecutor or the police (meaning cases that appear to be definable as worthy of investigation and prosecution within the conventional system). Indeed, the level of nonreporting seems to be on the rise. Although in our thinking we may still cling to the above-mentioned liberal state framework – as if the state still retains a monopoly in criminal justice matters – in reality, the criminal justice system has become one of 'the hundred tiny theatres of punishment' in our societies (Foucault, 1974).

'Justice' used to be a singular activity carried out by the state through the criminal justice system, but 'justice' is now being carried out by different private organisations to different people, in different ways, and on different occasions. Stuart Henry suggested that private policing is one component of the wider phenomenon of private justice. Formal justice systems function next to increasingly diversified and complex private justice systems: 'any human society does not posses a single legal system, but as many such systems as there are functioning units'.

We should be sensitive to the 'multitude of diffuse sources of power' (Henry, 1987), which is best captured by the concepts of legal pluralism and private justice. Depending on the nature of the crimes, in the Netherlands we find percentages of nonreporting between 40 and 80 or even 90 per cent. Internal fraud cases are dealt with internally through an elaborate system of 'private justice' arrangements. Employees are not reported to the police or regulators, but are fired or demoted, or else the employer and employee work out an arrangement for paying back the losses to the company. Insurance companies use investigation reports to reject claims or negotiate outcomes of claims filed by individuals or companies. The results of the Dutch research on private justice (2006) are shown in Table 1.

Arbitrary power

The argument against the use of 'private justice' is the fact that consumers, employees and corporations are being forced into binding arbitration, a quasilegal process that allows private individuals to pass final judgement on the disputes of the parties who hire them. Whereas the criminal and civil law systems are ostensibly transparent and lack conflicts of interest, private justice systems are by definition riddled with conflicts of interest. 'Judges', private authorities directing private investigations for solving private disputes, are by definition 'compromised judges'. Moreover, neither public transparency nor accountability exists concerning the use of investigative techniques and methods

Table 1 Reporting of crimes?

	Criminal charges %	**Private justice** %
Alcohol abuse	3	92
Use of drugs	9	83
Sexual harassment	7	80
Intimidation/violence between employees	11	73
Defrauding customers	34	51
Proprietary theft	38	47
Corruption	37	46
Theft of classified information	39	43
Sabotage	42	40
Forgery	40	37
Cooking the books	48	30
Extortion by means of threats	69	20

Report Private Justice in the Netherlands, Nyenrode Business University (2006)

used to gather or use information. Private security in the end is about power, accountability and democratic control, as is law enforcement by the state. Private justice by definition is exercised outside the public view. Ergo the exercise of power is less visible, less controllable and therefore more prone to unsafe and unsound practices than public policing. The argument not only holds for 'justice' but especially also the range of (il)legal activities to gather information to built up a 'criminal case'.

Dutch research on private investigations touches upon the informal exchanges of classified information between public and private officials; 'moonlighting', the use of social engineering techniques by private security officials to gather classified information through play-acting and posing methods, the setting up and exploitation of informant networks by private investigation firms investigating insurance fraud, and the use of infiltration techniques (Hoogenboom, 1987, 1991a, 1994a, 2001; Klerks, 2000; Dutch Data Protection Authority *College Bescherming Persoonsgegevens*, 2006).

In 'Corporate Espionage; Infiltration and Intelligence Work in the Private Sector', a case of corporate espionage is analysed. During the 1980s, Wackenhut, a private security firm, was hired by a consortium of oil companies operating in Alaska to spy on individuals active in the environmental movement. To that end, a bogus law firm was created (front store) manned with former law enforcement personnel and private detectives with experience in undercover work. The operation had all the characteristics of an infiltration normally associated with public intelligence and security forces. The operation involved the use of video surveillance, phone tapping, bugging devices, interception of mail and 'garbology' (searching through garbage). The case study is based on a U.S. Congressional report.

In 2004, the Dutch Data Protection Authority conducted an investigation into a trading information company (Dutch 'handelsinformatiekantoor') and unravelled an informal trade – often illegal – in personal data involving banks, insurance companies, social security departments, public police organisations, lawyers and solicitors. The people involved – two of whom were convicted in a criminal court – acted as information brokers using 'old boy' networks and paying for information or social engineering techniques.

Issues like these also pop up in other countries. In June 2001, *The Sunday Times* published an article on the private intelligence firm Hakluyt, with close ties to MI6, that spied on environmental campaign groups to collect information for oil companies, including Shell and BP. Hakluyt's agent, who posed as a left-wing sympathiser and film maker, was asked to betray the plans of Greenpeace's activities against the oil giants. One of his assignments coming from Hakluyt was to gather information about the movements of the motor vessel *Greenpeace* in the North Atlantic. Greenpeace claims the scandal has echoes of the *Rainbow Warrior* affair, when its ship protesting against nuclear testing in the South Pacific was sunk by the operatives of the French secret service in 1985. One of the perpetrators was the brother of Segolene Royal. Initial fervent denials were followed by some admission of guilt. The operatives were never formally prosecuted, nor have investigations with respect to governmental responsibility ever gone to any depth. A Dutch photographer died as a result of the explosion. Both BP and Shell admitted to hiring Hakluyt, but said they were unaware of the tactics used. Shell said it had wanted to protect its employees against possible attack. In sum, a plausible reason was given for the implausible denial of knowledge.

In *Battling Big Business*, Lubbers and her coauthors (2004) describe the tiny pressure group that campaigned against McDonald's and was infiltrated by at least seven private spies: indeed, at several meetings they even formed a majority! McDonald's hired two separate private security firms without informing them about each other. In another Dutch case, it has been revealed how a private security firm clandestinely gathered information on activists. Content filtered from the wastepaper basket surfaced at strategic moments in right-wing newspapers or on multinationals' desks. Lubbers also discusses the boundaries between corporate intelligence and government activities, which she argues are getting blurred. Though their goals may differ depending on their clients' needs, business intelligence agencies often use much the same surveillance modus operandi as do governments.

Unsafe and unsound practices: Growing interweaving, grey policing, hydraulic principles and revolving doors

An important implication of boundaries blurring is that public and private policing and security organisations can become functional alternatives for one another to operate in the grey areas and also to perform illegal tasks. Despite conflicts of interest and competition, public and private security can grow towards one another to perform actions together that they cannot or may not do themselves (Marx, 1987). Marx mentions the possibility of a 'hydraulic principle': if more democratic control and oversight is created concerning the public sector, then private alternatives are sought to ensure that certain things get done. The 'dirty work' is outsourced.

The new security architecture also creates 'revolving doors' between public and private sector through which personnel, experience, influence and power rotate. In 2006, the *New York Times* reported this phenomenon in a series chronicling dozens of national security officials who were closely involved in activities following 9/11 and who are now in different roles working on behalf of private companies that sell domestic security products, many directly to the federal agencies the officials once helped run. The concept of 'influence peddling' is often used in this respect. The traditional military-industrial complex is being reinvented along national security lines. The 'revolving door' manifests itself in contracts, studies, boards, commissions, retreats, seminars, conferences and lunches.

The Center for Public Integrity watchdogs have long criticised the 'revolving-door' between government and the private sector, particularly when former officials join businesses that they regulated while in office. Some are troubled by the 'revolving door' and think it is detrimental to the public's confidence in the country's political structure as well as its business structure. Other Washington observers say that there's nothing 'inherently unethical' about retired U.S. Defense Department officials working for private equities.

Unsafe and unsound practices: Mercenaries gone awry

Unsafe and unsound practices also come to the fore in the increased use of private contractors in warfare (Singer, 2003; Schumacher, 2006; Rasor and Bauman, 2007). Employees of the private military company CACI were involved in the Iraq Abu Ghraib prison scandal in 2003 and 2004. On October 27, 2005, a 'trophy' video, complete with postproduction Elvis music, surfaced to show private military contractors in Baghdad shooting Iraqi civilians. This sparked two investigations after it was posted on the Internet. The video has been linked unofficially to Aegis Defence Services. The man who is seen shooting at vehicles on this video in Iraq was a South African employee of the Aegis Victory team named Danny Heydenreycher. He had served in the British military for six years. After the incident, the regional director for Victory ROC tried to fire Heydenreycher, but the team threatened to resign if he did.

In 1999, a Racketeer Influenced and Corrupt Organizations Act (RICO) lawsuit was filed against DynCorp employees stationed in Bosnia, which found that 'employees and supervisors from DynCorp were engaging in perverse, illegal and inhumane behaviour and were purchasing illegal weapons, women, forged passports and were participating in other immoral acts'.

On April 5, 2005, Jamie Smith, CEO of SCG International Risk, announced the expansion of services from the traditional roles of PMCs – of protection and intelligence – to military aviation support. SCG International Air 'would provide air support, medevac (medical evacuation), rotary and fixed-wing transportation, heavy-lift cargo, armed escort and executive air travel to any location on earth'. This marks a unique addition and expansion of services to rival the capabilities of some countries' armies and air forces.

On March 27, 2006, J. Cofer Black, vice chairman of Blackwater USA, announced to attendees of a special operations exhibition in Jordan that his company could now provide a brigade-size force for low-intensity conflicts. According to Black, 'There is clear potential to conduct security operations at a fraction of the cost of NATO operations'.

In mid-May 2006, the Congolese police arrested 32 alleged mercenaries of different nationalities: 19 South Africans, 10 Nigerians and 3 Americans. Half of them worked for a South African company named Omega Security Solutions and the Americans worked for AQMI Strategy Corporation. The men were accused of plotting to overthrow the government but no charges were pressed: the men were to be deported to their home countries.

In her article in *Governance*, Ann Markusen (2003) describes the U.S. Pentagon efforts to outsource weapons, battlefield and base support operations and troop training, invoking competition-based savings and better quality and concluding that the current enthusiasm for privatisation is driven largely by commercial concerns and lobbying rather than real gains to the nation and citizens. She also argues that privatisation and outsourcing pose dangers of monopolisation and undue political influence, and that current contracting practices lack verification and mandatory evaluation safeguards to deliver promised results.

Unsafe and unsound practices in the intelligence community: The Jack Bauer culture and the ethics of intelligence

Jack Bauer is the main hero in the television series *24*. The plots revolve around terrorist issues. Rowlands, in *Everything I know I know from TV – Philosophy for the Unrepentant Coach Potato* (2005), uses Jack Bauer to draw attention to the moral and ethical dilemmas involved in the fight against terrorism. Does the end justify the means? James Jesus Angleton, head of the CIA's counterespionage section for many decades, described 'his' world as a wilderness of mirrors.[53] Within the new security architecture and especially with the emphasis on intelligence in many shapes and forms (intelligence-led policing, business intelligence, securitisation and so on), the governance of intelligence will become a prominent topic. For this reason, I will discuss the ethical dimensions of intelligence below. Most of the literature is on experiences, official reports and some academic literature, primarily in the United States. We should be cautious to draw any far-reaching conclusions on this. But because of the documented ironies, paradoxes and myths, the examples are used as a possible undertow in the new security architecture that could have effects on privacy, human rights and accountability issues. By far the most material is based on the so-called Church Committee in the United States. This was another time and place, and certainly another political and cultural context. However, lessons can be learned, I think, from some of these historical cases. Not so that history will repeat itself – this is seldom the case– but to raise (research) questions and draw attention to themes.

In recent academic intelligence studies, a certain shift can be witnessed away from the more traditional type of attention usually devoted to rules and regulations and procedural control mechanisms. The moral dimension, or the ethical dimension if you will, of intelligence operations has more and more occupied centre stage. Still, according to Perry, a 'substantive ethical analysis of intelligence operations themselves' is being missed grudgingly (Perry, 1995). Shulsky and Schmitt state that, at first sight, it may seem naive to bring up moral issues in 'a hard-headed field of national security' (Shulsky and Schmitt, 2002, 166 ff.). The authors nevertheless feel that it can and must happen. Steele is calling for an integration of 'overt, legal (and) ethical intelligence practices into every aspect of (...) operations' (Steele, 2003, 212).

The intelligence trade, so the argument goes, abounds at all times with small and large moral dilemmas. Field workers, or operatives, develop a psychological relationship with informers and agents in which deception, manipulation and emotional blackmail are part and parcel of the trade.[54] In American jargon, people with whom (criminal) intelligence operatives in the field develop a relationship are known as 'assets'. They are, of course, somewhat different than the average citizen as far as motivation, reliability and morality are concerned: 'White swans don't swim in the sewers'. This metaphor justifies the Australian operational cop code stating that 'you either play by the rules or you lose'. In short, the relationship with sometimes 'close-to-the-ground' figures is an essential part of the intelligence process (Norris and, Dunningham 2000, 385–412).

Within CIA, ideas have been developed on the 'psychology of betrayal': what type of person is one dealing with? Ideological considerations are apparently not high on the list of motives that drive the 'assets' and/or defectors although these would be in line with the 'human failure' model' and the fact that everyone has their price. Instead, it is more about personal issues ('the stuff of soap operas'): broken marriages, mistresses, 'wrong' sexual preferences, drinking and gambling problems, stagnating careers or money issues (Marbes, 1995, 71 ff.). Psychopathic character tendencies are also mentioned. In laymen's terms, people demonstrating them are 'chronic sons-of-bitches' who are unable to develop emotional ties and for whom concepts such as loyalty, friendship or moral boundaries have no meaning. They have narcissistic tendencies, they are unaware of their arrogance and lack a sense of self-mockery and humour. The CIA author quoted here delicately points out that these personalities are on occasion also found amongst the 'good guys': lawyers, district attorneys, professors and, of course, intelligence officers.

In any analysis, 'his master's voice' ('intelligence to please') versus providing objective analysis reports forms an important issue. Here, too, moral and ethical questions play an important role. 'Intelligence to please' points to the question whether analysis reports are (un) consciously written to satisfy political wishes or whether the service provides independent and objectives reports. How independent is the service when it comes to political pressure?

The ethical dimension also features strongly in 'fieldwork'. Much has been written in the American context on covert operations in which, as part of foreign policy, political propaganda is distributed alongside economic manipulation and/or coups. How far can and may one go? Reisman and Baker discuss the legitimacy of such actions in the context of (inter)national law, with a focus on bombings (such as the bombing of the Greenpeace vessel *The Rainbow Warrior* committed by French secret services in 1985) and liquidations (Reisman and Baker, 1992).

A possibly even greater 'assault' on ethics by a service occurs when political authorities hand out assignments for the benefit of their own (party-) political interests. This is, of course, illegal in Western democracies, yet various American presidents have given such orders. President Johnson, for example, asked the FBI to investigate Barry Goldwater, his opponent during the elections in 1964 (Andrew, 1995). More recently in France, the judiciary has indicated that judges in France have been tapped in corruption investigations. Who is better able to describe the moral price that has to be paid than John Le Carré? In *The Secret Pilgrim* we find: 'Please don't ever imagine you'll be unscathed by the methods you use. The end may justify the means if it wasn't supposed to, I dare say you wouldn't be here. But there's a price to pay, and the price does tend to be oneself'.

Moral transgressions

In 1976, the U.S. Church Commission reported to the American Congress on 'Intelligence activities and the rights of American citizens'. The commission addressed the American intelligence and security services' counter-intelligence programme between 1936 and 1976.[55] It mainly dealt with the period of the Cold War, the McCarthy committee, the rise of the civil rights movement, student protests and large-scale social opposition to the war in Vietnam, particularly on college campuses. The objective of the Counter Intelligence Programme (Cointelpro) was 'to neutralize' American political dissidents. Cointelpro was not aimed at foreign espionage activities, but at American citizens. The Church Commission formulated three critical questions and assumptions:

- How can fundamental freedoms of citizens be guaranteed in the light of governmental intelligence and security activities;
- Despite the fact that finding a balance in this context is difficult, it must be found, and;
- A rejection of the idea that traditional American principles of rights, justice and fair play do not have a place in the battle against the enemies of freedom.

The commission concluded that

- Intelligence activities have grown to include citizens who in no sense can be defined as a threat to the democratic rule of law as well as to citizens who were guilty of nonpolitical crimes (commune criminality);
- In too many cases, intelligence activities lost sight of their primary target, including far-reaching breaches of privacy, and infringed upon civil rights on a large scale (the right of association and assembly and the freedom of speech);
- Domestic intelligence activities threatened to undermine democratic society and to fundamentally change its character.

The report refers with common consent to a quote by the Attorney General Harlan Fiske who said in 1924 that 'when a political system transgresses its boundaries, it represents a threat to the correct maintenance of the law and of human freedoms. We must cherish the latter above all (...). A secret police may threaten a free government as it bears the seeds of the abuse of power within itself. These are in no sense always seen, yet understood'. The Church Commission report abounds with letters being opened and photographs, intercepted telegrams, the creation of index systems for storing files on American civilians and the creation of lists of people who in the case of a 'national emergency' should be arrested.

The use of informers is the most penetrating intelligence technique. On the basis of a selective sample compiled by the commission, it concluded that an informant or agent was involved in 83 per cent of cases. These informers' only role is to provide information. Agents manipulate the environment in which they operate. Electronic surveillance occurred in only 5 per cent of cases. Of course the informers collect information, but a number of them also act as 'agent provocateur', inciting citizens and groups to perform (violent) actions to bring them into disrepute and/or to provoke arrests.

The Church Commission also noted that a large proportion of the counterintelligence activities occurred in the forefront of criminal procedures. The rights of a suspect in a criminal investigation differ considerably from those who are the subject of intelligence operations. The Code of Criminal Procedure allows the legitimacy of tracing activities to be contested. Information collection by intelligence and security services is lacking a similar system of checks and balances.

The forefront contains a number of problems. First of all, there is the problem of choice: what criteria are needed for a citizen to become a 'target'? In this context, the Church Commission points to the vitally important relative **indeterminacy of concepts** such as 'national security' or 'subversion'. These 'broad labels and sweeping generalizations' led to many innocent civilians becoming the target of counterintelligence activities. Secondly, one thing follows another: once a choice has been made, intelligence activities develop their own internal dynamic. A tendency grew to add increasing amounts of information to the files. In addition, information was added that had nothing directly to do with the original objective (political dissidence). Thirdly, great pressure developed (un)consciously to use the information collected against the target. After all, the file had been put together for a reason.

Moral boundaries were crossed particularly severely in the way information was used. On a large scale, targets' employers were informed about 'misbehaviour' with the objective of having the target fired. This often occurred anonymously. Many a career was shattered in this way. An alternative to this was writing anonymous letters to spouses with the objective of upsetting marriages and of unsettling the 'target' in a psychological sense. Another technique used was falsely, again anonymously, labelling civilians who were active in civil rights or other political movements as government informers. Often, the (prominent) role of the target was then undermined because they were no longer trusted by their sympathisers. Yet another variety was the distribution of misinformation within a political group in order to stir up political animosity within these groups (manipulation). Finally, agents provocateurs made provocations inducing civilians to make statements or perform actions that they had not originally planned. For these moral transgressions, U.S. citizens paid a price. Civilians were unjustly the target of surveillance activities and thereby unjustly discredited. As a result, constitutional guarantees and values were threatened. Above all, the democratic process was disrupted.

The commission also looked at costs in a literal sense. Cointelpro was not only costly from a figurative perspective, it was also expensive in dollars and cents. In 1976 alone, the FBI had a budget of seven million dollars for counterintelligence, twice the sum paid out in the same year for criminal informants. It is estimated that, over the years, the FBI spent eighty million dollars on domestic surveillance. The actual costs are far higher because, since the mid-1960s and early 1970s, the CIA, NSA and other military intelligence services were involved in the programme also.

The Church Commission questioned Cointelpro's returns: 'the usefulness has been questionable in serving the legitimate goal of protecting society'. The criterion that the committee used in this instance was the number of criminal convictions. Between 1960 and 1974, the FBI performed five hundred thousand different investigations into individual civilians and political groups. In no case did it lead to a criminal investigation, let alone conviction, on the basis of laws related to national security ('planning or advocating action to overthrow the government'). The General Accounting Office has stated that, in 1974, the FBI performed 17,528 'domestic intelligence' investigations. This was followed by legal proceedings in 1.3 per cent of these cases. Even more humiliating is the fact that these 17,528 investigations provided marginal knowledge on activities aimed at undermining the authorities (about 2 per cent). Moreover, part of the information was obtained illegally.

The commission listened to both sides of the argument. According to the FBI, Cointelpro was necessary for countering terrorism, social unrest and protest, 'subversion' and foreign espionage activities. The commission countered the idea that the programme entailed 'grave risks of undermining the democratic process'.

Self-reflection

Because confidentiality and the uncomfortable relationship between professionals and political-administrative authorities mean that there is a large degree of autonomy, it is important that services look at themselves critically. How can this be organised? As an example, we use an investigation held within the CIA (Pekel, 1998). Between February and March 1996, Pekel interviewed more than 50 officials. The basis for his investigation was the notion that the ethical calibre of an organisation, including the CIA, is intrinsically linked to the quality of its leadership and particularly to its organisational culture. Unethical behaviour can sometimes be explained by character deficiencies of individual officers, but far more often there are many more structural causes in the implicit, and sometimes explicit, cooperation of third parties (colleagues and/ or management). One step further is the notion that there is not only cooperation, but also a stimulation of unethical behaviour. In this case, the unethical behaviour is a reflection of values and standards in the organisation itself that are often expressed through the use of language and through behavioural patterns. This collective forms a service's operational (sub)culture. And this culture is then the nurturing ground for unethical activities, while at the same time covering them up.

Many of the CIA officials who were interviewed found that the organisation demonstrated too much of a passive attitude towards ethical dilemmas. Certain areas of the CIA had developed behavioural codes and had successfully organised a number of workshops on the issue. The general complaint, however, was that it did not address the actual dilemmas. In particular, so the argument goes, people remained stuck in abstract legal discussions. Other characteristics of the organisational culture found by Pekel included the impossibility of expressing criticism or discussing failed operations, and the promotion of officers precisely on the basis of moral transgressions ('a long tradition at the Agency of promoting people who have demonstrated effectiveness *at the expense of integrity'*).

Pekel called for

- The creation and guarantee of participation and communication procedures within which discussions are possible and criticism can be expressed publicly ('speaking truth to power');
- Possibilities to engage in discussions on mistakes and failures;
- The promotion of officers who have demonstrated that they assume ethical positions and/or made a critical contribution – of which the symbolic value is severely underestimated;
- The implementation of an ethics programme for all officers that includes not only politically correct discussions on rules and regulations and mission statements, but also role games and games in which (historical) case studies are used.

The security paradox

The development of tension between order and freedom is unavoidable in society. Espionage is the second-oldest profession. Joseph Fouché, Napoleon's minister for police distinguished between *haute police* (political intelligence) and *baisse police* (maintaining law and order, maintaining public peace and offering assistance). Post 9/11, the (inter)national focus on *haute police* has greatly increased. There are distinct threats with respect to the democratic rule of law by what is being referred to as 'new' or 'catastrophic terrorism'. According to Oliver Cromwell, there are certain great occasions in which some men are called to great service for the state. They are excused from the moral rules that apply to the layman concerning the way in which they perform these services. But is this actually true?

Since 9/11, we have seen an ongoing public discussion on the benefits, necessity and future of the intelligence and security services. More and more, men and women are being called upon for increasingly great(er) services. Are they excused from existing moral boundaries? Of course, the politically correct answer is 'no'. But does this do justice to the 'Rough Justice' situations in Guantanamo Bay, Iraq and Israel? What about the recruitment of informers and infiltration activities? What about the large-scale automated collection of information? The existing legal and moral boundaries are being stretched. The Church Commission did not challenge the right of existence of the intelligence and security community, but in the first sentence of the final report it raised the question as to how the fundamental freedoms of civilians can be guaranteed in periods in which there is a greater demand for the state to guarantee our safety. This vital question still remains of topical interest.

The intelligence and security debate

In 'naive' societies such as our own, the threats of terrorism are often reduced to headlines and (background) articles. There is an increasing awareness, however, that innovative and creative solutions are required to anticipate infringements of the (inter)national democratic rule of law. This will require a political debate on the future of intelligence and security services. A structural component in this discussion must be the moral quality of both the leadership and individual intelligence officers. After all, the history of the (inter)national intelligence community abounds with examples of blurring moral boundaries that in turn elicit major questions regarding the quality and the (un)intended consequence of the work.

There is broad (inter)national consensus on the necessity of combating terrorism. The same consensus ruled during the Cold War. The intelligence and security community has an important role in combating terrorism, and this role is being expanded. During the time of the Church Commission's investigation, it was generally accepted that there was a threat to the democratic rule of law, and the intelligence and security community was mobilised.

The American Civil Liberties Union and the Electronic Frontier Foundation point to (un)intended consequences of new antiterrorism legislation that greatly resemble the findings of the Church Commission:

- Assessment of civilians on the basis of unknown criteria;
- Too much faith in the quality of the information systems (misspelling someone's name could have major consequences);
- The 'one-thing-follows-another' effect: (digital) information collection could develop its own dynamic whereby an increasing amount of data is unveiled;
- A possible shift in objectives from terrorism to violence, drugs, criminality, tax evasion, critical scientists, research journalists and/or children who have eloped;
- The question whether civilians have the right of inspection, correction or appeal;
- Discriminatory tendencies;
- The possible abuse of (digital) systems for political objectives.

In my considered opinion, the most important lesson presented by the Church Commission is that *haute police* fulfils a necessary and vital political function. At the same time, *haute police* demands surgical precision. This was the case in the past and still applies today. Cointelpro has shown that professionals may well lose this type of precision. It has made room for shotgun ammunition tactics: we'll just wait and see if we hit anything.

12
Myths in Policing and Security

Introduction

In many ways, policing and security arguments, debates and public discussions are mixed with myths, rhetoric, operational codes and other 'necessity language' actually masking institutional ineffectiveness. The introduction to this book mentioned my interests in two valuable concepts that were to be addressed in the final parts of the book: varieties of the 'myth system' and the 'operational code'. 'Myth systems' refer to the formal front that governments and corporations present to the outside world and the 'operational code' indicates the actual informal – and sometimes covert – rules of the game: what really happens on the shop floor, in operations and in implementation? Somehow, the interface between the two 'systems' has to be managed, and only when this has been exposed, can we obtain a glimpse of the true lie of the land.

In this chapter, I will briefly discuss some of the myths about terrorism, but also a number of security myths, information-sharing myths and crime-control myths. Why this chapter and why here almost at the end of this long and winding road through public policing and other assorted new developments, which together 'create' a new security architecture? Because I have an interest in ironies, paradoxes, double-loop arguments and irrationalities within the emerging new security architecture. And, more in general, I have an interest in the differences between what we see front stage and what actually happens backstage.

At front stage, different plays are enacted and played out day after day. Not all things are what they seem. What the planners, officials and operational executives in the new security architecture do is invariably accompanied by much talk. Talk (or what I call 'necessity languages') has many functions. One of them is to maintain and increase the self-confidence, worth and interests of those who work in the system to protect them from criticism and to suggest that they are doing all right in a difficult world (Cohen, 1985). The people who produce 'necessity languages' are all 'mounting a complex sociodrama for each other and their respective publics (...) all this is to give the impression that social problems (crime, mental illness, pollution, etc.) are not totally out of control' (Cohen, 1985).

I find inspiration for this chapter in Goffman's (1959) analyses of social life in terms of play acting and performing roles, speaking lines and in general adopting a role the audiences expect. In *The Presentation of Self in Everyday Life,* he uses the imagery of the theatre in order to portray the importance of human – namely, social – action. In the centre of the analysis lies the relationship between performance and front stage. An actor performs in a setting that is constructed of a stage and a backstage; the props at either setting direct his action; he is being watched by an audience, but at the same time he is an audience for his viewers' play. According to Goffman, the social actor has the ability to choose his stage and props, as well as the costume he would put on in front of a specific audience. The actor's main goal is to keep his coherence and adjust to the different settings offered him. This is done mainly through interaction with other actors. A major theme that Goffman treats throughout the work is the fundamental importance of having an agreed-upon definition of the situation in a given interaction in order to give the interaction coherency. In interactions, or performances, the involved parties may be audience members and performers simultaneously; the actors usually foster impressions that reflect well upon themselves and encourage the others, by various means, to accept their preferred definition. Goffman acknowledges that, when the accepted definition of the situation has been discredited, some or all of the actors may pretend that nothing has changed if they find this strategy profitable to themselves or wish to keep the peace.

Front-stage myth systems in this Goffman perspective are created and perpetually reinforced: the war on terror, the war on crime, the plethora of security measures, the introduction of more and more security technology, the introduction of new organisations like Home Land Security or the Terrorism Coordinators and the ongoing slow motion process of centralisation within the public policing systems. Does this all make society safer, more secure? Is crime – as Durkheim writes – endemic to society, and do we need crime not actually to wage war with, but as a myth that binds society together? Let us probe underneath the surface of some of these theatres of war.

But before we enter this road of 'debunking', a cautionary word to begin: The caution lies in the sketchlike way I deal with some of these issues. If there is one chapter in this book in which the 'essaylike' character is visible, it is this one. Much more work is needed on this topic to further 'debunk' some of the pretensions and 'glamorisations' of policing and security. This I will keep for my next publication. Here I just want to introduce some initial doubts, raise some eyebrows, generate some discomfort and formulate future research questions on what I like to call the pretence of all these 'necessity languages'.

Myths on terrorism

We seem to living in an 'Age of Rage' in which new folk devils and moral panics are created. For instance, the Al Qaida Myth: instead of demonstrating a tightly knit organisational structure, Al Qaida seems to be a patchwork of youngsters around the world who are in a process of self-radicalisation. In many cases, these youngsters are 'frighteningly normal' with middle-class backgrounds and relatively high levels of education. Jessica Stern writes on Al Qaida in terms of ideological or belief systems. Stern says that the Bush administration focused almost exclusively on a military war against terrorists and that it was failing in the equally vital war of ideas in the Muslim world just as rancour toward the United States rose sharply in the shadow of the U.S. occupation of Iraq. Stern continues to say that these wars may cultivate even more fertile ground for terror attacks in the Middle East, especially in pro-Western countries such as Turkey. She believes that 'we are not paying nearly enough attention to the psychological aspects of the war on terror. We should not worry exclusively about people who are prepared to pick up a gun. We should be equally worried about people who are going to open their doors and provide logistic support – terrorists do require support in the broader population. Iraq is absolutely pouring fuel on the fire' (http://dissidentvoice.org).

Stern also states that 'to win this war, we need to understand that we are fighting an idea, not a state. Military action minimally visible and carefully planned and implemented may be necessary to win today's battles. But the tools required in the long run to win the war are neither bombs nor torture chambers. They are ideas and stories that counter the terrorist narrative – and draw potential recruits away from the lure of jihad (www.boston.com). The Jihad is a global fad (Stern, 2006) and fads appeal to young people around the world. Triggers for self-radicalisation not only have roots in religious arguments and belief systems but root causes also include (perceived) inequity in different parts of the world. Other authors mention the societal and political reactions towards immigrants, the Muslim community and terrorism. The paradox here is the idea that stricter policies, repression and increasing surveillance will foster behaviour the new security architecture deems to prevent, control and 'fight'.

Zbigniew Brzezinski, former U.S. national security adviser, describes the current climate in terms of an 'atmosphere of fear' (*Washington Post*, 2007). What we are witnessing is the institutionalisation of superficial thought and a false sense of insecurity: assessed in broad but reasonable context, terrorism generally does not cause much damage, and the costs of terrorism very often are the results of hasty, ill-considered and overwrought reactions (Mueller, 2004).[56] Mueller sees 'hyperbolic overreactions' after 9/11. It would seem reasonable, Mueller argues, for those in charge of our safety to inform the public about the dangers of flying, for instance. Quoting an *American Scientist* article: the chance of getting killed in one nonstop airline flight is about 1 in 13 million (even taking the September 11 crashes into account), whereas automobile driving is far more dangerous. In the twentieth century, more than 3 million Americans were killed in automobile incidents. However, people tend to feel safer driving a car because then they are in control. The 3,000 deaths in the 9/11 crashes inspire more grief and fear than the 100,000 deaths from car accidents since then. There is a 'lottery paradox' at work: fear of terror may be something like playing the lottery except in reverse. The chances of winning the lottery or dying from terrorism may be microscopic, but for monumental events that are, or seem to be, random, one can irrelevantly conclude that one's chances are just as good, or bad, as those of anyone else (Mueller, 2004).

Security myths

In 2007, the *Security Journal* devoted its twentieth-anniversary issue to answer the following question: what do we actually know about security management and its effects? Practitioners and academics studying security unravelled a number of myths in this field of security studies. Gill concludes: 'Probably the most disappointing thing about the study of security is that, in some respects at least, it has progressed remarkably little since the first volume of the *Security Journal* in 1989' (Gill, 2007). 'A plethora of research has shown that all too often security measures do not work (...) Security has been compromised by poor understanding of the problem (...) and implementation failures (are) extremely common'.[57]

Gill is backed by Button (2007): 'Going back to the main findings of the last 20 years being poor standards of professionalism, the agenda we need is a more regular and sophisticated analysis of security'.[58] Another author, Giever (2007), shares the same critical approach to what has actually been achieved in security: 'I think the most important thing we have learned is how little we actually know. I really do not think the discipline of security has matured yet. We are very much in the infancy stage of development'.[59]

I find these startling conclusions from academics and practitioners on security especially in the context of decades of growth and product diversification. Are 'security' systems only supplying a false sense of security? Are investments in security only for the front stage, and do those of us at back stage have any clue as to what works and what doesn't work?

Bruce Schneier cuts right to the heart of the matter: 'You take off your shoes in the airport. You scan the supermarket's 'preferred customer' card to get the sale price. You claw your way through tamper-resistant packaging for a couple of aspirin. You accept all these inconveniences in the name of security. But are you any safer?'[60]

Schneier raises simple and troublesome questions and makes statements such as the following:

- Why data mining will never protect us from terrorists;
- How your stone-age brain affects what you fear and what security measures you accept;
- Why computer security is fundamentally an economic problem;
- Whether you can really trust a Trusted Traveler;
- If sacrificing your privacy has made you more secure;
- Why refusing drivers' licences to illegal immigrants actually reduces security;
- The industry power struggle over controlling your computer;
- Why we overestimate some risks and underestimate others;
- Why national ID cards won't make us safer, only poorer.

Schneier, Gill, Giever and Button challenge our notions and perhaps illusions of security at every level. Compare, for instance, the growing criticism of the use and effects of CCTV.

Technology myths

Our culture at times seems to be overawed by science. Manning (1992a, 1992b, 1996) describes the disappointing results of various technological innovations such as CAD systems, attempts to reduce response time, car locator and tracking systems, crime mapping, techniques and management information systems. He concludes: 'Such research is often inconclusive or suggests that new technologies have less effect on police practices than their proponents predict or prefer' (Chan, 2003).

Technology must overcome vast cultural barriers before becoming integrated in the hearts and minds of practitioners. Technology operates in a social context, and its meaning is perceived differently by people in different social and organisational positions (Manning, 1992a). The impact of a specific technology on social life is often determined by factors beyond its specific technical capacity – psychological, social, political or cultural factors (Chan, 2003). Moreover, availability of computerised information systems does not guarantee that what is entered is complete, accurate and timely. Research shows 'widespread and varying interpretations (...) wrong classifications and an error rate of between 15% and 65% (Chan, 2003).

Gary Marx (1991) writes about 'technofallacies'.[61] Again, a much-needed research agenda can be written on the flip side of the 'technopoly' chapter. Among all the fallacies represented by policing and security technologies, Marx highlights four.

The fallacy of novelty. This fallacy entails the assumption that new means are invariably better than the old. Decisions are often based on newness rather than on data suggesting that the new will work or that the old has failed. The symbolism of wanting to appear up-to-date is important.

The fallacy of intuitive appeal or surface plausibility. This entails the adoption of a policy because 'it sure seems as if it would work.' The emphasis is on commonsense 'real-world' experience and a dash of wish fulfilment in approaching new programmes. In this ahistorical and anti-empirical world, evaluative research has little currency.

The fallacy of the free lunch or painless dentistry. This fallacy involves the belief that there are programmes that will return only good results without any offsetting losses. It ignores the existence of low-visibility or longer-range collateral costs and fails to recognise that any format or structure both channels and excludes.

The fallacy of technical neutrality. This involves the assumption that technology per se is morally and ethically neutral; that any piece of machinery can have both good and bad implications *depending on how it is used.* This fallacy can stop critical thought. It ignores the fact that the technology is always developed and applied in a social context that is never neutral.

In the future, we should deal with a number of these fallacies to address issues of political control, accountability, civil rights and efficiency issues. The big story of 'technopoly' and the like and the use of excellent Hollywood movies like *The Matrix, Enemy of the State* and *Minority Report* as examples of the (near) future of policing and security are relevant to understand some of what is happening. But, we also need little stories on what's happening at the ground.

Information-sharing myths

Under the surface data, information and intelligence sharing is essentially a political process. 'No matter how sophisticated the computer system is, it cannot make officers share information they want to keep to themselves (...) There is evidence that the introduction of information technology has not substantially changed this reluctance to share information' (Sheptycki, 2003; Chan, 2003; Hoogenboom, 2009). Sheptycki (2003) cites 'intelligence hoarding', and 'information silos' as structural characteristics of police intelligence. However, research findings are not conclusive. Chan (2003) refers to two studies that found 70 per cent and 83 per cent of the respondents stating that information technology has led to increased information sharing between police officers. Much more research is needed here because empirical findings are relevant for the supposedly large-scale and intrusive data mining taking place. Perhaps we have a much too rational idea about information sharing and the political, bureaucratic, sociological and cultural dimensions involved are vastly underestimated. The history of policing and security is abundant with turf wars, nonintervention and strategic evasion. In many ways, information is a form of 'capital' for individuals, departments, organisations and countries. Within the public sector, we find 'guerre des flics' (Ponsaers and Hoogenboom, 2004; Marx, 1988; Fijnaut, 1979); between the public and private sector, we find that much of the internal crime is not followed by filing a criminal complaint (private justice); and of course we have the 'tensions' between high and low policing (Brodeur, 1983 and 1999; Matassa and Newburn, 2003).

There is an evident need to do much more theoretical and empirical research into information-sharing processes and especially the cultural barriers involved here. Probably the most relevant theoretical dimensions are the concepts of 'field and habitus' used by Chan (2003) in combination with literature on police culture (van der Torre, 1999).

Information sharing is in many ways limited to individual goals and interests, legal frameworks; organisational interests and the fact that, within the new security architecture (or networks), different interests (national security, law enforcement, civil law and commercial) are not always, and sometimes never, in alignment (Hoogenboom, 2009). The complexity of 'information sharing' is in dire need of more academic scrutiny. If neglected, the 'big stories' of 'the surveillance society', 'Orwellian scenarios' or my use of 'unbounding' and 'blurring boundaries' will lose much of their meaning and only have a ideological (or political) meaning and appeal. What is needed here is old-fashioned empirical research.

Crime-control myths

Real police work is crime work, at least this is the image of policing in the media, the popular culture and in many political debates. This view 'has remarkable currency, given that the public police actually spend a tiny fraction of their time dealing with crime or something that could potentially be made into a crime' (Ericson, 1982). The essence of public policing is 'reproducing order', according to Ericson. Policing involves a wide range of nonrepressive strategies dealing with a variety of behaviour.

Low policing is not about crime but about services rendered to the public and reproducing order in microsocial interactions. Public policing on the local level is essentially dealing with 'the asshole – creep, bigmouth, bastard, animal, mope, rough, jerkoff, clown, scumbag, wiseguy, phoney, idiot, shithead, bum, fool, or any of a number of anatomical, oral, or incestuous terms – a part of every policeman's world' (Van Maanen, 1978). Conventional wisdom equates police work with crime work, which is a myth perpetually reinforced by the police themselves, moral entrepreneurs, politicians, some academics and of course the media and popular cultural images in movies, television series and novels (Reiner, 1992). A sound – comparative and cross-cultural – empirical basis exists for the primary noncrime-related character of everyday policing. Patrol police work is not primarily or essentially about crime prevention or law enforcement (Kelling et al., 1974; Wilson and Bolland, 1978; Chan and Ericson, 1981; Ericson 1982).

Most of the genuine crime the police are called upon to handle is minor. And crime the general public associates policing with – such as homicide, aggravated assault, robbery and forcible rape – is a fraction of the reality of policing. And, of course, the police also deal with crime but the macro effect on the levels of crime in society is marginal: 'The reason is that all of the major factors influencing the presence or absence of crime are factors over which police have no control whatsoever. Police can do nothing about the age, sex, racial or ethnic distribution of the population. They cannot control economic conditions, poverty, inequality, occupational opportunity, oral, religious, family, or secular education; or dramatic, social, cultural or political change' (Klockars, 1988).

War on drug myths

The UN strategy on drugs over the past decade has been a failure, a European commission report claimed in March 2009 on the eve of the international conference in Vienna that plans to set future policy for the next ten years. Referring to the United Nations' existing strategy, the authors declared that they had found 'no evidence that the global drug problem was reduced'. They write: 'Broadly speaking, the situation has improved a little in some of the richer countries while for others it worsened, and for some it worsened sharply and substantially, among them a few large developing or transitional countries.' The policy had merely shifted the problem geographically, the authors claimed; 'Production and trafficking controls only redistributed activities. Enforcement against local markets failed in most countries'.

These are damaging conclusions about the war on drugs that has been waged for more than three decades now. As early as 1995, the *British Medical Journal* devoted an editorial on the failing war on drugs. To quote the psychiatrist Thomas Szasz, drugs have taken over the leading role of sex in the 'morality play of human existence'. Civilians are no longer morally threatened by the lure of sex, but they are threatened by the ever-present morally devastating effects of drugs. For decades now, politicians, moral entrepreneurs and, in their wake, law enforcement agencies around the world have been 'hooked' on drugs. Large numbers of criminal investigations are directed at drug production, drug trafficking and drug consumption. Around the world the prison system – especially in the United States – is disproportionately populated by people (mostly men from nonwhite backgrounds) convicted for drug felonies. Yet production and consumption of drugs does not decline, and despite all the law enforcement efforts, drug prices around the world have been declining in the last decade, which seems to indicate that the supply of drugs is abundant and the war on drugs 'useless'.

Of course, this is not true for the political and otherwise symbolic meaning of the war on drugs, yet the symbolism has no effect whatsoever on the drug production and use. In this sense, the war on drugs is, in the view of Goffman, 'a stage' on which politicians produce necessity language for audiences (voters) who cannot deal with, or aren't interested in, the backstage realities of the war on drugs. A large number of studies debunking the drug myth – including *Drug Crazy. How We Got Into This Mess & How Can We Get Out* (Gray, 1996); *The War on Drugs Is Lost; Smoke and Mirrors; The War on Drugs and the Politics of Failure* and *Drug War Politics. The Price of Denial* – have no effect on the political (and moral and symbolic) realities of the war on drugs, Yet many of the players (in the Goffman sense of the word) are very well aware of the conclusions about the actual effects of all the efforts. As the UN report of 2009 indicates, there are no real effects. Writing on the 'useless' war on drugs, the *Financial Times* reporter Clive Crook (April 12, 2009) states: 'How much misery can a policy cause before it is acknowledged as a failure and reversed? The U.S. "war on drugs" suggests there is no upper limit. The country's implacable blend of prohibition and punitive criminal justice is wrong-headed in every way: immoral in principle, since it prosecutes victimless crimes, and in practice a disaster of remarkable proportions. Yet for a U.S. politician to suggest wholesale reform of this brainless regime is still seen as an act of reckless self-harm.' However, South American politicians, centre stage actors in the war on drugs, have moved beyond 'an act of reckless self harm'. After a year of researching, interviewing experts, holding meetings and debates, the Latin American Commission on Drugs and Democracy published its final report in early 2009 evaluating the current drug policy and its impacts on the region. Their findings are devastating: the first conclusion is titled 'A Failed War'. The commission concludes: 'Prohibitionist policies based on the eradication of production and on the disruption of drug flows as well as on the criminalization of consumption have not yielded the desired results. We are further than ever from the announced goal of eradicating drugs' (www.drugsanddemocracy.org).

Ironies, myths and paradoxes

As mentioned in the introduction to this book, I intended to introduce ironies, paradoxes, double-loop arguments and irrationalities within the emerging new security architecture. Although, as my arguments go, we can trace increasing cooperation – and even interweaving – between different security domains or 'silos', we also find many contradictions, tensions and conflicts of interests. Privatisation, militarisation, internationalisation and securitisation are in many ways based on broad and sweeping generalisations (Bowling and Newburn, 2006). The story of the new security architecture unfolds itself at different levels, in different time frames, and it involves many paradoxes. In this chapter, some myths have been introduced. What do we know about the effects of the war on drugs, the war on crime and all the security measures, programs, technology and manpower involved? Does it 'work' or are we made to believe all the 'necessity languages' involved? What is real, what is front stage and what is backstage? Increasingly, some researchers and commentators touch upon these mythical undertows: things are not what they appear to be. Some fascinating questions have to be formulated here for future research.

Epilogue: Conversations with Clifford Shearing (II)

Introduction

When I first started researching private policing in 1986/1987, hardly any literature was available. Much of the early writings on private security were completed by Clifford Shearing and Philip Stenning. As true pioneers, they ventured outside the criminal justice system, and I read and used much of their work compiled in the 1980s. They were a constant inspiration. Jan van Dijk, then director of the scientific research department of the Ministry of Justice I worked for at the time, once made a cynical remark about the number of Shearing and Stenning references I made. But it was the same Jan van Dijk who made it possible for me to cross the Atlantic to deliver my first-ever speech: a presentation to be held in 1987 at an academic conference in Montreal. After my speech, someone came up to me and introduced himself: Philip Stenning. I met Clifford Shearing briefly in 2006 at a Mannheim seminar organised by the London School of Economics.

Clifford Shearing keeps crossing my path: from my early work on privatisation through my research and lectures on policing to the more recently developed nodal security perspective. He has been an inspiration and, in many ways, a role model. This chapter is written as a 'conversation' with him, not to sing his praises even more loudly – I think I have made my point in this respect – but because of the German saying 'was sich liebt, das neckt sich', the quarrel of lovers is the renewal of love. In conversing with him here, I introduce five themes on which I differ in opinion. Only through a 'clash of opinions' can we move forward on the bumpy roads we walk to understand something of the bewildering world of policing and security.

Conversation 1

'Jack Daniels, straight please'

Much of Shearing and Stenning's early work on private security stresses the concept of 'loss prevention' as the main objective of private security as opposed to criminal justice objectives. Crime in a private context is fundamentally different from crime in the public sector, because 'crime' is only defined as 'crime' when losses occur. Shearing and Stenning have stripped preventive and repressive actions carried out by private individuals from normative connotations expressed by the public sector and the criminal justice system.

The definition of what exactly constitutes 'crime' differs over time and is dependent on its context as well as the power relations exhibited within it. This would explain why the private sector so often fails to file criminal complaints. As discussed in previous chapters, the private sector and the criminal justice system operate in 'multiple realities'. Let me illustrate this. During my university studies, I took up all sorts of odd jobs to make a bit of money. For a number of months, I worked with some of my fellow students; my weekend job with a fruit company involved packaging fruit for supermarkets. Every Saturday afternoon, the general manager would take out a few cases of beer, which we drank rather fast, not really limiting ourselves. A private security guard would sometimes include our hall in his rounds. Every now and then, he was treated to a can of beer by the general manager. Every Saturday, we would all walk out of this mass private property with somewhat more alcohol in our systems than the public police would generally allow. And every Saturday I would observe the general manager driving by in his car, greeting the security guard standing at the gate and wishing him a good weekend. To me, this anecdote is meaningful for understanding the nature, function and paradoxes of private security. Private security goals, objectives, means and mentalities fundamentally differ from those related to public policing.

My point here is that some of the original and groundbreaking insights of the early Shearing and Stenning work have become somewhat 'diluted', such as the actual meaning of the more pragmatic (commercial) definition of crime and the original meaning of private justice (Shearing and Stenning, 1987a). Also, for instance, the concept of 'loss prevention' as distinct from the criminal justice system is no longer – or, at best, to a lesser extent – part of the current discourse. *Private Policing*, edited by Shearing and Stenning (1987a).

Reiss problematises the intrusion of privacy; in three different chapters Henry, South and Weiss chronic storical role played by private security in social conflicts (for instance, in labour disputes); Marx touches on the integrity of the criminal justice system, which could wcll bc jcopardised in cases of close interweaving between the public and private sectors; and Reichman writes on the widening webs of surveillance in networks of insurance company investigators and the police. In their foreword entitled 'Reframing Policing', Shearing and Stenning are at their finest: 'after a long period in which the phenomenon of private policing was almost totally ignored' they now see a change. Order, they argue, is no longer a prerequisite of the state: today, order (keeping) is supplemented by different forms of private order keeping structures and processes. Still, and in my view this is what has become diluted, 'these are in some cases inconsistent with or even in conflict with the public order proclaimed by the state'. The 'inconsistency' argument is stressed even more in the following quotation: 'The irony is that it is the liberal frame itself (with its emphasis on the relative right of "individuals", especially property-owning ones) that has legitimated the development of huge multinational corporations into powerful private authorities whose very existence, and activity, mock the liberal frame'.

In the 1990s and the first part of the twenty-first century, these sharp edges have become less pronounced in the academic debate. In the Netherlands, research on private security – if done at all – mostly limited itself to the uniformed guards (Van Steden, 2007), and hardly any more probing research is currently being done into in-house security functions and activities and/or the private investigation market, which is estimated by the Ministry of Justice to vary between 500 and 1,000 (small) companies. The Dutch Privacy Authority has unravelled a case in which a private information company traded in illegal information (social security information, debts, criminal records). Both supply and demand in this market were determined by legitimate corporations such as financial institutions and law firms. Even the Dutch State Advocate, prosecuting for the state, was found to be one of the buyers of information. Although cases and incidents like this surface every now and then, no academic research programme has as yet structurally focused on the privatisation of security. Even a report from the Dutch Advisory Committee on International Relations indicating that the Dutch military presence in Afghanistan has become 'too dependent' on private contractors and that operations could thus become affected has not sparked much public debate or received any real academic interest.

The 'diluted' argument also applies to new – and fashionable – languages used nowadays to conceptualise policing in the 'postmodern society' in terms of 'nodal governance' and 'nodal security'. I will bring this up further along the way in this chapter.

Conversation 2

What happened to Disneyland?

Private Policing (1987) ends with a powerful metaphor featuring Disneyland. In 'Say "Cheese": The Disney Order that is not so Mickey Mouse', Shearing and Stenning describe and analyse the contours of a brave new world in which social control has become embedded in daily routines. 'This is where the fun begins', the authors promise. Next, they take us through the Disneyland system with a 'series of smiling young people' who guide us through the park softly and gently with the aid of 'visible road markings', 'guard rails' and 'physical barriers' to 'assign people into corrals'. Disneyland handles large crowds of people in 'a most orderly fashion', and control strategies are friendly and benevolent. Moreover, social control thus 'becomes consensual'.

I have always considered this a strong metaphor touching upon the undertow of changes in social control – away from the inclusion by the criminal justice system through incarceration in the prison system and into the direction of exclusion. Especially in the private sector, social control is exercised by background checks of (new) personnel, due diligence investigations of potential business partners, alcohol and drug testing of employees (in the United States), supplying personal information to obtain (health) insurance and mortgages, monitoring employees' Internet and e-mail behaviour and the widespread introduction of surveillance cameras, not only in the private sector but also by the state in the public domain. All these examples may be termed consensual because they form part of civil contracts between an employer and an employee or, in the case of insurances and mortgages, because they form part of a civil contract between financial institutions and civilians and companies. Also safety and security policies concerning mass private properties (sports stadiums, shopping malls, recreational areas, gated communities) stipulate searches and/or identification of visitors, for instance. Again, this is voluntary.

Bayley and Shearing (1996) are very much concerned with the ongoing 'pluralisation' of policing and the supposed = 'end of the monopoly by the public police', but they are much less concerned with the overall changes in social control in society. This is especially evident because public and private policing are treated as distinct categories, as a result of which the undertow of continuous interweaving between both sectors is largely ignored.

My point here is that developments within public policing as well as the private security market deserve academic scrutiny. Still, due to the fact that around the world the state itself is creating the largest demand for private security, the interpenetration (blurring) is more or less neglected. Thus, a metaphor like the Disney metaphor loses much of its power. The overall consequences of changes in policing and security (or social control) as discussed in the *Technopoly* chapter, for instance, or the information related to airline passengers travelling to the United States that is supplied by European airlines, credit card companies and government agencies indicate that other conceptual lenses, so to speak, have to be put in place to understand what is happening on the ground. In this respect, the new field of surveillance studies is of particular interest. Academics from a variety of backgrounds and areas of study are exploring the technology push in data gathering and data exchanges, ranging from marketing, computer sciences and Internet monitoring to law enforcement and intelligence. Zureik and Salter's (2005) *Global Surveillance and Policing. Borders, Security, Identity* is an excellent introduction into this new field as is Haggerty and Ericson's (2006) *The New Politics of Surveillance and Visibility*. Glimpses of Disneyland can be found in both publications. Surveillance has been made to cohere with a number of institutional agendas, including rational governance, risk management, scientific progress, and military conquest. Haggerty and Ericson write about the fact that 'people are broken down into a series of discrete informational flows which are stabilized and captured according to pre-established classificatory criteria'. Individuals at every location in the social hierarchy are now scrutinised, but at each level this monitoring is accomplished by different institutions with the aid of different technologies for quite unique purposes. This of course is one part of the story. The other part includes the interweaving of different information systems. Both stories are applicable, but both lack a sound empirical basis, which we should address.

Conversation 3

What's happening on the ground?

Wood and Shearing (2007), write that 'there is still much we don't know about the range of formal and informal aspects, or for instance the governance of commercial military service provision (...) It remains necessary to undertake a kind of explanatory "mapping" of the governance regime as it currently exists (...) This would provide a sound empirical basis for then assessing regulatory failures, weaknesses and limitations of the system as a whole'.

Wood and Shearing address the need for checks and balances in the exercise of policing and security in a pluralised world. This is something I wholeheartedly agree with, but it is especially their remark about the provision of 'a sound empirical basis' that I find illuminating and disturbing at the same time. Ever since the early work by Shearing and Stenning on privatisation and more recently the 'discovery' of regulatory agencies, inspectorates and specialised investigative agencies working for department academics have hardly demonstrated any beginning of thorough, sound and methodical empirical research into these domains. This holds true for the great majority of criminologists and police researchers around the world.

As a result, much academic writing may be termed superficial, anecdotal and abstract. The criminal justice system remains the centre of the universe of academic research and in the cathedral of criminology we worship the output of this system: crime as registered by the public police. Inspired by anomalies that no longer fit the existing paradigm, academics intuitively construct new jargon for new developments. For more than two decades now, the jargon pendulum has moved back and forth between privatisation, plural policing, the police extended family, interweaving, hybridity, the regulatory state, fragmentation of policing and security and, more recently, nodal governance and nodal security.

Much of the literature lacks 'a sound empirical basis'. We find ourselves stuck in the middle of broad and sweeping statements on 'disciplinary power' quoting Foucault over and over again or, multilateral institutions (Drahos, 2004) and today's nodal security. In my view, the new lingo does not really make things any clearer. I have difficulties reading sentences like 'nodes relate to one another, and attempt to mobilize and resist one another, in a variety of ways so as to shape matters in ways that promote their objectives and concerns' (Wood and Shearing, 2007). The same can be said about 'ruptures coexisted with continuities, blending explicit and self-proclaimed ruptures with unspoken continuities and so giving rise to very complex legal and institutional constellations and hybridizations', unreservedly quoted by Wood and Shearing (2007).

The issue here is this: why not negotiate access to Stansted Airport or Heathrow Airport, for instance, or Manchester or Liverpool harbour, or the upcoming London Olympics to study *on the ground* what kind of agencies are involved in safety and security arrangements and subsequently research their respective roles and functions, how they interact, how information is dispersed, who authorises different arrangements, who is responsible and how conflicts are managed. The nodal language – due to the lack of empirical insights – has esoteric, almost scientific 'religious' connotations that cloud what's happening on the ground.

I strongly believe in the use of small-scale, bottom-up empirical (case) studies evaluating security arrangements in shopping malls, in semi-public domains where private guards, municipal officials and the police interact and also in the use of small-scale in-depth studies of actual 'nodes'. For instance, in the Netherlands, new hybrid structures have come into existence such as the Financial Expertise Centre (FEC) in which financial regulators, customs, the fiscal investigation agency, the police and the intelligence service exchange information and negotiate possible interventions. This may truly be termed a 'node' as we find it in the literature on policing and security today. It is important to realise here that publications such as *Imagining Security* (Wood and Shearing, 2007) and *Nodale orde* for the Netherlands hardly contain any examples of or references to empirical realities. Of course, Shearing incorporates his field study of networks in South African communities, and this is illuminating and interesting in many ways, but I am convinced that, to understand nodal security, a larger number of more diverse case studies have to be undertaken (van Steden, 2007).

Let me return to the concept of 'nodes' to illustrate the current issue. Nodes have been created in the United States, the United Kingdom, the European Union and in countries like Australia under the umbrella of 'homeland security' departments: structures or processes in which information is shared across the public-private divide and also across the different countries' many law enforcement and regulatory bodies. In the Rotterdam harbour, the Harbour Expertise Centre (ECH) combines law enforcement information from the police and information from specialised investigative agencies (for instance, the fiscal investigation agency). Across the Atlantic, the El Paso Intelligence Centre analyses drug-related intelligence from the military, customs, DEA, FBI and a number of other agencies in the war on drugs in the Caribbean and South America. Another 'node' worth mentioning is the obligation formulated by the EU and placed on its member states to keep records of all Internet behaviour demonstrated by citizens for a period of 6 to 18 months, depending on the country. The content of e-mails and Internet surfing is not retained, but instead the 'nodes' involved (Internet providers and ISP-addresses). One of the more pervasive 'nodes' being scrutinised by the intelligence community is the global financial network of the Society for Worldwide Interbank Financial Telecommunication (SWIFT). In 2004, media attention was focused on the fact that the CIA was monitoring global financial transactions carried out by the SWIFT system located in Brussels. The European Parliament adopted a resolution on July 6, 2006, asking EU governments, the commission and the European Central Bank 'to explain fully the extent to which they were aware of the secret agreement' between the Belgium-based SWIFT and the authorities of the United States. According to reports that have been at least partly confirmed by the United States, the data concerning millions of daily international money transfers are forwarded to the United States, where they are subject to data mining procedures. On the U.S. side, the scheme, which is part of the 'war on terrorism', is operated jointly by the CIA and the Treasury Department.[62] In sum, if we really wish to make the concept of 'nodes' an empirical reality, there are many dozens of case studies begging to be carried out.

Conversation 4

Beware of Greeks bearing new conceptual gifts

The concept of *chronocentrism* is the doctrine that what is current must somehow be superior to what went on before; it proposes that ideas, scholars and scholarship inevitably become stale and discredited over time.[63] I will argue that the rise and attraction of new concepts like the 'fragmentation or pluralisation of policing', 'the end of the monopoly' and, more recently, nodal governance and nodal security fit the definition of chronocentrism. Rock (2005) uses 'chronocentrism' to indicate that criminology has proceeded in a series of fits and starts that are marked by radical discontinuities, a recurrence of new beginnings and a quest for the seemingly distinctive under the spell of a chronocentristic bias. Looking back to classics in policing in Chapters 1 and 2, we can see that undertows within policing come the surface once again. Contrary to much of the fashionable change, the languages of undertows can be labelled as centralisation and nationalisation. Looking more closely under the surface, these dynamics within public policing are accompanied by organisational, strategic, tactical and operational changes within policing that are strengthening intelligence-led policing, criminal investigation structures (including forensic sciences), public order keeping and closer cooperation with the intelligence and security services. Fictional policing is much more about community policing, reassurance policing and restorative policing. In Chapter 2, I made a distinction between five levels of policing. Conventional wisdom equates public policing with the friendly unarmed bobby and other images of community-oriented policing. This first level of policing is vital in many ways, but clinging to catchy phrases in a neophiliac way clouds actual changes in manpower, organisational structures, information processes and public order keeping potential on the other four levels. Actually, what we mostly research in public policing (community-oriented policing and varieties of this concept) is a 'limited' part of policing in terms of manpower, budgets, operational capacities and innovations taking place (technopoly argument). What criminology and police research actually studies is part of a broader picture, and this part is actually becoming smaller.

The recent 'discovery' of a multitude of (semi-)public agencies and private sector actors performing police functions also has neophiliac tendencies and characteristics. For instance, one tends to neglect the fact that many of these agencies and actors have a long-standing history (sometimes more than a century) and have been the subject of many, if forgotten, academic studies. Moreover, these studies are richer in their theoretical foundations because of the explanations they give for different functions, goals, interests, cultures and operational styles of public policing, administrative policing and private policing than much of the current fashionable language. In many ways, nodal governance and nodal security are new labels for ongoing processes of gradual interweaving of different forms of policing. Next to centralisation/nationalisation and the changes in operational processes within public policing, another long-term trend becomes visible under the surface of changes: the gradual interweaving between public policing and other 'nodes'. This is not something that started with the nodal language, but much earlier.

For this reason, the use of these concepts is useful in two ways: first, for policy makers and practitioners. For them, the new concepts seem to have a function as a motivational strategy. For instance, what were called increasing cooperation in the justice system (*ketensamenwerking*) and public-private cooperation in the eighties and nineties have been revitalised using new labels.

Second, nodal governance and nodal security in the academic community 'forces' us to rethink the very notion of policing. Policing increasingly takes place in hybrid organisations and processes in which boundaries between public administration, public policing, regulatory agencies and private security are blurring.

My argument here is we should be wary of the never-ending academic and consultancy addiction to ever-new concepts – not only the concepts mentioned above but also the never-ending supply of new policing concepts like 'signal policing', 'intelligence-led policing', 'reassurance policing' and, more recently, 'restorative policing'.

In the end, to describe and analyse policing, a limited number of concepts are relevant. Public policing can only be understood in the context of the state, in which the function of policing is public order keeping and law enforcement. What distinguishes public policing from regulation by administrative agencies and regulatory agencies and private security is the legal monopoly on violence. This not only includes violence in the strict sense of the word but also the exercise of legal powers (stop and search, electronic surveillance, arrest and so on).

Things change and stay the same. Underneath neophilia, public policing has not fundamentally changed in the last two centuries. Public order keeping, criminal investigations, (political) intelligence gathering and the interaction with the general public on a daily basis date from the decades in which Sir Robert Peel introduced 'the blue-coated' worker continuity. Of course, changes occurred in training and education and more technology influenced working processes, but the basic function did not change. For instance, the recent 'discovery' both within public policing itself and the academic community of 'intelligence-led policing' strikes me as somewhat awkward in light of the structural nature of intelligence gathering in the history of policing. In many ways, public policing is and has always been about intelligence: for political reasons, public order keeping, investigations and, in many ways, also to inform and involve the general public in crime prevention.

Conversation 5

The State, policing and security: Interweaving, unbounding and the 'eminence grise, a shadow entity lurking off-stage'

In 'The Transformation of Policing? Understanding Current Trends in Policing Systems' (2002), Jones and Newburn challenge much of the language used in referring to change in policing. I agree with them in many ways.

During the first decade of the twenty-first century – especially after 9/11, the Madrid and London bombings, and two political murders involving Dutch politician Pim Fortuyn and artist and film director

Theo Van Gogh – the Dutch state reemerged in further shaping law enforcement and intelligence. In a few years' time, the Dutch intelligence service AIVD raised staff numbers from around 550 people to more than 1,500, cooperation between the AIVD and the regional police forces was strengthened and, on a regional level, the regional intelligence forces cooperating with the AIVD showed significant growth (300 per cent). A National Coordinator for Counterterrorism was appointed (with an organisation and staff of 100 functionaries) to coordinate preventive measures, conduct exercises, mobilise the private sector and inform the general public about these issues.

Undertows in public policing follow the currents described in Chapters 1 and 2: a gradual centralisation, increasing investments in information processes, new and more powerful antiterrorism laws and the redirection of manpower into specialised antiriot teams, interregional and national investigation squads. In 2005, the Dutch regional police structure was evaluated, which led to a new proposal (the 2007 Police Act) discussed in Parliament in December 2008. The law has not been passed yet, but it has already led to enhanced pressures on interregional cooperation and greater leverage for new information systems, thus making it possible to share criminal intelligence across regional forces. These recent changes in policing are in line with historical analyses of the political function of the police, the subsequent dynamics within the police system and the structure and primary processes in policing on the ground. In many ways, these undertows have not been prominent in police research and criminology. From this perspective, we can understand also the undertows in policing and security in which, at different levels and on different themes (national security, crime prevention, criminal investigations, crowd control and so on), public policing has become part of 'hybrid' organisational structures in which cooperation with regulators, specialised investigative agencies and private security is a dominant trend.

The state has never left the stage – contrary to much of the change and transformation language. 'The End of Public Policing' is nowhere in sight. Admittedly, policing is currently involved in a process of pluralisation, but the prediction that 'future generations will look back on our era as a time when one system of policing ended and another took its place' does not fully acknowledge the undertows in policing. I find the very prediction somewhat missing the undertows in policing and security, because the state (public policing, regulatory agencies and the intelligence community) is more present the ever. We have to scratch below the surface of many a text in policing and security studies.[64] And although privatisation is visible everywhere and on a global scale, it is the state that is presently creating the largest demand for private security. It can safely be stated that private security in many of its forms and manifestations is actually becoming part of public policing: from the guarding of police stations and criminal courts to crowd control in sports and pop concerts to the guarding of government agencies to parts of the security checks in airports and harbours and in some cases to the hiring of private forensic accountants, IT-specialists and private investigators for internal fraud cases. The same can be seen in the domain of private military companies being hired by the state for operations around the world in troublesome areas.

Around the world, states have enacted money-laundering laws with obligations for financial institutions to give information on suspicious financial transactions to national financial intelligence units. Other examples are the EU laws and regulations requiring telecom companies and Internet providers to store information on different forms of communication for periods between 6 and 18 months.

In the Netherlands, increasingly hybrid expertise centres are created in which police, financial regulators, customs, Marechaussee (military police) and specialised investigative agencies in the field of environmental crime, identity fraud, illegal immigration and financial crimes cooperate. In the Rotterdam harbour, the police share information in the Harbour Expertise Centre with fiscal, social security and environmental investigative agencies from different ministries; at Schiphol Airport, the Marechaussee has set up a Expertise Centre for Identity fraud, sharing information with a number of regulators, specialised investigative agencies, the police and also financial institutions because of their expertise in this area. The dominant governance model for policing and security is driven by notions like multiagency cooperation and multitasking. The traditional governance model in policing and security was – and, in many ways, still is – organised along vertical lines of authority and primary processes. Gradually, however, we witness the emergence of horizontal forms of cooperation in terms of information sharing, multiagency crime analyses and more coordination in operations. The future of policing is hybrid both in terms of organisational structures but increasingly also on strategic, tactical and operational levels.[65]

'Much current criminology tends to exaggerate the degree of change, and underplay the extent of continuity, in seeking to explain the transformations taking place in contemporary policing systems' (Jones and

Newburn, 2002). I used this quote in the beginning of this study. And I very much agree with it. Crawford (2006) also challenges the idea of a 'post-regulatory state' in a network society comprising a multitude of agencies more or less performing policing tasks. Quoting Hawkins (1984), Crawford sees the state in governing security as 'a kind of *eminence grise*, a shadow entity lurking off-stage'. Crawford juxtaposes authors who write about the demise of the state and the end of its monopoly in drawing attention to 'state anchoring': far from showing state withdrawal, the British state 'is engaged in ambitious projects of social engineering in which the deployment of hierarchy, command and interventionism are prevalent. I agree with Crawford. Yes, of course, on one level fragmentation of policing and security is taking place. But looking more closely at some of the undertows, we find many 'nodes' actually being created by the state (and different policing agencies). In this way, the police become part of different organisational networks through which the information position is gaining in quantity and quality. The more prominent presence of the 'eminence grise' also shows itself in the trend to control ('discipline') some of the policing taking place outside the criminal justice system. Because the many (semi-)public and private organisations that now make up the 'new architecture' of policing and security function within democracies and are bound by the rule of law, the state has a responsibility for upholding the law. Next to 'horizontal' cooperation, the state also restructures 'vertical' relationships.

What has somehow disappeared from much of the 'horizontal' language of networks, nodal security, institutional fragmentation and public-private arrangements are 'vertical' relations and responsibilities. The 'eminence grise' is actually also looking over the shoulder of private security entrepreneurs. If a private uniformed guard uses excessive force, the public police will investigate a complaint; if a financial institution does not comply with antimoney-laundering laws, the public prosecutor can start a criminal investigation, and if an environmental inspectorate does not adequately deal with enforcement, the inspectorate (or responsible functionaries) can be prosecuted. Crawford emphasises this point using Braithwaite: 'when the cooperative approach fails, the regulator escalates up the pyramid'.

Cooperation, voluntary compliance and other 'soft' ways of influencing citizens and corporations – or even public officials – are to be pursued in what is called 'smart regulation'. Nevertheless, command and sanctions do not disappear altogether: command and coercion remain available in the background as a tool of last resort.

Our research agenda for the near future should include research questions on the way 'the state, the *eminence grise*, a shadow entity lurking off-stage' is actually integrating all sorts of policing, regulation and private security for a number of traditional state objectives: national security, public order keeping, law enforcement and regulation of financial markets. The state and public policing seems to be in a transitional phase in which policing is being reconfigured in many ways. Not only is the police system itself undergoing new phases in the gradual process of centralisation and nationalisation but in the wake of this, more cooperation is being organised with a multitude of agencies and corporations, sometimes under contract, sometimes voluntary and sometimes based on legal obligations.

Perhaps there is more 'truth' in the lucid prediction by Fijnaut (1985) that the future of policing lies in the emergence of a differentiated public police force in which regulation, specialised investigative agencies and private security are becoming integrated than much of the language in vogue on the demise of the state and the ' disappearance' of public police. What has also been neglected, or at least downplayed, is the monopoly on violence by the state ever present in social conflicts and in times of crisis and calamities. On one level, there is 'truth' in Shearing's quote that there is nothing the police does that is not being done by others too. But on a deeper level, a distinctive characteristic of the state is not only its monopoly on violence, but also the exclusive exercise of powers based on the criminal code. Yes, violence is exercised by others, for instance, PMCs, and yes, 24/7 investigations are carried out by private security agencies. But still, they all lack the legal authority of the state, and the state can and actually does intervene when non-state actors transgress legal boundaries, as indicated by criminal cases against PMCs, private investigators and private intelligence cases.

To close: Curiosity and undertows in policing and security

In John Irving's novel *The World According to Garp*, we encounter two scenes in which a young child is warned before taking a swim in the Atlantic Ocean: 'beware of the undertow', for undertows are dangerous to the unwary. In 12 chapters and a conversation with Clifford Shearing, I have described and analysed 'undertows' in policing and the broader security structures in our societies.

Somewhere along the way I quoted Gary Marx, who urged me to 'write all the time, on everything and everywhere'. This is what I do more or less. Not only because of Gary but also because it has become part of my professional life as an academic. I accompanied Maurice Punch on a number of occasions to Mannheim Lectures at the London School of Economics. During one of these visits, I bought George Orwell's (2004) essay 'Why I write'. I was curious, as a sort of writer, why he wrote, and perhaps to find some reason for why I write. I never actually had given this any systematic thought. I just moved from project to project, article to article and book to book. I liked it, and I still do. But why?

Sheer egoism is the first reason Orwell offers. Writers have 'a desire to seem clever, to be talked about, to be remembered after death, to get your own back on the grown-ups who snubbed you in childhood, etc., etc.' (p. 4). He continues, 'It is humbug to pretend this is not a motive, and a strong one. Writers share this characteristic with scientists, artists, politicians, lawyers, soldiers, successful businessmen – in short, with the whole top crust of humanity' (p. 5). I can relate to this in some ways although I have no ambition at all 'to be remembered after death', and I certainly have no grudge against anyone 'who snubbed' (p. 5) me in childhood. Actually, my memories are vague here.

Aesthetic enthusiasm is Orwell's second reason. The sheer pleasure of structuring a text, finding words and phrases, toying with form and content is something I recognise very much. For instance, I wrote *The Sopranos* chapter (Chapter 7) with enthusiasm arising from the experiment of writing it like a play. I felt some sort of 'aesthetic enthusiasm' from writing, and the bottle of Barolo at hand was useful here too. 'Above the level of a railway guide, no book is quite free from aesthetic considerations' (p. 5), according to Orwell.

Historical impulse is Orwell's third reason. He has 'the desire to see things as they are, to find out true facts and store them up for the use of posterity' (p. 5). I am not really interested in posterity, but I can relate to the 'desire to see things as they are, to find true facts' (p. 5). Curiosity still is a motivation to look into the history of policing, to understand undertows and use some of this knowledge to understand why public policing is integrating other forms of policing. I am curious to formulate new research questions. I am curious to probe underneath the surface, and that is why I started and finish with 'undertows'.

Finally, Orwell mentions a political purpose. And, he uses the word *political* in the widest possible sense. Orwell talks about a 'desire to push the world in a certain direction, to alter other peoples' idea of the kind of society that they should strive after. Once again, no book is genuinely free from political bias' (p. 5).

I recognise this reason as well. At the same time, I understand the relativity of 'writing all the time, on everything and everywhere'. First of all, there are other things in life besides writing. And, second, the actual possibilities of 'pushing the world in a certain direction' are not that abundant and easy to accomplish. Of course, Orwell has done this in his ways, but academics? Yet 'politics' in the 'widest possible sense' is of course present in the execution of this book. Prof. A. C. t' Hart was one of my doctoral professors. He wrote *Instrumentaliteit en rechtsbescherming* (Instrumentality and civil rights protection) in which he traced the norms and values underlying the state and criminal law. The state and the rule of law in democracies are primary systems to safeguard us from arbitrary power exercised by people in power. The rule of law was an answer to the Absolutist Ancien Regime and the medieval feudal society before that. I have this curiosity for the way democracies formulate answers for national security, crime control and regulating society. Control, regulating, monitoring, the exercise of violence in public order settings and investigations of (organised) crime are all legitimate activities. But the 'politics' in *The Governance of Policing and Security. Ironies, Myths and Paradoxes* comes to the surface in the chapters on the governance of security (Chapter 5) in which the location of power and accompanying accountability structures in the governance of policing and security networks is questioned. Do the existing checks and balances created for public policing suffice in a 'new world' of security networks and growing interweaving of public policing and other assorted 'policing' and security organisations? 'Politics' is also present in the chapters 'Ironies, Paradoxes and the Seven Plagues of Policing and Security (Chapter 8), 'Unsafe and Unsound Practices (Chapter 11) and 'Myths in Policing and Security' (Chapter 12). In all three chapters, I draw attention to possible unwanted and unforeseen undertows in the new 'security architecture'. Power corrupts; absolute power corrupts absolutely.

Notes

1. I started this project three years ago with Maurice Punch. We travelled together to LSE for Mannheim Lectures on some occasions and discussed policing issues in many other places (mostly Pakistani restaurants in London and Amsterdam). I have always considered Maurice, together with a handful of other scholars, as a role model. Sometimes I refer to them in lectures as 'my heroes'. I was proud to work with Maurice, and we had stimulating times. Somewhere along the line, we disentangled ourselves from this book and chose different avenues, projects and interests. I owe Maurice for a number of themes, angles and arguments in this book. Without him, the book would have looked much different. I dedicate the book also to Gary Marx, whose work I keep returning to. He showed me also the importance of experimenting with academic rules, regulations and formats: narrative knowledge through art, pop music, poetry, novels and cartoons can be very powerful and useful. Although academic hardliners disagree with some (or most) of this 'frolicking', there are many ways to tell academic stories. Therefore, I've put Maurice and Gary – outta respect (as the Mafia saying goes) – at a table in Tony Soprano 'headquarters', the nightclub Bada Bing, in an experiment with academic form and content: here's to you guys!
2. E. Ericson and K. D. Carriere, 'The Fragmentation of Criminology', in *The Futures of Criminology*, ed. D. Nelke (London: Sage, 1992).
3. Van Maanen (1987) quotes a veteran patrolman: 'I guess what our job boils down to is not letting the assholes take over the city. Now I'm not talking about your regular crooks...they're bound to wind up in the joint anyway. What I'm talking about are those shitheads out to prove they can push everybody around. Those are the assholes we gotta deal with and take care of on patrol...You take the majority of what we do and it's nothing more than asshole control'. (p. 224).
4. As of 1985, I have been involved in police research and police education at the Dutch Police Academy and in consultancy services related to law enforcement. Also, I have spoken with many police officers of all levels and listened to their accounts. In writing this chapter, I started thinking whether or not I have heard any reports on how individuals have built community relations as compared to reports about incidents, specific actions and, in general, events that seem to be pivotal points in the professional histories of these many hundreds of officers. I can't recall one single community relation account as opposed to dozens of reports on large-scale riots, for instance, those witnessed during the coronation of Queen Beatrix in 1980, moments in high-profile criminal investigations or the period of squatter riots in Amsterdam. As Reiner (1992) argues, police culture is action driven and carries a strong sense of mission. The context in which factional policing takes place is limited to specific and concrete incidents of which policing on the ground has an unlimited supply.
5. 'The reason is that all of the major factors influencing the presence or absence of crime are factors over which police have no control whatsoever.

Police can do nothing about the age, sex, racial or ethnic distribution of the population. They cannot control economic conditions, poverty, inequality, occupational opportunity, oral, religious, family, or secular education; or dramatic, social, cultural or political change' (Klockars, 1988).

6. Even when 'community policing' is successfully organised, the question remains if the public is actually aware of this. Does the public perceive 'community policing' in the same way as the relatively small number of community officers and/or police researchers perceive its importance? Also, can 'community policing' function on a 24/7 basis in its original manner and in line with its underlying philosophy without being swept aside in the ad hoc, incident-driven need to maintain the law and reproduce order? Research in one specific force conducted in 2003 indicated that only 40 per cent of the population was aware of the existence of special community policing officers in their neighbourhood. One of the explanations put forward was the fact that visibility of these officers was adversely affected because from time to time they were appointed members of an investigative team and were subsequently relieved from their community policing duties (www.politie.nl/zuid-holland-zuid).
7. NWO is the Dutch national organisation for academic research (www.nwo.nl).
8. Smeets and Dutch authors like Terpstra (2007) and Stokkom (2007) are doing wonderful work on 'new uniforms' and the fragmentation of the surveillance function. However, this touches on the area of privatisation. A uniformed guard is the most visible aspect of privatisation and, in many ways, the least troublesome – from a perspective of accountability. Much more interesting are the shifting locations of power that come not from the uniform but from the civil contracts between employer and employees, or insurance company and insured; from information positions through data mining, business intelligence or investigations by private eyes or private forensic accountants and/or private IT specialists. In many ways, the private sector exercises power from its offices; uniformed guards are used for entry controls but they have no relationship whatsoever with the other aspects of private security.
9. 'ArmorGroup provides single-source solutions to identify, reduce and resolve exceptional risks in complex, sometimes hostile, environments. To achieve this we have in excess of 7,600 highly trained, experienced personnel in over 26 countries. Global reach is what distinguishes ArmorGroup – we have people where they are needed most' (www.armorgroup.com)
10. 'The diversity of Northbridge Services Group ensures that we have the capability to provide a varied range of electronic, photographic, and human intelligence. We have the expertise in place to ensure that the intelligence is confidentially gathered and professionally analyzed' (different websites of private military companies show intelligence is provided as a service).
11. Report of the Committee on Interior and Insular Affairs of the U.S. House of Representatives, Alaska Pipeline Service Company Covert Operation. Washington, 1992.
12. 'Covert operations' is American jargon for illegal or clandestine operations often related to public intelligence services.

13. G. T. Marx, 'An Ethics for the New Surveillance,' *The Information Society*, vol. 14, no. 3 (1998).
14. I do not limit 'narrative knowledge' to the field of literature only. In the broadest sense of the term, art (paintings, poems, rap texts, graffiti, films, sculptures, music, and so on) tells a story. As such, art and all its expressions offer insight – insight that often differs from rational knowledge because it has the ability to touch people emotionally. It is precisely for this reason that narrative knowledge is in many ways superior to academic know-how.
15. For a psychological analysis of the show, see M. Yacowar, 2003. He starts the book with a quote by Dr Melfi: 'This fantasy of yours has meaning'. Fully in line with traditional psychoanalysis, sexual passion and death wishes are used as explanations for behaviour. On page 56, he explains the skill of cunnilingus.
16. Patrick van Calster derived part of his analysis from anthropology, in particular the work by George Herbert Mead, in which Mead emphasises interactions (or social relationships). Mead looks for explanations for social reality in actual social interaction. He states that the meaning of an action lies not in the action itself, but rather in the reaction to the action. Social beings communicate through gestures, movements, touch, sound, exterior displays, and smell. There is ongoing action and reaction (interactions).
17. M. de Galan, 'There's a Horse's Head in Your Bed: The American Mafia's Been Bled Dry by Hollywood', *NRC,* March 18, 2005.
18. http://www.ministerievanjustitie.nl/b_organ/nhg/nieuws/campagne_amk.htm
19. http://www.novatv.nl/index.cfm?fuseaction=videoaudio.details&reportage_id=1667. See also: http://www.medischefouten.org/. Accessed on March 2008.
20. 'I posit that, in each society, the production of language is concurrently checked, selected, organized, and redistributed by a range of procedures that are aimed at allaying their powers and force, managing their contingency character, and avoiding their pressing, frightful materiality' (Foucault, 1988, p. 37). Elsewhere, Foucault also eloquently discusses 'muzzling' speech. Foucault, and Foqué in his footsteps, 't Hart, Gutwirth, Van Calster and ŽiŽek: they all counteract with narrative knowledge.
21. Gutwirth, 1989. The quote is by V. Havel (Havel, 1990, p. 15).
22. In various episodes, Tony retreats to his television set where he watches old thrillers from the 40s and 50s with actors such as Jimmy Cagney and Humphrey Bogart. References to *The Godfather* are made throughout the series. Maurice Yacowar includes an appendix in *The Sopranos on the Couch: Godfather to the Sopranos,* in which the influence of *The Godfather* trilogy in the series is analysed systematically. Influences are not only found in the choice of music, but also in the dialogue.
23. N. Postman, *Technopoly. The Surrender of Culture to Technology* (New York: Vintage Books, 1993).
24. © 2007, The Center for Public Integrity. All rights reserved. IMPORTANT: Read our privacy policy and the terms under which this service is provided to you. 910 17th Street, NW, 7th Floor, Washington, DC 20006. Tel. (202) 466–1300.

25. Mark P. Mills is a founding partner of Digital Power Capital, which invests in securities technologies, and coauthor of *The Bottomless Well* (Basic Books, 2005).
26. A number of these examples have been taken from the EU Report Technologies of Political Control, Straatsburg, 1997.
27. Chen, H. Fei-Yue Wang Zeng, D. Manage "Intelligence and security informatics for homeland security: information, communication, and transportation". Inf. Syst. Dept., Univ. of Arizona, Tucson, AZ, USA; This paper appears in: Intelligent Transportation Systems, IEEE Transactions on Publication Date: Dec. 2004 Volume: 5, Issue: 4.
28. Across large enterprises, predictive intelligence technology is being used for a stunningly broad set of applications. Sports teams are using it to predict when star athletes might get injured. Banks use it to detect money laundering and insider trading. Retailers are forecasting demand down to the store and item level. Manufacturers use it in product design and to forecast equipment failure. Drug companies use it to develop drugs and then figure out what marketing programmes will cause doctors to write more prescriptions.
29. Readers are referred to the website of the American Civil Liberties Union: www.aclu.org/privacy.
30. Donatella della Porta, 'Corruption, Clientelism, and Maladministration: Notes on the Dynamics of Corrupt Exchanges in Italy; Corruzione, clientelismo e cattiva," *Quaderni di Sociologia*, vol. 37, no. 5 (1993): 31–50.
31. P. Klerks, 'Big in Hashish. Theory and Practice of Organized Crime,' *Samson* (2000): 40.
32. D. Downes and Paul Rock, *Understanding Deviance. A Guide to the Sociology of Rule Breaking* (Oxford: Oxford University Press, 2007), 254.
33. A. Block, 'The Serious Crime Community in Oil en Banking,' *Journal of Financial Crime*, vol. 207 (1997): 4.
34. Criminal Intelligence Service Canada, 1999. Available at www.cisc.gc.ca.
35. www.usseaportcommission.org.
36. J. M. Waller and V. Yasmann, 'Russia's Great Criminal Revolution: The Role of the Security Services,' *Journal of Contemporary Criminal Justice*, vol. 11, no. 4 (December 1995): 111–128.
37. 'Who's Clean?,' *Newsweek* (September 6, 1999): 22.
38. W. N. Grigg, 'Dirty Cops in the Former Soviet Union Running Both Sides of the Law,' *The New American*, vol. 3, 1996: 236–245.
39. 'Organized Crime in the Netherlands; Report Based on the WODC Monitor by E. R. Kleemans, E. A. I. M. van den Berg and H. G. van de Bunt, with cooperation from M. Brouwers, R. F. Kouwenberg and G. Paulides (Ministry of Justice: Den Haag, 2002).
40. F. Bovenkerk and Y. Yesilgöz, De Maffia van Turkije (Turkey's Mafia). Amsterdam: Meulenhoff, 1998, 212–57.
41. V. Ruggiero, 'War Markets: Corporate and Organized Criminals in Europe,' *Social and Legal Studies,* vol. 5, no. 1 (March 1996): 5–20.
42. F. Battistelli, 'Arms and Corruption; Armi e corruzione,' *Critica Sociologica*, vol. 106 (July/October 1993): 33–42.
43. Adam Graycar, 'Trafficking in Human Beings,' presented at the International Conference on Migration, Culture and Crime, Israel, July 7, 1999.
44. A. Johnson, *Yakuza: Past and Present.*

45. Robert Delfs, 'Feeding on the System: Gangsters Play Increasing Role in Business and Politics." *Far Eastern Economic Review* (November 21,1991): 28.
46. 'More Eyes On Yakuza's Role in Japanese Economy,' Japan Economic Institute, May 8, 1992. See also David E. Kaplan and Alec Dubro, *Yakuza: The Explosive Account of Japan's Criminal Underworld* (Reading, MA: Addison-Wesley Publishing Co., 1986).
47. 'Drugs, Law Enforcement and Foreign Policy Subcommittee on Terrorism, Narcotics and International Operations,' Committee on Foreign Relations, United States Senate, 1989, S. Prt. 100–165, chaired by Sen. John Kerry of Massachusetts.
48. R. Stich, *Defrauding America* (Alamo: Diablo Western Press, 1994).
49. 'Causes and Cures: National Campaign on the Narcotics Epidemic: Final Report,' Washington D.C., 1991, 9.
50. For a discussion on the CIA's role in the drug trade, go to http://www.narconews.com/darkalliance and navigate to the web page Cocaine Importing Agency. This website is maintained by Gary Webb, the author of *Dark Alliance. The CIA, The Contras, and the Crack Cocaine Explosion.* In her foreword, U.S. Congresswoman Maxine Waters writes: 'It may take time, but I am convinced that history is going to record that Gary Webb wrote the truth. brings to light one of the worst official abuses in our nation's history. We all owe Gary Webb a debt of gratitude for his brave work. On the cover we find the following comment: 'This updated paperback edition of Gary Webb's *Dark Alliance* features revelations in just-released reports from the Department of Justice, internal CIA investigations, and a new cache of recently declassified secret FBI, DEA, and INS files—much of which was not known to Webb when writing the first edition of this book. Webb further explains the close working relationship that major drug traffickers had with U.S. Government agencies—particularly the DEA—and recounts the news of the past year regarding this breaking story'.
51. As explained in the introduction of this book, this project originally was set up as a collaborative effort with Maurice Punch whom I greatly admire and regard as a professional friend. It turned out we chose different paths to pursue, but much of the inspiration and ' undertows' on accountability can be directly traced back to Maurice Punch.
52. It is of interest here to note that not were only individual officers prosecuted for a number of offences, but also that the French government was subsequently prosecuted and convicted by the ECHR for the cruel and degrading treatment of Selmouni.
53. From 1954 to 1974, James Jesus Angleton was responsible for counterespionage within the CIA. Angleton was both loved and hated. He was loved for his intelligence and drive. He was hated for his excessive mistrust. The Cold War and the McCarthy period left deep traces in his mind. Each defector was a valuable source of information for the CIA's intelligence services. Angleton trusted none of them and saw plots and schemes everywhere. See: 'The Angleton Archive by the Center for the Study of National Security' (www.jamesjesus.com) Also see www.cia-on-campus.org/yale.edu/henwood: 'Its landscape is "a wilderness of mirrors" ("In a wilderness of mirrors. What will the spider do?") – a phrase from T.S. Eliot's *Gerontion* that Angleton quoted frequently'. D. C. Martin, 'Wilderness of Mirrors: Intrigue, Deception, and

the Secrets that Destroyed two of the Cold War's most important agents', Guildford: Lyons Press (2003).

54. 'Emotional blackmail is a powerful form of manipulation in which people close to us threaten to punish us for not doing what they want. Emotional blackmailers know how much we value our relationships with them. They know our vulnerabilities and our deepest secrets. They are our mothers, our partners, our bosses and co-workers, our friends and our lovers. And no matter how much they care about us, they use this intimate knowledge to give themselves the payoff they want: our compliance' (see Forward and Frazier, 1998).
55. See also the final report of the select committee to study governmental operations with respect to intelligence activities (Church Commission), Washington, 1976, and in particular the chapter 'Political Abuse of Intelligence Information'.
56. J. Mueller, 'A False Sense of Insecurity? How Does the Risk of Terrorism Measure Up Against Everyday Dangers?,' *Regulation* (Fall 2004): 42–6.
57. M. Gill, 'The Challenge for the Security Sector,' *Security Journal*, vol. 20, no. 1, Special Issue: 20th Anniversary (2007).
58. M. Button, 'Developments in Security,' *Security Journal*, vol. 20, no. 1, Special Issue: 20th Anniversary (2007).
59. D. Giever, 'Security Education – Past, Present and the Future,' *Security Journal*, vol. 20, no. 1, Special Issue: 20th Anniversary (2007).
60. http://www.schneier.com/book-sos.html.
61. G. T. Marx, 'Critique: No Soul in the New Machine: Technofallacies in the Electronic Monitoring Movement,' *Justice Quarterly*, vol. 8, no. 3 (September 1991).
62. http://www.euractiv.com/en/security/parliament-wants-information-swift-cia-data-transfer/article-156625. See also http://www.indymedia.ie/index.php. Accessed on October 2008.
63. P. Rock, 'Chronocentrism and British Criminology,' *British Journal of Sociology*, vol. 56, no. 3 (2005): 473–91.
64. I. Loader, 'Necessary Virtues: The Legitimate Place of the State in the Production of Security,' www.libertysecurity.org (April 19, 2005)
65. This in no way means that all these hybrid organisations and processes are aligning in harmony. Conflict, turf wars and strategic evasion are at times pervasive. In 'Nodale Politie in de Rotterdamse havens' (Nodal policing in the Rotterdam Harbour), 2009, I describe and analyse the interweaving taking place, but also stress the fact that cooperation is at times difficult to organise. There are 'nodal barriers' (differences in interests, legal powers, cultures and so on), and cooperation constantly has to be negotiated. I use the concept of 'negotiated order' for this.

Bibliography

Aalberts, T. E. (2009). 'A Dangerous Triangular Relationship? Failed States, Organized Crime and Transnational Terrorism.' *Justitiele Verkenningen*, 3: 65.

Andrew, C. (1995). *For the President's Eyes Only: Secret Intelligence and the American Presidency from Washington to Bush*. London: Harper Collins.

Aniskiewicz, R. (1994). 'Metatheoretical Issues in the Study of Organized Crime.' *Journal of Contemporary Criminal Justice* 10(4): 314–24.

Bakker, J. C. M., B. Hoogenboom, R. N. J. Kamerling and M. Pheiffer (2006). *Facetten van fraude & fraudebestrijding*, Forensische studies deel 11. Den Haag: Sdu.

Battistelli, Fabrizio (1993, July/October). 'Arms and Corruption; Armi e corruzione.' *Critica Sociologica* 106: 33–42.

Baugher, Th. R. (1996/1997). 'Swans Swimming in the Sewer; Legal Use of Dirty Assets bij CIA.' *International Journal of Intelligence and Counterintelligence* nr. 4: 435–71.

Baum, D. (1996). *Smoke and Mirrors: The War on Drugs and the Politics of Failure*. New York: Back Bay Books.

Bayley, D. (1994). 'What Do the Police Do?' in *Police for the Future*, ed. D. Bayley. New York: Oxford University Press 187.

Bayley, D. and C. Shearing (1996). 'The Future of Policing.' *Law & Society Review* 30(3), 585–606.

Bayley, D. and C. Shearing (2001). *The New Structure of Policing: Description, Conceptualization, and Research Agenda*. Washington: Ministry of Justice.

Beck, U. (1986). *Riskogesellschaft*. Frankfurt an Main: Suhrkamp.

Bertram, E., Moms Blachman, Kenneth Sharpe, and Peter Andreas. (1996). *Drug War Politics. The Price of Denial*. Berkely: University of California Press.

Bittner, E. (1970). *The Functions of Police in Modern Society*. Boston, MA: Northeastern University Press.

Block, A. (1997). 'The Serious Crime Community in Oil en Banking.' *Journal of Financial Crime* 4: 207–221.

Boissevain, J. (1974). *Friends of Friends: Networks, Manipulators and Coalitions*. Oxford: Basil Blackwell.

Bourgeois, Ph. (1995). *In Search of Respect. Selling Crack in El Barrio*. Cambridge: Cambridge University Press.

Boutellier, H. (2004) *The Safety Utopia: Contemporary Discontent and Desire as to Crime and Punishment*. Dordrecht: Kluwer Academic Publishers

Boutellier, H. and B. van Stokkom (1995). 'Consumptie van veiligheid; van verzorgingsstaat tot veiligheids- staat.' *Justitiële Verkenningen* 21(5).

Boutellier, H. (2007). *Nodale orde*. Amsterdam: VU Press.

Bovenkerk, F. and Y. Yesilgöz (1998). *De Maffia van Turkije*. Amsterdam: Boom Publishing.

Bovens, M. (1998). *The Quest for Responsibility: Accountability and Citizenship in Complex Organizations*. Cambridge: Cambridge University Press.

Bowling, B. and J. Foster (2002). 'Policing the Police' in *The Oxford Handbook of Policing*, ed. M. Maguire, R. Morgan and R. Reiner, 3rd ed. Oxford: Clarendon Press.

Bowling, B. and T. Newburn (2007). 'Policing and National Security.' Presented at London-Columbia Police, Community and Rule of Law Workshop, London, March 16–17, 2006.

Boyd, B. (2009). *On the Origin of Stories. Evolution, Cognition, and Fiction*. Cambridge, MA: The Belknap Press of Harvard University Press.

Braithwaite, J. (1985). *To Punish or to Persuade. Enforcement of Coal Mine Safety*. Albany: State University of New York Press.

Braithwaite, J. (1989). *Crime, Shame and Reintegration*. Cambridge: Cambridge University Press.

Braithwaite, J. and P. Petit (1990). *Not Just Deserts: a Republican Theory of Criminal Justice*. Oxford: Clarendon Press.

Braithwaite, J. (2002). *Restorative Justice and Responsive Regulation*. New York: Oxford University Press.

Brink, G. van (2007). *Van waarheid naar veiligheid: twee lessen van een door angst bevangen burgerij*. Amsterdam: Sun Uitgeverij.

Brodeur, J. P. (1983). 'High and Low Policing: Remarks about the Policing of Political Activities.' *Social Problems* 30(5): 507–20.

Brodeur, J. P. (1999). 'Cops and Spooks: The Uneasy Partnership.' *Police Practice and Research: An International Journal* 1(3): 1–25.

Broer, W. and C.D. van der Vijver (1984). *Een wijkteam dat moest wijken*. Den Haag: Ministerie van Binnenlandse Zaken.

Broer, W. and C.D. van der Vijver (1985). *Team Policing*. Den Haag: Ministerie van Binnelandse Zaken.

Buckley (1996). 'The War on Drugs is Lost.' *National Review*, 35–48.

Button, M. (2007). 'Developments in Security.' *Security Journal* 20(1), 35–41. Special Issue: 20th Anniversary.

Buuren, J and W. van der Schans (2003). *Keizer in lompen. Politiesamenwerking in Europa*. Breda: Papieren Tijger.

Calster, P. van (2005). 'Georganiseerde Criminaliteit als Emergent Fenomeen van Complexe Wisselwerkingsprocessen.' PhD diss., Brussels: Free University.

Chambliss, W. J. (1998). *On the Take: From Petty Crooks to Presidents*. Bloomington: Indiana University Press.

Chan, J. and R. Ericson (1981). *Decarceration and the Economy of Penal Reform*. Toronto: Centre of Criminology, University of Toronto.

Chan, J. (1996). 'Changing Police Culture.' *British Journal of Criminology* 36(1): 241–256.

Chan, J. (2003). 'Police and New Technologies' in *Handbook of Policing*, ed. T. Newburn. Cullompton, U.K.: Willan Publishing, 655–79.

Christie, N. (1993). *Crime Control as Industry*. London: Routledge.

Clarke (2001). *Business Crime. Its nature and Control*. Cambridge: Polity Press.

Cohen, S. (1985). *Visions of Social Control. Crime, Punishment and Classification*. Cambridge: Polity Press.

Cools, M. (2005). 'Nog een rondje ondernemingen pesten of oude en nieuwe vormen en gedachten inzake criminalisering, inspectie en controle,' in *De suggestie van toezicht en handhaving*, ed. A. B. Hoogenboom and M. Pheijffer. Breukelen: Nyenrode Press.

Cools, M. (2009). 'André Cools and Agusta: A Belgian Affair.' *Justitiele Verkenningen*, 3: 36–52.

Coolsaet (2007). *Macht en waarden in de wereldpolitiek*. Brussel: Academia Press.

Crawford, A. (1996). 'The Spirit of Community: Rights, Responsibilities and the Communitarian Agenda.' *Journal of Law and Society* 23(2), 247–62.

Crawford, A. (2005). *Plural Policing: The Mixed Economy of Visible Patrols in England and Wales*. The Policy Press.

Crawford, A. and Mathew Jones (1995). 'Inter-Agency Co-Operation and Community-Based Crime Prevention: Some Reflections on the World of Pearson and Colleagues.' *British Journal of Criminology* 35(1), 17–33.

Crawford, A. and S. Lister (2004a). 'The Patchwork Shape of Reassurance in England and Wales: Integrated Local Security Quilts of Frayed, Fragmented and Fragile Tangled Webs?' *Policing: An International Journal of Police Strategies and Management* 27(3): 413–30.

Crawford, A. and S. Lister (2004b). 'The Extended Police Family: Visible Patrols in Residential Areas. Notes from the Marketplace.' *Policing and Society* 16 (2): 116–132.

Criminal Intelligence Service Canada (1999). www://cisc.gc.ca/.

DeFilippi, R. J. and M. B. Arthur (1998). 'Paradox in Project-Based Enterprise: The Case of Film Making.' *California Management Review* 40(2): 125–39.

Delfs, R. (1991, November 21). 'Feeding on the System: Gangsters Play Increasing Role in Business and Politics.' *Far Eastern Economic Review*, 28.

Downes, D. and Paul Rock (1990). *Understanding Deviance. A Guide to the Sociology of Rule Breaking*. Oxford: Oxford University Press.

Drahos, P. 2004. 'The Regulation of Public Goods,' 7 (2004) *Journal of International Economic Law* 7(2), 321–39, ISSN:1369–3034.

Drugs, Law Enforcement and Foreign Policy, Subcommittee on Terrorism, Narcotics and International Operations, Committee on Foreign Relations, United States Senate, 1989, S. Prt. 100–165, chaired by Sen. John Kerry of Massachusetts.

Ehrman, M. and R. J. Lundman, eds (1996). *Corporate and Governmental Deviance*, 3rd ed. New York: Oxford University Press.

Ellroy, J. (1990) *L. A. Confidential*. New York: Random House.

Engelen, D. (1995). *Geschiedenis van de Binnenlandse Veiligheidsdienst*. Den Haag: SDU.

Enhus, E. and P. Ponsaers (2005). 'Onmacht tot cultuurverandering – Politiehervorming in België.' *Tijdschrift voor Criminologie*: 47–56.

Ericson, R. (1982). *Reproducing Order: A Study of Police Patrol Work*. Toronto: University of Toronto Press.

Ericson and Haggerty (1997). *Policing the Risk Society*. Toronto: University of Toronto Press.

Ericson, R. and K. Carriere (1994). 'The Fragmentation of Criminology' in *The Futures of Criminology*, ed. D. Nelken. London D. Reidel Publishing Company.

Ericson. R. V. and C. D. Shearing (1996). 'The Scientification of Police Work,' in *The Knowledge Society: The Growing Impact of Scientific Knowledge* on Social Relation, ed. G. Bohme and N. Stehrs. Dordrecht: D. Reidel Publishing Company, 129–59.

Ericson, R. V. and K. D Carriere (1993). 'Community Policing as Communications Policing,' in *Community Policing*, ed. Dieter Dolling and Thomas Feltes. Holzkirchen: Felix Verlag.

Fijnaut, C. (1979). *Opdat de macht een toevlucht zij? Een historische studie van het politie-apparaat als een politieke instelling.* Antwerpen: Kluwer Rechtswetenschappen.

Fijnaut, C. (1998). 'De politie onderzocht. Kantekeningen bij het rapport Politie in wetenschap.' *Justitiële Verkenningen*, 8–16. Den Haag: Ministerie van Justitie.

Fijnaut, C., E. G. M. Nuijten-Edelbroek and J. L. P. Spickenheuer (1985). *Politiële misdaadbestrijding : een studie van het Amerikaanse, Engelse en Nederlandse onderzoek aangaande politiële misdaadbestrijding sedert de jaren '60.* 's-Gravenhage: Staatsuitgeverij.

Fijnaut, C. and N. Van Helten (1999, 89 e.v.). 'De 'bovenbouw' van het reguliere politieapparaat: het KLPD, de KMAR en de BVD', in *Politie. Studies over haar werking en organisatie,* ed. C. Fijnaut, E. Muller and U. Rosenthal.

Fijnaut, C and N. Van Helten (1999). 'De bovenbouw van het reguliere politieapparaat: het KLPD, de KMAR en de BVD', in *Politie. Studies over haar werking en organisatie,* ed. C. Fijnaut et al. Alphen aan den Rijn: Samson Uitgeverij.

Foqué, R. and A. C. 't Hart (1990). *Instrumentaliteit en rechtsbescherming; grondslagen van een strafrechtelijke waardendiscussie.* Arnhem: Gouda Quint/Kluwer Rechtswetenschappen.

Forward, S. and D. Frazier (1998). *Emotional Blackmail: When the People in Your Life Use Fear, Obligations and Guilt to Manipulate You.* North Yorkshire, U.K.: Quill.

Foucault, M. (1976). *De orde in het vertoog.* Meppel: Boom.

Foucault, M. (1988). *De orde van het spreken.* Meppel en, Amsterdam: Historische Uitgeverij.

Foucault, M. (1990). *Discipline, toezicht en straf. De geboorte van de gevangenis.* Groningen, the Netherlands..

Garland, D. (2001). *The Culture of Control: Crime and Social Order in Contemporary Society.* Oxford: Oxford University Press.

Gentry, C. (1992). *J .Edgar Hoover: The Man and the Secrets.* New York: W.W. Norton.

Giever, D. (2007). 'Security Education – Past, Present and the Future.' *Security Journal* 20(1): 43–52. Special Issue: 20th Anniversary.

Gill, M., ed. (2006). *The Handbook of Security.* Houndmills, U.K.: Palgrave Macmillan.

Gill, M. (2007). 'The Challenge for the Security Sector.' *Security Journal* 20(1): 52–56. Special Issue: 20th Anniversary.

Goffman, E. (1959). *The Presentation of Self in Everyday Life.* Harmondsworth, U.K.: Penguin.

Gounev, P. and T. Bezlov (2009). 'Organized Crime, Corruption and Politics in Bulgaria.' *Justitiele Verkenningen*, 3–12.

Graaff, B. de and C. Wiebes (1992). *Gladio der vrije jongens. Een particuliere geheime dienst in Koude Oorlogstijd.* Den Haag: SDU.

Graaff, B. de and C. Wiebes (1992). *Spion in de tuin. King Kong voor en na zijn dood.* Den Haag: SDU.

Graaff, B. de and C. Wiebes (1997). *Villa Maarheeze.* Den Haag: SDU.

Grabosky, P. N. (1996). 'The Future of Crime Control.' Paper for the Australian Institute of Criminology Outlook Seminar, Canberra, Australian Capital Territory.

Grabowsky, P. (1989). *Wayward Governance.* Canberra: Australian Institute of Criminology.

Granovetter, M. (1973). 'The Strength of Weak Ties.' *American Journal of Sociology* 83: 1287–303.

Gray, M. (1996). *Drug Crazy. How We Got Into This Mess & How Can We Get Out.* New York: Doubleday.

Graycar, A. (1999). 'Trafficking in Human Beings.' Presented at the *International Conference on Migration, Culture and Crime*, Israel, July 7, 1999.

Grigg, W. N. (1996). 'Dirty Cops in the Former Soviet Union Running Both Sides of the Law.' *The New American* 4: 52–60.

Gutwirth, S. (1985). *Dostojevski criminoloog ? Een bio-bibliografische speurtocht naar de criminologische inzichten van de Russische schrijver.* Antwerp: Kluwer/Gouda Quint.

Gutwirth, S. (1989). 'Kreten uit de ondergrond; Dostojewski, Foucault en criminology.' *Tijdschrift voor criminologie* nr. 2: 129–51.

Haggerty, K. D. and R. V. Ericson (2006). *The New Politics of Surveillance and Visibility.* Toronto: University of Toronto Press.

Hauber, A. R. (1994). *Stadswachten: Effectiviteit, draagvlak en organisatorische aspecten.* Den Haag: Ministerie van Justitie, Stafafdeling Informatievoorziening, Directie Criminaliteitspreventie.

Havel, V. (1990). *Pogingen om in de Waarheid te leven.* Amsterdam.

Hawkins, K. and J. M. Thomas (1984). 'The Enforcement Process in Regulatory Bureaucracies,' in *Transcarceration: Essays in the Sociology of Social Control*, ed. J. Lowman, R. Menzies and T. Payls. Washington: Sage.

Hinton, M. S. (2005). *The State and the Streets.* Boulder, CO: Riener.

Hoogenboom, A. B. (1985). *Bijzondere opsporingsdiensten en politie. Een exploratief onderzoek naar de handhaving van de bijzondere wetgeving in Nederland.* Ministerie van Binnenlandse Zaken: Den Haag.

Hoogenboom, A. B. (1986). *Privatisering van de politiefunctie. Een literatuurstudie over de particuliere veiligheidsindustrie.* Ministerie van Binnenlandse Zaken: Den Haag.

Hoogenboom, A. B. (1987). *Particuliere recherche. Een verkenning van enige ontwikkelingen.* Den Haag.

Hoogenboom, A. B. (1988). 'Des paradoxes du contrôle d'etat sur l'industrie de la securité privee: la legitimation et la naisance d'un complexe d'organismes policiers?' *Deviance et Societe* 12(4): 391–400.

Hoogenboom, A. B. (1988). 'Honderden Kleine Theaters van Bestraffing; de verspreiding van de politiefunctie,' *Delikt en Delinkwent*, nr. 5 429 e.v.

Hoogenboom, A. B. (1988). *Particuliere recherche. Een verkenning van enige ontwikkelingen.* WODC-publicatie: Den Haag.

Hoogenboom, A. B. (1991). 'The Mining Police: Dutch Private Security in a historical perspective' in Robert, Ph. And C. Emsley *Geschichte und Soziologie des Verbrechens.* Pfaffenweiler, 85 e.v.

Hoogenboom, A. B. (1991a). 'Grey Policing. A Theoretical Framework.' *Policing and Society* 2: 17–30.

Hoogenboom, A. B. (1991b) 'The Mining Police: Dutch Private Security in Historical Perspective,' in *Geschichte und Soziologie des Verbrechens*, ed. Ph. Robert and C. Emsley. Pfaffenweiler, Germany: Centaurus Verlaggesellschaft, 85–100.

Hoogenboom, A. B. (1994). *Het Politiecomplex. Over de samenwerking tussen politie, bijzondere opsporingsdiensten en particuliere recherche.* Arnhem.

Hoogenboom, A. B. (1994a). 'Politiepoëzie.' *Recht en kritiek* nr. 1: 46–66.
Hoogenboom, A. B. (1994b). *Het Politiecomplex. Over de samenwerking tussen politie, bijzondere opsporingsdiensten en particuliere recherche.* Arnhem: Gouda Quint.
Hoogenboom, A. B. (2000). *Schaduwen over Van Traa.* Lelystad: Servicecentrum Uitgevers.
Hoogenboom, A. B. (2006a). *Operationele betrokkenheid. Prestatiesturing en bedrijfsvoering Nederlandse politie. Politie en Wetenschap.* Den Haag: Elsevier Overheid.
Hoogenboom, A. B. (2006b). 'Grey Intelligence.' *Crime, Law and Social Change* 45: 373–81.
Hoogenboom, A. B. (2006c). *Operationele betrokkenheid.* Den Haag: Politie en wetenschap.
Hoogenboom, A. B. (2007). 'G. van den Brink. Van waarheid naar veiligheid: twee lessen van een door angst bevangen burgerij' in *Delikt en Delinkwent.* Kluwer Publishing.
Hoogenboom, A. B. (2008). 'Fictional and Factual Policing: The Case of Reassurance Policing,' in *Reflections on Reassurance Policing in the Low Countries,* ed. Eastom, M. et al. Den Haag.
Hoogenboom, A. B. (2009). *Spelers op zoek naar regels en scheidsrechters. Inwinning openbare orde informatie door de RID.* Den Haag.
Hoogenboom, A. B. (2010). *The Governance of policing and security. Ironies, Myths and Paradoxes.* London: Palgrave Macmillan.
Hoogenboom, A. B. (2010). *Politie in de newterksamenleving.* Dordrecht: SMVP.
Johnson, L. and C. Shearing (2003). *Governing Security: Explorations in Policing and Justice.* London: Routledge.
Jones, T. and T. Newburn (2002). 'The Transformation of Policing? Understanding Current Trends in Policing Systems.' *British Journal of Criminology* 42(1): 129–146.
Kaplan, D. E. and A. Dubro (1986). *Yakuza: The Explosive Account of Japan's Criminal Underworld.* Reading, MA: Addison-Wesley Publishing Co.
Katz, J. (1988). *Seductions of Crime. Moral and Sensual Attractions in Doing Evil.* New York: Basic Books.
Kelling, G. L., T. Pate, D. Dieckman and C. E. Brown (1974). *The Kansas City Preventive Patrol Experiment.* Washington D.C.: Police Foundation.
Kleemans, E. (1998). *Georganiseerde Criminaliteit in Nederland. Rapportage op basis van de WODC-Monitor.* Den Haag: WODC.
Klerks, P. (2000). *Groot in de hasj: theorie en praktijk van de georganiseerde criminaliteit.* Arnhem: Gouda Quint.
Klockars, C. B. (1988). 'The Rhetoric of Community Policing,' in *Community Policing: Rhetoric or Reality,* ed. J. R. Greene and S. D. Mastrofski. New York: Praeger.
Kraska, P. and V. Kappelaer (1997). 'Militarizing American Police: The Rise and Normalization of Paramilitary Units.' *Social Problems* 44(1): 96–112.
Kuhn, Th. (1962). *The Structure of Scientific Revolutions.* Chicago: University of Chicago Press.
Latour, B. (1987). *Science in Action.* Cambridge: Harvard University Press.
Levitt, S. and S. J. Dubner (2005). *Freakonomics: A Rogue Economist Explores the Hidden Side of Everything.* New York: William Morrow/HarperCollins.
Loader, I. (1997). 'Policing and the Social: Questions of Symbolic Power.' *British Journal of Sociology* 48(1): 1–18.

Loader, I. (2000). 'Plural Policing and Democratic Governance.' *Social and Legal Studies* 9(3), 323–45.
Loader, I. and N. Walker (2001). Policing as a Public Good. Reconstructing the Connections between Policing and the State,' *Theoretical Criminology* 5(1), 9–35.
Loader, I. and N. Walker (2006). 'Necessary Virtues: The legitimate Place of the State in the Production of Security,' in *Democracy, Society and the Governance of Security,* ed. J. Wood and B. Dupont. Cambridge: Cambridge University Press.
Loader, I. and N. Walker (2007). *Civilizing Security.* Cambridge: Cambridge University Press.
Lubbers, E. (2004). *Battling Big Business. Countering Greenwash, Infiltration and Other Forms of Corporate Bullying.* Carlton, Australia: Scribe Publications.
Lyon, D. and Zureik, E. (eds.) (1996). *Computers, Surveillance and Privacy.* Minneapolis: University of Minnesota Press.
Maanen, J. van (1978). 'The Asshole,' in *Policing: A View from the Street,* ed. P. K. Manning and J. Van Maanen. Santa Monica, CA: Goodyear Publishing, 221–38.
Maanen, J. van (2005). 'The Asshole,' in *Policing. Key Readings,* ed. T. Newburn. Cullompton: Willan.
Maas, P. (1974). *Serpico.* London: Collins.
Manning, P. K. (1977). *Police Work.* Cambridge, MA: MIT Press.
Manning, P. K. (1992a). 'Information Technologies and the Police,' in *Modern Policing: Crime and Justice, A Review of Research,* ed. M. Tonry and N. Morris. Chicago: University of Chicago Press.
Manning, P. K. (1992b). 'Technological Dramas and the Police: Statement and Counterstatement in Organizational Analysis.' *Criminology* 30(3): 327–46.
Manning, P. K (1996). 'Information Technology in the Police Context: The "Sailor" Phone.' *Information Systems Research* 7(1): 52–62.
Marbes, W. (1992). 'The Psychology of Treason,' in *Inside CIA's Private World: Declassified Articles from the Agency's Internal Journal 1955–1992,* ed. H. Bradford Westerfield. Washington: Spooks Publishing.
Markham, G and M. Punch (2007a). 'Embracing Accountability: The Way Forward.' *Policing. A Journal of Policy and Practice* 1(3): 300–8.
Markham, G. and M. Punch (2007b). 'Embracing Accountability: The Way Forward—Part Two.' *Policing: Journal of Research and Practice* 1(4): 1–9.
Markusen, A. R. (2003). 'The Case Against Privatizing National Security.' *Governance* 16(4): 471–501.
Marx, G. T. (1987). 'The Interweaving Of Public And Private Police Undercover Work,' in *Private Policing,* ed. C. Shearing and P. Stenning. Newbury Park: Sage, 172–93.
Marx, G. T. (1988). *Undercover: Police Surveillance in America.* Berkeley: University of California Press.
Marx, G. T. (1990). 'The Case of the Omniscient Organization.' *Harvard Business Review* (2): 4–7.
Marx, G. T. (1997, February/March). 'Of Methods and Manners for Aspiring Sociologists: 37 Moral Imperatives.' *The American Sociologist* 2: 52–72.
Marx, G. T. (1998). 'An Ethics for the New Surveillance.' *The Information Society* 14(3): 171–185.

Marx, G. T. (2001). 'Murky Conceptual Waters: The Public and the Private.' *Ethics and Information Technology* 3(3), 157–69.
Marx G. T. (2002). 'What's New About the "New Surveillance"? Classifying for Change and Continuity.' *Surveillance and Society* 1, 9–29.
Marx. G. T. (2007). 'Rocky Bottoms and Some Information Age Techno-Fallacies.' *Journal of International Political Sociology* 1: 83–110.
Marx, G. T. (2009). 'A Tack in the Shoe and Taking of the Shoe: Neutralization and Counterneutralization Dynamics.' *Surveillance & Society* 3: 295–306.
Matassa, M. and T. Newburn (2003). 'Policing and Terrorism,' in *Handbook of Policing,* 467–500.
McLauchlin, E. and K. Murji (1995). 'The End of Public Policing. Police Reform and the New Managerialism,' in *Contemporary Issues in Criminology,* ed. Noaks, L. et al. Cardiff.
Mead, G. H. (1934). *Mead, Mind, Self, and Society.* Chicago: University of Chicago Press, xv–xvi.
Mills, M. P. (2005). *The Bottomless Well.* New York: Basic Books.
Mollen Commission (1994). *Report of the Commission to Investigate Allegations of Police Corruption and the Anti-Corruption Procedures of the Police Department.* City of New York: Mollen Commission.
Morselli, C. (2000). 'Contacts, Opportunities and Crime; Relational Foundations of Criminal Enterprise.' PhD diss., Montreal University, Montreal.
Nadelman, E. (1994). Cops Across Borders: The Internationalization of U.S. Criminal Law Enforcement. Pensylvania: University Park.
Napoleoni, L. (2004). *NV Terreur. De nieuwe economie van de terreur.* Amsterdam: de Arbeiderspers.
Nelken, D. (1994). Introduction and 'Reflexive Criminology?' in *The Futures of Criminology,* ed. D. Nelken. London: Sage.
Newburn, T. (1999). *Understanding and Preventing Police Corruption: Lessons from Literature.* London: Home Office.
Newburn, T. (2003a). *Handbook of Policing.* Cullompton, U.K.: Willan Publishing.
Newburn, T. (2003b). 'The Future of Policing,' in *Handbook of Policing.*
Newburn, T. (2005). *Policing. Key Readings.* Cullompton, U.K.: Willan Publishing.
Neyroud, P. (2005). 'ACPO and the NPIA: A New Professional Future.' Presentation to ACPO, June. London, U.K.
Nogala, D. (1989). *Polizei, Avancierte Technik und Soziale Kontrolle.* Pfaffenweiler: Pfaffenweiler Verlag.
Norris, C. and C. Dunningham (2000). 'Subterranean Blues: Conflict as Unintended Consequences of the Police Use of Informers.' *Policing and Society* nr. 4: 385–412.
O'Hare (2004). *No Place to Hide.* Washington: Universal.
O'Neill, O. (2002). *A Question of Trust: BBC Reith Lectures.* London: BBC.
Orwell, G. (2004). *Why I Write.* London: Penguin Books.
Paoli, L. (2009). 'The Political-Criminal Nexus in Italy: 150 Years of Relationships Between Mafia and Politics.' *Justitiele Verkenningen,* 3: 12–20.
Pavarini, M. (1994). 'Is Criminology Worth Saving?', in *The Futures of Criminology,* ed. D. Nelken. London: Sage.

Pekel, K. 'Integrity, Ethics, and the CIA: The Need for Improvement.' Available at https://www.cia.gov/library/center-for.../v41i5a05p.pdf.

Peper, B. (2002). *Na 11–09-01. Veiligheid een schaars goed*. Breukelen: Nyenrode Press.

Perry, D. L. (1995, spring). 'Repugnant Philosophy: Ethics, Espionage, and Covert Action.' *Journal of Conflict Studies*, 3: 38–52.

Ponsaers, P. and R. De Cuyper (1980). *Arbeidsinspektie: Overheidszaak of privé-aangelegenheid?, Interuniversitaire Reeks Criminologie en Strafwetenschappen*. Antwerpen: Kluwer.

Ponsaers, P. and B. Hoogenboom (2004). 'Het moeilijke spel van wortel en stok – Organisatiecriminaliteit en handhavingstrategieën van bijzondere inspectie- en opsporingsdiensten', in *Tijdschrift voor Criminologie*, SISWO, Amsterdam, 2.

Ponsaers, P. and M. Easton (2008). 'Community (oriented) Policing Reassured: Significance within the Flemish Context,' in *Reflections on Reassurance Policing in the Low Countries*, ed. M. Easton et al. Den Haag: Boom.

Popper, K. (1945). *The Open Society and Its Enemies*. Londen: Routledge.

Port, M. van de (2001). *Geliquideerd; criminele afrekeningen in Nederland*. Amsterdam: Meulenhoff.

Porta, Donatella della (1993). 'Corruption, Clientelism, and Maladministration: Notes on the Dynamics of Corrupt Exchanges in Italy; Corruzione, clientelismo e cattiva.' *Quaderni di Sociologia* 37(5): 31–50.

Postman, N. (1993). *Technopoly. The Surrender of Culture to Technology*. New York: Palgrave.

Powis, R. E. (1992). *The Money Launderers. Lessons from the Drug Wars – How Billions of Illegal Dollars Are Washed Through Banks & Businesses*. Cambridge: Cambridge University Press.

Punch, M. (1985). *Conduct Unbecoming; The Social Construction of Police Deviance and Control*. London: Tavistock.

Punch, M. (1995). 'Grievous Business Harm: Exploring Corporate Violence.' *European Journal on Criminal Policy and Research* 3(2).

Punch, M. (2003). 'Rotten Orchards: '"Pestilence", Police Misconduct and System Failure.' *Policing and Society* 13(2): 171–96.

Punch, M. (2006). *Van 'alles mag' naar 'zero tolerance': Policy transfer en de Nederlandse politie*. Dordrecht: SMVP.

Punch, M. (2009). *Police Corruption. Deviance, Accountability and Reform in Policing*. Cullompton, U.K.: Willan Publishing.

Punch, M. (2009). 'Why Corporations Kill and Get Away with It: The Failure of Law to Cope with Crime of Organizations,' in *System Criminality in International Law*, ed. P. A. Nollkaemper and H. van der Wilt. Cambridge: Cambridge University Press.

Rabaska, A. and P. Chalk (2001). 'Colombian Labyrinth: The Synergy of Drugs and Insurgency and Its Implications for Regional Instability.' Santa Monica, CA: RAND Corporation. Available at http://www.rand.org/publications/MR/MR1339/. Accessed on February, 2008.

Rasor, D. and R. Bauman (2007). *Betraying Our Troops. The Destructive Results of Privatizing War*. New York: Palgrave MacMillan.

Reenen P. van (1978). 'Het ijzeren politiebestel,' in *Het politiebestel. Opstellen over het Nederlandse Politiebestel*, ed. P. Van Reenen. Arnhem: Gouda quint, 1978.

Reenen, P. van (1979). *Overheidsgeweld. Een sociologische studie van de dynamiek van het geweldsmonopolie*. Alphen a/d Rijn: Samson uitgeverij.
Reenen, P. van (1985). 'Liberal Policing in the Interventionist State.'*Police Studies* 2.
Reenen, P. van (1987). 'Het ijzeren politiebestel,' in *Het Politiebestel,* ed. P. van Reenen. Arnhem: Gouda Quint.
Reiner, R. (1992). *The Politics of the Police*. Oxford: Oxford University Press.
Reiner, R. (2002). 'The Organisation and Accountability of the Police,' in *The Handbook of the Criminal Justice Process*, ed. M. McConville and G. Wilson. Oxford: Oxford University Press, 21–42.
Reiner, R. (2007). 'Neophilia or Back to Basics? Policing Research and the Seductions of Crime Control.' *Policing & Society* 17(1), March, 89–101.
Reisman, D. (1979). *Folded Lies*. New York: Free Press.
Reisman, W. M. and J. Baker (1992). *Regulating Covert Action: Practices, Contexts and Policies of Covert Coercion Abroad in International and American Law*. Washington: Yale University Press.
Reiss, A. J. (1987). 'The Legitimacy of Intrusion into Private Space,' in *Private Policing,* ed. C. D. Shearing and Ph. Stenning. Newbury Park, CA: Sage Publications, 19–44.
Report of the Committee on Interior and Insular Affairs of the U.S. House of Representatives, Alaska Pipeline Service Company Covert Operation. Washington, 1992.
Rock, P. (2005). 'Chronocentrism and British Criminology.' *British Journal of Sociology* 56(3): 473–792.
Rowlands, M. (2005). *Everything I Know I Know from TV – Philospohy for the Unrepentant Coach Potato*. London: Ebury Press.
Ruggiero, V. (1996, March). 'War Markets: Corporate and Organized Criminals in Europe.' *Social and Legal Studies* 5(1): 5–20.
Ruggiero, V. (2003). *Crime in Literature. Sociology of Deviance and Fiction*. London: Verso.
Schneier, B. (2008). *Schneier on Security*. Washington: Wiley.
Schumacher, G. (2006). *A Bloody Business. America's War Zone Contractors and the Occupation of Iraq*. St. Paul, MN: Zenith Press.
Seaport Commission Report. Available at www.USSeaportcommission.org
Shearing, C. and Stenning (1983). 'Private Security:Implications for Social Control.' *Social Problems* 5, 493–503.
Shearing, C. D. and J. Wood (2003). 'Nodal Governance, Democracy and the New 'Denizen.' *Journal of Law and Society* 30(3):237–245.
Shearing, C. D. and P. C. Stenning (1987a). *Private Policing*. Newbury Park, CA: Sage Publications.
Shearing, C. D. and Ph. Stenning (1987b). 'Say "Cheese". The Disney Order That Is Not So Mickey Mouse,' in *Private Policing*, 317–24.
Sheptycki, J. (2003). *Review of the Influence of Strategic Intelligence on Organised Crime Policy and Practice*. Final Report. London: Home Office.
Sherman, L. W. (1974). 'Becoming Bent: Moral Careers of Corrupt Policemen,' in *Police Corruption: A Sociological Perspective,* ed. L. W. Sherman. New York: Doubleday.
Shulsky, A. and G. J. Schmitt (2002). *Silent Warfare. Understanding the World of Intelligence*. Washington: Brassey Inc.
Siegel, D. (2009). 'Crime and Politics in Russia.' *Justitiele Verkenningen*, 3: 73–81.

Simon (2007). *Governing Through Crime. How the War on Crime Transformed American Democracy and Created a Culture of Fear.* Oxford: Oxford University Press.

Skolnick, J. H. and D. H. Bayley (1986). *The New Blue Line: Police Innovation in Six American Cities.* London: Free Press.

Sousa Santos, de (2006). *Reinventing Democracy : Grassroots Movements in Portugal.* London: Routledge.

Sparrow, M. (2000). *The Regulatory Craft. Controlling Risks, Solving Problems and Managing Compliance.* Washington, D.C.: Brookings Institution Press.

Steden, R. van (2007). *Privatizing Policing. Describing and Explaining the Growth of Private Security.* Boom Juridische Uitgeverij: Den Haag.

Steele, R. (2003). 'Information Peacekeeping & the Future of Intelligence,' in *Peacekeeping Intelligence: Emerging Concepts for the Future,* ed. B. Jong and W. Platjes. Oakton, VA: OSS International Press.

Steele, R. (2005). *Information Operations: All Information, All Languages, All the Time.* Washington: OSS.

Stern, J. (2003). *Terror in the Name of God: Why Religious Militants Kill.* New York: Harper Collins Publishers.

Stern, J. (2004a). *Terreur in de naam van God.* Utrecht: het Spectrum.

Stern, J. (2004b). 'How the war in Iraq has damaged the war on terrorism.' Available at http://dir.salon.com/opinion/feature/2004/04/07/terrorism. Accessed on 22 November 2008.

Stokkom, B. van (2007). *Godslastering, discriminerende uitingen wegens godsdienst, en haatuitingen.* Den Haag: WODC.

Stuart Henry (1987). *The Informal Economy.* New Haven: Sage.

Sutherland, E. (1983). *White Collar Crime. The Uncut Version.* New Haven, CT: Yale University Press.

Taussig, (1993). *Mimesis and Alterity: A Particular History of the Senses.* New York: Doubleday.

Terpstra, J. (2006). 'Veiligheidszorg als publiek goed bij een gedeelde verantwoordelijkheid', in *Gedeelde verantwoordelijkheid voor veiligheidszorg,* ed. L. Gunther Moor and R. Johannink. Dordrecht, the Netherlands: SMVP.

Terpstra, J. (2007). *Wijkagenten en hun dagelijks werk. Een onderzoek naar de uitvoering van gebiedsgebonden politiewerk.* Den Haag: Reed Business.

Toffler, A. (1990). *Powershift: Knowledge, Wealth and Violence at the Edge of the 21st Century.* New York: Bantam Books.

Torre, E. van der (1999). *Politiewerk. Politiestijlen, community policing, professionalisme.* Alphen aan den Rijn: Samson.

Veld, R. in 't, F. A. Beemer, W. de Haan, F. Mertens, E. Romein, and M. van Roost (2002). *Vooruitgang of regendans? Evaluatie Beleids-en Beheerscyclus Politie.* The Hague: Bestad Consultancy and Berenschot Procesmanagement.

Veldt, R. (2002). *Vooruitgang of regendans? Evaluatie Beleids- en beheerscyclus Politie.* Den Haag: Berenschot.

Vold, G. and T. Bernard (1986). *Theoretical criminology,* 3rd ed. New York: Oxford University Press.

Waller, J. M. and V. Yasmann (1995, December). 'Russia's Great Criminal Revolution: The Role of the Security Services.' *Journal of Contemporary Criminal Justice* 11(4).

Weber, M. (1962). *Basic Concepts of Sociology.* New York: Citadel Press.

'Who's Clean?' (1999, September 6). *Newsweek*, 22.
Wilensky H. L. (1967). *Organizational Intelligence. Knowledge and Policy in Government and Industry* Washington: Sage.
Wilson, J. Q. and B. Boland (1978, spring). 'The Effect of Police on Crime.' *Law and Society* 5: 156–172.
Winlow, S. (2001). *Badfellas: Crime, Tradition and New Masculinities.* Oxford: Berg Publishers.
Wood, J. and C. Shearing (2007). *Imagining Security.* Cullompton, U.K.: Willan Publishing.
Yacowar, M. (2003). *The Sopranos on the Couch: Analyzing Television's Greatest Series.* London: Continuum International Publishing Group.
Zaitch, D. (2002). *Trafficking Cocaine: Colombian Drug Entrepreneurs in the Netherlands.* The Hague: Kluwer Law International.
Zoomer, O., S. Nieuwkamp (2004). *Economische belangen; barrières voor preventie en bestrijding van (georganiseerde) criminaliteit.* Dordrecht: Stichting Maatschappij, Veiligheid en Politie (SMVP).
Zureik, E. and M. B. Salter (2005). *Global Surveillance and Policing. Borders, Security, Identity.* Cullompton, U.K.: Willan Publishing.

Index